CURIOUS TALES
of
OLD EAST YORKSHIRE

Howard Peach

Published by Sigma Leisure – an imprint of
Sigma Press, 1 South Oak Lane, Wilmslow, Cheshire SK9 6AR, England.

British Library Cataloguing in Publication Data
A CIP record for this book is available from the British Library.

ISBN: 1-85058-749-3

Typesetting and Design by: Sigma Press, Wilmslow, Cheshire.

Cover Design: Graham Beech

Cover photographs: large picture: under the Humber Bridge; smaller pictures, clockwise from top left: King Billy on Lowgate, Hull; Riverhead at Driffield; Kilnsea mirror; gatehouse at Burton Agnes Hall; The Beverley Imp, St Mary's *(all photographs by Howard Peach)*

Location Map: Morag Perrott

Printed by: MFP Design & Print

Foreword

by Rt. Hon. David Davis MP
Member of Parliament for Haltemprice and Howden, East Yorkshire

The East Riding of Yorkshire is a part of England largely unknown to our fellow countrymen. Off the beaten tracks of the A1 and M1, it is less populous than the West Riding, and with the exception of seaside resorts like Bridlington, less visited by tourists than the more fashionable North Riding. In many ways the East Riding is England's secret garden.

Yet it is very much a cockpit of English history, and can lay serious claim to being a birthplace of English individualism. It was at Stamford Bridge, in the East Riding, that the English won their battle of 1066 – and arguably against a tougher opponent than the Norman usurper, William. Harald Hardrada, killed by the English at Stamford Bridge, was at the time viewed as the greatest soldier in Europe.

Later battles were less successful, if more principled. When Henry the Eighth sequestered the monasteries, many of his more devout subjects were horrified, particularly here in the North of England. Robert Aske, of Aughton, in the East Riding, led the famed Pilgrimage of Grace to London to protest. Aske bravely stood up to Henry, and was repaid by being hanged in chains at Clifford's Tower in York.

Others were equally principled, but perhaps more skilful, and certainly more effective. William Wilberforce, the phenomenal campaigner for the abolition of slavery, and in moral terms probably the greatest man of his day, went to school in Pocklington, and represented the area in Parliament. It is extraordinary to think that this man from this quiet rural area of England should have effectively banished slavery from Great Britain, and via the intercession of the British Navy, from much of the rest of the world as well.

These men, who have left an indelible mark on history, were but the most prominent of the highly individualistic men and women who have populated the East Riding down the centuries. This excellent book describes brilliantly many such people and their often-idiosyncratic traditions, and in doing so Howard Peach gives marvellous human texture to the history of the county.

Why this is an area of such strong characters and traditions is hard to know. Perhaps it is because, being on the north bank of the Humber, we are on the main invasion route into England, and our characters reflect the people who met on our land and the battles they fought there. Certainly we are visibly an amalgam of Anglo-Saxon and Viking stock, as is obvious from our language and, from the names we give to our people and places. Visitors still ask me why we call streets "gate", and why so many of our villages end in "thorpe" or "stead".

Yet this cannot explain us by itself. Some of the East Riding's most distinctive history pre-dates event the Anglo Saxon invasions, or indeed even the Romans. The boats found at Ferriby, and particularly at Hasholme (see Chapter 12), are clear indicators that this part of the world was a hive of activity and trade in the Iron Age long before the Romans arrived. So the tradition of commercial enterprise that built Hull over many centuries, that led to railway kings like Hudson in the last century, and that populates the county with many self-made millionaires today, goes back over more than two thousand years.

So the East Riding carries many distinctions and many secrets. This book, with its encyclopaedic range over so much of our local history, does a fine job of elucidating and illuminating what makes up the people of the East Riding today. "Curious Tales of East Yorkshire" is undoubtedly an interesting and often amusing read. More than that, however, reading it might, just, even lead you to understand quite what it is that makes this particular brand of Yorkshireman tick.

David Davis MP

Preface

East Yorkshire amply rewards those who take time to explore its rich heritage. Our parents and grandparents lived through unprecedented and far-reaching changes in social welfare, education, transport and technology. They witnessed also huge reductions of such traditional workers as blacksmiths, joiners, farmworkers, needleworkers and domestic servants. Pitchforks, milking stool, toasting fork, mangle and chamber pot have become museum pieces or, indeed, collectors' items.

Paradoxically, while the old ways are in danger of being forgotten there is a widespread nostalgia for things of the past. Family history is a growth industry, as almost any visit to a local studies library shows. So many customs, beliefs, happenings teem with interest and are worth recording – plus, of course, the variety and unpredictability of human nature across these Broad Acres, where "nowt so queer as folk" is a matter of common observation and remark.

This present labour of love comprises 14 chapters, most of which unfold in approximate chronological sequence. The first three (Events, People, Buildings and Artefacts) hopefully provide a basic structure for cover-to-cover reading, but there will be opportunities galore for indiscriminate browsing. And while there is a sprinkling of light-hearted and amusing material, many more serious tales are offered which could become base lines for further research. Moreover, the author's own photographs could facilitate the use of the book as, in part, a tourist's guide.

Acknowledgements

In preparing this book I have consulted many writers from different periods. To list them all would be a very lengthy exercise and I hope that my select bibliography will at least be serviceable in indicating some of my main sources. I would like to record here the always-cheerful assistance given by the staff of the Local Studies sections of the Hull and York Central Libraries and the Beverley Reference Library. Another vital repository of information has been the open-access shelves of the Guildhall Road library (Hull) of the University of Lincolnshire and Humberside. Various officers of the East Riding of Yorkshire Council have been generous with help and advice, and in making available, for example, records of oral interviews with old people whose thoughtful and often moving reminiscences are invaluable for anyone wanting a richer understanding of the past.

From scores of conversations and correspondences, I am especially grateful to Mike Smith, WEA tutor in local history for numerous insights and recommendations; to George Billaney for his recollections of the Ottringham area of Holderness; to Roger Billington (Butlins Archivist); and to John Curtis and George Nellist for allowing me to draw directly on their personal experiences.

For permission to use copyright illustrations (and in many cases for additional information) I am indebted to the following: Miss M. Campling; John Dunning; East Riding of Yorkshire Council Library and Information Services; Filey Town Council Archives Service; Frederick France; Glasgow City Council Cultural and Leisure Services; Mrs. M. Grice; Hornsea Museum; Patrick Howlett; Mrs D. Hughes; Humberside Police; the Christopher Ketchell Collection; Kingston upon Hull Central Library, Local Studies Section; Kingston upon Hull Museums; Geoff Lumb; Miss M. Milner; Museum of Rural Life, University of Reading; the Royal National Lifeboat Institution; Richard Traves; Dr J.E.S. Walker; John Wheeler; Edvard Winkler.

My thanks are due also to these persons and organisations for allowing me to quote from their publications or resources:

Beverley Guardian and Driffield Post (contemporary news reports).

Janice and Peter Crowther: 'The Diary of Robert Sharp of South Cave: Life in a Yorkshire Village 1812 – 57' (OUP for The British Academy, 1997).

East Riding of Yorkshire Archives Service, with special reference to parish records and school log books.

Mrs Doreen Lawrence, for lines from 'The Launch of the Hornsea Lifeboat', written by her brother, Arthur Jarratt.

Smith Settle Ltd. (Publishers) for Walter Turner's 'The Good Awd Tahmes' from 'A Century of Yorkshire Dialect', edited by Arnold Kellett and Ian Dewhirst (1997).

Finally I should like to thank the Rt. Hon David Davis MP for his kind introduction to my book.

Howard Peach

Contents

Chapter 1	Events	1
Chapter 2	People	13
Chapter 3	Buildings and Artefacts	27
Chapter 4	Churches and Religious Life	38
Chapter 5	What A Way To Go!	56
Chapter 6	Superstitions and Sayings	71
Chapter 7	Customs	82
Chapter 8	Children and Schools	99
Chapter 9	Punishments	110
Chapter 10	Disputes	122
Chapter 11	Domestic Doings	133
Chapter 12	Communications	144
Chapter 13	Alfresco	159
Chapter 14	Miscellany	172
	Bibliography	181

THE OLD EAST RIDING

Chapter 1

Events

The Battle of Stamford Bridge

The year 1066 marks one of those county events that rank also as national history. King Harold's half-brother, Tostig, had been expelled from Northumbria, where he had ruled tyrannically, and had won the support of Harold Hardrada of Norway. Some 300 ships carrying 60,000 men rounded Spurn, and sailing up the Humber as far as Riccall, disembarked to march on York. Intercepted at Fulford they roundly beat the combined forces of Morcar and Edwin of Mercia.

Harold had to move north with all possible speed. Reaching Tadcaster, he learnt that the Northmen were massing near Stamford Bridge. Messengers were sent to try to negotiate a peace. Generous terms were offered. Tostig was invited to consider not only the return of Northumbria, but a third of Harold's Saxon kingdom.

The next part of the dialogue is worth savouring.

"And what," demanded Tostig, he of the curled lip, "what will you give Hardrada?"

"Seven feet of English earth", was the reply. "Or eight, allowing for his size".

Tostig was contemptuous.

"Then it's war. Either we die with honour or we win a great victory".

Finally, the Saxons won. The story of the critical spearing of the giant Viking who blocked the bridge is told in Chapter 7. Hardrada was doubtless buried in the promised seven feet of East Yorkshire earth; and Tostig, with poetic justice was despatched by his royal brother's own sword. Further to a truce, the remnant of the Viking horde was promised safe conduct back to their ships on condition that they never returned.

The celebrations were short-lived. Harold soon had to march to the south coast to try to counter the invasion of William of Normandy. On that unlucky 13th October, he met his come-uppance.

The Harrying of the North

After the Norman Conquest was largely complete serious dissident problems arose in York, and a special force of Norman soldiers was sent to relieve the situation in 1068. The following year the garrisons in two fortified castles were besieged; and the Conqueror, thoroughly enraged, decided on severe retribution, "by the splendour of God".

"Scorched earth" orders were given. Contemporary accounts tell of devastation from the Humber to the Tees, with villages systematically looted, torched, men, women and children slaughtered, crops and animals destroyed, the countryside fit only for wild beasts and robbers. Wolves and wild dogs, it was said, licked the bones of the dead.

According to the Domesday Book (1086) very many places were vastly reduced or laid waste. Keyingham, for example, worth £8 in the time of Edward the Confessor (1042-66) was now valued at 30s. Market Weighton was down from £20 to £3. "Belebe" (Bielby) on the Wolds dropped from £56 to £8. But there is uncertainty, and dispute among historians, as to the overall scale of damage.

It is understandable that William wanted to spare Beverley. Nevertheless, one leader, Toustain, ventured into the church where his horse stumbled and fell, breaking the trespasser's neck and distorting his limbs. The incident was thought to be a sign of the displeasure of the founder, John of Beverley. There was no point in struggling against the Divine – so Beverley was left alone.

William took a more pragmatic line. He was crowned at York and spent Christmas there. A castle was built at Skipsea and given to Drogo de la Beuvriere as a reward for his services at Hastings (See Chapter 10).

King's Town

By the end of the 13th century the settlement of Wyke, consisting of perhaps 60 houses near the mouth of the River Hull, was secure as the possession of Meaux Abbey. Meaux was becoming prosperous by the export of wool to Flanders, some 2,000 sacks being sent annually between 1279 and 1299. Indeed, a century earlier the Abbey had contributed wool towards the ransom of King Richard I, held by the Emperor Henry VI. By 1279, a collector of the King's Customs had been appointed, and Wyke had won the right to a weekly market and an annual fair.

Further potential was seen by Edward I: Wyke would make a strategic base for his wars with Scotland. In 1299 a charter for King's Town-upon-Hull granted the right to a warden and bailiffs; a twice-weekly market; the right of freemen to buy and sell; freedom from property tolls; a gallows and a prison! King's Town was one of six permitted to establish a mint. After London and Boston it was the third most important port in the realm.

In 1332 a further charter granted by Edward III allowed Kingston-upon-Hull to elect its own mayor, the first being William de la Pole, merchant and moneylender extraordinary (see Chapter 2).

The Black Death

Up to one-third of the population may have perished in the bubonic plague of 1349. Huge blackening boils producing foul-smelling pus generally indicated death within seven days. According to the Chronicle of Meaux, the only Cistercian Abbey in the East Riding, the living were scarcely enough to bury the dead, and numbers fell from 49 to seven (see Chapter 10 re the disputed succession as abbot).

With priests in demand to comfort the dying, mortality rates in the church were high. It was circumstantially likely that at Walkington William Dareyus died of the plague. Building stopped at critical points. In Holy Trinity, Hull, the transepts are older than the choir. At Patrington the main building was complete by about 1340, but the spire was added half a century later.

Further outbreaks followed in 1361, 1369 and 1451, wiping out the village of Flotmanby near Hunmanby.

Ravenspur and the Royals

Whereas Ravenser Odd was a temporary island (emerging c1200 but overwhelmed again by 1360), Ravenspur was situated on the Spurn mainland. Remote from the corridors of power, this sea-swept settlement was none the less the scene of a number of significant kingly comings and goings. In 1310 Edward II called on Ravenspur to provide a ship and crew against Scotland; and 22 years later Edward Balliol embarked here, with 2 000 men-at-arms, to claim the Scottish throne. A ship and 28 marines were provided by Ravenspur to assist Edward III at the siege of Calais.

Two later arrivals, however, showed some remarkable parallels. On 4th July 1399, Henry Bolingbroke landed at Ravenspur with 60 men from France, having earlier been banished by his cousin, Richard II. He had come to reclaim the "estate" of his father, John of Gaunt, and was immediately joined by the Earls of Northumberland and Westmorland. Recalled from Ireland, where yet again there were troubles, Richard found his support waning as Bolingbroke advanced. He was consigned to the Tower of London and abdicated in favour of his rival, soon to be proclaimed King Henry IV.

On 11th March 1471 Edward Plantagenet, ruler for the past ten years, landed at Ravenspur from Flushing. Only a few months earlier he had been driven out by "Kingmaker" Richard Neville and various Lancastrian supporters. His landing on this part of the coast was, admittedly, accidental, his vessel having been driven there by storm winds. Opposed briefly by Sir John Westerdale, Vicar of Keyingham, who was speedily arrested, Edward won support at Beverley and York. He then marched south, defeated Neville at Barnet and won again at Tewkesbury. Once again, the throne was his, and Lancastrian hopes were dashed – for a time – in these interminable Wars of the Roses.

Suppression of the Monasteries

Henry VIII had three main reasons for wanting to destroy the monasteries. They were corrupt, reduced in terms of numbers of monks and long past their heyday. They were part of the empire of the Roman Catholic Church, and the king, as self-appointed Supreme Head of the Church of England would brook no rival. And, of course, he was greedy for the material wealth of the monasteries.

Royal Commission inquiries found plenty to criticise. Numbers were indeed well down. Meaux Abbey had an abbot and 24 monks. The Augustinians at Warter Priory numbered a prior and 10 canons, while Haltemprice had but 9 canons, plus 40 servants and boys.

Scandals had multiplied, with evidence of financial mismanagement and irregular secular visitors. Ribaldry attended stories emanating from the Gilbertine Priory at Watton, accommodating canons and nuns living in separate quarters ... Superstition and credulity walked hand in hand. Parts of the Holy Cross were claimed by Haltemprice, Howden Minster and Nunkeeling Nunnery. The Girdle of St Mary, a talisman for helping childbirth, was available at Kirkham and Haltemprice. The latter institution claimed also an arm of St George. Howden's sacred relics included dust from the mortal remains of John the Baptist, a hair of the Blessed Virgin, a piece of Christ's cradle and the hand of St John the Evangelist.

So Henry sold off the monasteries which were thoroughly looted of treasures and furnishings. Nuns and canons were pensioned off. Christina Burgh, prioress of Nunkeeling, for example, surrendered her trust on 10th

The seal of Haltemprice Priory

September 1536, receiving a pension of £8 a year. Haltemprice went to Sir Ralph Ellerker of Risby, and the Swine Nunnery to Sir Thomas Gresham, a London merchant.

Compared to monastic remains in the West and North Ridings, this East Riding has little to show. Only Kirkham Priory has any substantial remains. The prior's house at Watton was spared and is privately occupied. Of the great houses at Haltemprice and Meaux nothing survives but bumps and hollows. At Bridlington the splendid Bayle Gate is now a museum and the priory church flourishes.

Pilgrimage of Grace

The suppression of the monasteries gave rise to serious protests which began in Lincolnshire and soon spread to East Yorkshire. One of the leaders was Robert Aske of Aughton Manor. A rally at Beverley found common cause with others around Market Weighton and a force estimated at 40,000 massed on Skipwith Common. Joined by Lord Darcy of Templehirst they marched on York, which fell to them on 16th October 1536.

Through the mediation of the Duke of Norfolk, Aske pleaded for a royal review of their grievances. Henry met a deputation at Windsor and offered vague reassurance. The revolt was over. The arrests and trials were about to begin. Darcy was beheaded on Tower Hill, 30th June 1537. Sir Robert Constable, who had fought against the Scots at Flodden (1513), alongside his aged father, Marmaduke was hanged at Hull's Beverley Gate on Friday, 6th July. His gibbeted remains were still evident when the king visited the town four years later. Aske was hanged on Clifford's Tower, York on 28th July, and his body gibbeted. William Wood, Prior of Bridlington, had been intimidated locally and his life threatened if he failed to supply the rebels with mounted retainers. After much agonising he acceded – and was beheaded and quartered at York on 21st September.

Skidby Expects

By 1584 deteriorating relations with Spain forced England to look to the dangers of possible invasion. As with Dad's Army of a later era, Skidby summoned 36 able-bodied men to organise its defences. A Muster Roll detailed four pikemen, five billmen, two calevars (light musketeers), two archers plus 23 labourers, several of whom had a bow and half a sheaf of arrows. Thomas Avice and William Attmar, however, had only a bow. How they would have fared against foreign opposition can be no more than conjecture.

Royalty Rebuffed

King Charles I had cause for concern about the arsenal left in Hull by the Royalist army in 1641. Accordingly, he wrote to the military governor, Sir John Hotham announcing his intention to join his son, James, Duke of York who was already in the town. Both Houses of Parliament had invested Hotham with full authority to maintain and retain the guns and ammunition in all circumstances.

The governor's dilemma was obvious. On the morning of 23rd April 1642 he called a meeting at his residence, now Ye Olde White Hart Inn, in a panelled room subsequently dubbed the Plotting Parlour. Mayor Henry Barnard was for welcoming the king. A majority of others, including Peregrine Pelham

Sir John Hotham

Charles I locked out at the Beverley Gate, Hull. Based on the painting by Joseph Parrocel (1704-81)
(Courtesy of Hull Museums)

MP were opposed. After the four gates to the town were shut, the large royal party duly arrived to contemplate their exclusion. The governor appeared on the wall above the Beverley Gate to greet his king and to try to explain his divided loyalties. Luncheon refreshments were passed down, but the drawbridge stayed up.

Charles was very angry. After intermittent fruitless parleying, royal heralds pronounced Hotham a traitor. The Duke of York then joined his father who retreated to Beverley at about 5pm. Parliament, through the Governor of Hull, had defied the king. Civil War was imminent.

But as the storm clouds gathered Sir John Hotham's support for the Roundheads wavered. A Royalist siege of Hull for three weeks in July was a nightmare. As secret talks were held, Parliament became suspicious and threw a guard around the governor's residence. Hotham escaped, only to be arrested near his home at Scorborough. Consigned to the Tower for 17 months he was beheaded on 2nd January 1645, the day after the same fate befell his son, Captain John Hotham, court-marshalled for complicity.

Royalty Entertained

The queen of England might seem an unlikely gun-runner, but that was the situation when Dutch arms were landed at Keyingham Creek, for onward transmission to her husband at York. On 23rd February 1643, having landed in a storm at Bridlington, bringing money to buy more munitions, she was found temporary shelter in a house on the Quay. She was awakened by Roundhead ships firing at Dutch vessels in the bay, and had to escape quickly. Crouching in a ditch, Henrietta Maria realised she had left behind her little dog, and despite all the dangers of flying shrapnel, insisted on going back to fetch it.

After a quieter night spent on a farm at Burton Fleming, the queen was welcomed at Boynton Hall. Here, the story goes, she abused all trust by stealing their silver, replacing it with a portrait of herself.

Henrietta: Queen of Charles I

Town Taking Day

Well into the 20th century, to the joyful tolling of the church bells, Hull school children were given an extra day's holiday on 4th December. On this day in 1688 the Protestants of the town took the Citadel from the Catholic governor, Lord Langdale, fearing a plot to seize the town. Hull declared enthusiastically for William of Orange and the Protestant cause (see Chapter 3, King Billy).

Moonlit Naval Battle

John Paul Jones was a marauding American privateer active off the Yorkshire coast during the early years of his country's War of Independence (1776-83). There were fears that he would not be contented indefinitely to fire salvos at Rolston Hall, the residence of William Brough, Marshall of the High Court of Admiralty. Then came the moment. His flagship, *Le Bonhomme Richard* turned south from Scottish waters to intercept a Baltic merchant convoy escorted by two English vessels, the *Countess of Scarborough* and *HMS Serapis* under Captain Richard Pearson. On 22nd September 1779 exchanges of fire brought hundreds of sightseers to the coast and cliffs near Flamborough Head. Musket and cannon lit up the night sky, and there was tremendous cheering when the American suffered a direct hit.

But Pearson suffered heavier casualties when the two ships became locked together, and hand-to-hand fighting ensued. The convoy, meanwhile, escaped. Although Pearson at last had to surrender his sword, Jones had won a Pyrrhic victory. *Le Bonhomme Richard* sank, and its crew was transferred to the *Serapis*. Realising that an English fleet was on its way, Jones took the captured prize to France.

Although court-marshalled, Pearson was honourably acquitted, receiving the freedom of Hull and Scarborough. A knighthood followed and he was appointed as lieutenant-governor of Greenwich Hospital.

Jones received the congratulations of his President, Benjamin Franklin and honours from Louis XVI of France. Posterity has remembered him as "Father of the American Navy".

Further to the battle, Hull tightened its defences, especially at the Citadel; and for the duration of hostilities an English naval presence was more conspicuous between the Humber and the Tyne.

The Wold Newton Meteorite

About 3 o'clock on the misty afternoon of 13th December 1795 John Shipley, a farm worker, paused in the field and hearing an unfamiliar whirring sound, looked up and about him. A few moments later there was a tremendous impact nearby and John instinctively flung up his arms to protect his face from flying soil. When he cautiously opened his eyes a huge smouldering hole, five feet across, lay but a few yards away. He had narrowly avoided being hit by a meteorite. "Heaven and earth have come together!' he whispered.

Abandoning his plough, and accompanied by a carpenter and groom who had been occupied some 70 yards distant, John ran to report to his boss, Major Edward Topham. They all went back to investigate and eventually prised out a rock of volcanic appearance measuring some 30 inches across. Realising its importance Topham had it sent for investigation by Sir Joseph Banks, President of the Royal Society. The rock, weighing 56lb, and thought to be some 4.5 billion years old was transferred to the Natural History Museum.

Four years later, on the spot where it landed, adjacent to Wold Cottage Farm south-west of Wold Newton, Major Topham built a brick obelisk commemorating the event. Soldier, playwright, journalist and sportsman, renowned across the Wolds for greyhound breeding and coursing, Topham was an enterprising and popular landlord. Thanks to his initiative, the meteorite remains the oldest to fall in Britain for which a considerable sample is still available for study.

Beware the French

Between 1797 and 1805 there were continuous fears of a possible French landing in Holderness. French vessels hovered around the Humber estuary. A pilot, William Croft, had his boat captured by a French privateer in February 1793, though happily he was released unharmed. In villages like Hornsea and Patrington, wagons stood ready in the market place to evacuate women and children westwards. Housewives were advised to keep bundles of essential clothing immediately to hand. Cattle, too, were to be driven away and in an emergency stackyards were to be burned.

On 14th August 1805 – just before Trafalgar – a warning beacon was accidentally fired near Pontefract and West Riding militias, mistaking this for an invasion signal, poured into the areas around York and Howden. When it became clear that there was no chance of shooting the enemy, the Wessies settled for the hospitality of a number of hostelries east of the Derwent before returning home.

Return of the Swan

Having set sail in March 1836 the Hull whaler "Swan" had become frozen up in the Davis Strait, west of Greenland. Captain Dring's strategy was to ration the food, especially meat and biscuits, and to organise hunting expeditions.

These gave the crew exercise and a sense of purpose. Regular prayer meetings helped to keep up morale.

All whaling ships hoped to be back in Hull for the October Fair, but it was not unusual for a ship to be months late. For families, however, the uncertainty was stressful, with growing fears of scurvy aboard as fruit and vegetables were used up, or of the ship's timbers cracking under pressure from the ice.

By midsummer 1837 Hull had accepted the worst. On Sunday afternoon, 2nd July a memorial service was organised on Dock Green officially to mourn the loss. A collection raised £47 for the bereaved. Just before the first hymn was about to start, a sudden hubbub grew along the dockside as a man came running. Rumour – and hope – were enough. The Swan had been identified in the estuary and was approaching. There was a rush for places and vantage points. Just before 5pm came the first sightings, accompanied by tremendous cheering, and not a few tears. Set up against the foremast was the huge jawbone of a whale. As they emerged on the north side of the Old Dock, the survivors looked thin and exhausted. Twenty-five of their comrades had died including eleven Shetlanders, two from Grimsby and seven from Hull.

So the rejoicings were mixed. One lady, believing herself to be a widow, had just re-married. Suddenly she found herself with a choice of husbands.

The Cholera Outbreak 1849

The three months of cholera in Hull that started in August resulted in the deaths of some 1860 townsfolk, 507 in the second week of September. Seven hundred were buried in a mass grave in the Spring Bank Cemetery. In his "Fifty Years Recollections of Hull" the Rev John Sibree described the cemetery as looking like a ploughed field. On that most dreadful Sunday, 9th September he officiated at 12 burials before lunch and 31 afterwards. From all the approaching streets corteges converged. He portrayed in detail the agony of his visits – the discoloured flesh, the cramps of the near-dying; the victim with doubled-up knees who could not be laid out and for whom a triangular box had to be built. Fear was everywhere. Faithful pastors put themselves severely at risk in ministering to the afflicted. Open air services were conducted in the market place. Hope for deliverance lay only in God.

Dr (later Sir) Henry Cooper and his scientific colleagues pointed to the greatest incidence of mortality in low-lying and poorly drained areas, like the courtyards only a few steps from the High Street: "open ditches with offensive impurities", as the Hull Advertiser had delicately put it (27th July, 1849). There was a desperate need for slum clearance, partially to be recognised in the Kingston upon Hull Improvement Act, 1854; and drastic changes in the conditions of water supply. Parts of Sculcoates were still drawing drinking water from the seriously contaminated River Hull.

"That Uninteresting Town"

Corruption in Parliamentary elections was such that in 1832 Hedon was disfranchised and incorporated into the Holderness constituency. Beverley was no better. Ann Routh's House in Toll Gavel, the Liberal headquarters, provided for voters to enter at the front door to be bribed, and then to be directed to a waiting cab at the back door for the very short journey to Walkergate and the poll.

The hustings were noisy and occasionally violent. Unpleasant missiles were thrown. When the novelist Anthony Trollope contested the election as a Liberal in 1868 he found little to cheer him, and later came to describe Beverley as "that most uninteresting town". Tramping the lanes and mounting the hustings were "the most wretched fortnight" of his life. Refusing to stoop to bribery he polled only 740 votes. Possibly his plight attracted a degree of public sympathy. At the declaration a riot developed, the stage was attacked and all four candidates fled.

Beverley, too, was disfranchised. And it can hardly be doubted that the unseemly proceedings here contributed to the introduction of the Secret Ballot four years later.

The Great Bridlington Storm

Just before dawn on Friday, 10th February 1871 a huge storm gathered on the north-east coast. It rapidly gained in ferocity. Ships that had put out the previous day tried desperately to reach the comparative safety of Bridlington Bay. The two lifeboats, *Harbinger* and *Robert Whitworth* were on full alert.

The *Delta* from Whitby was in peril. Lowered boats were immediately swamped. For a time the captain obstinately clung to the rigging. Even the lifeboat was beaten. The *Harbinger* rowed through mountainous seas, but six of its crew were lost.

Altogether, 70 men were drowned and 30 ships were wrecked. A mass funeral was arranged at the Priory Church. For 120 years, Fishermen's Sunday, earmarked as nearest to the 10th February, was commemorated, with tributes paid at the churchyard memorial.

The Baccarat Affair

This society house party scandal would never have happened had not Edward, Prince of Wales switched his attentions from the hapless Christopher Sykes of Brantinghamthorpe a few miles away, to Tranby Croft at Anlaby the home of Arthur Wilson JP, merchant, shipowner, philanthropist and Master of the Holderness Hunt.

Among the guests travelling to Hull early in September 1890 was a guards officer, Lt. Col. Sir William Gordon Cumming, who knew the Prince well enough to gain admission to the special train. Both were looking forward to a game or two of baccarat after dinner, neither being aware that their host, probably with good reason, had previously banned the game. But Edward loved it well enough to bring his own counters. And when he expressed a wish to play, Wilson, embarrassed, withdrew from the company, leaving his wife Mary in charge.

She and her guests became outraged as the military man systematically cheated, manipulating the counters and adjusting his stakes. During the second evening, 9th September Gordon Cumming was exposed, obliged to sign a document admitting impropriety – and shown the door. He was later cashiered by the army and thereafter ostracised by high society.

Arthur Wilson continued to prosper, becoming High Sheriff of Yorkshire in 1901, the year Edward succeeded to the monarchy.

The Russian Outrage

In 1904 the Hessle Road fishing community found itself at the centre of a nasty international incident. On 22nd October the Russian Baltic Squadron fired on the Hull fishing fleet, somehow mistaking it for the Japanese enemy – in the Dogger Bank area! One trawler, the *Crane* was sunk, its crew managing to scramble into other boats. George Smith, the skipper and William Leggett, third hand, were killed; and Walter Whelpton, skipper of the *Mino* died the following May.

The funeral of the two fishermen on 27th October was the biggest occasion of its kind ever seen in Hull, with the streets lined with mourners all the way from Hessle Road to the Western Cemetery. The nation shared the grief. In London the Russian embassy was stoned and telegrams were exchanged between King Edward VII and his cousin, the Czar Nicholas II. Although a Paris tribunal awarded the sum of £65,000 in compensation, the Russian officers concerned were not punished.

At the junction of Boulevard and Hessle Road, the statue of Captain George

The *St Mino* and crew *(Courtesy of Hull Central Library, Local Studies)*

Smith, unveiled on 30th August 1906, stands proudly looking over the home scene he loved so well.

Captured by a German Sub

On the foggy morning of Saturday, 5th May 1917, off Robin Hood's Bay, the *Edith Cavell*, a Filey herring coble, was intercepted by the German submarine UB21. Skipper George Hunter and his four crew members were taken aboard and obliged to watch explosives set on their vessel. Almost immediately, however, the U-Boat had to dive to avoid a British naval patrol.

The German lieutenant, Franz Walther was sympathetic towards his prisoners and treated them well. He asked the youngest, 14-year-old George, son of the skipper, what he would otherwise have been doing at home on the Sunday. "Sunday school, sir", the lad replied. On this occasion, he didn't quite make it.

Suspected of carrying contraband goods to Scarborough or Hull, a Swedish steamship was bombarded by the Germans, killing five of the crew of nine. The survivors and the five Filey men were transferred to two lifeboats, with adequate provisions, and told to row for England. This was early on the Sunday afternoon. Their position was approximately 80 miles east of Tynemouth, and eventually they beached at Newton on the Northumberland coast. From Newcastle George and his men caught a train back to Filey, where the entire town turned out to welcome them.

There was an intriguing sequel and astonishing coincidence. Years later, Filey's celebrated "Walking Parson", Canon A.N. Cooper came across Franz Walther, now a lay pastor in a German church. Reminiscences were exchanged, and later George Hunter was pleased to receive greetings from his former captor. George died in 1952 at the age of 77.

The Hull Blitz

Zeppelin raids in 1915 and 1916 had demonstrated Hull's vulnerability to aerial attack, although the actual damage was relatively minor. During the Second World War, however, the River Humber was a huge natural landmark, leading to inland cities and other objectives. Hull itself was a prime target, referred to obliquely in deliberately bland news reports as "a town on the north-east coast". The docks and central areas suffered colossal damage, the high point being 7/8th May 1941. The statistics are chilling – 800 alerts; 82 raids; 1,200 people killed and over 3,000 injured; only 5,945 houses out of 86,715 within the city boundaries escaped damage or worse. Over 152,000 citizens were made homeless. Whole streets were reduced to rubble. Renowned shops like Hammonds were devastated. Factories and the railways were hit time and again. Among the buildings of architectural distinction lost was the Royal Institution (Cuthbert Brodrick, 1853/54) on Albion Street, blasted on 24th June 1943. Amidst all the stoicism and pride in "taking it", the sober boast was "No ship from this port ever missed the tide".

Chapter 2

People

"King Beyond the Humber"

William le Gros was an apt name for the corpulent Lord of Holderness. A religious man, he had once vowed to make a pilgrimage to Jerusalem, but on gaining too much weight to mount his horse, asked to be set free from this undertaking in return for founding a number of religious houses. Of these the most important was the Cistercian Abbey of Meaux in 1151, which became renowned for its pioneering of land drainage and sheep farming, sending prodigious amounts of wool to Flanders. He was instrumental also in creating the port of Hedon. During his regular Channel crossings William derived comfort from thinking of all the prayers being offered for his safety by the monks owing him allegiance.

When necessary, William was capable of decisive action. William Fossard, a young adventurer indebted to the Jews of York, had the temerity to seduce le Gros's sister – and fearful of many possible consequences, prudently fled. Furious, le Gros pulled down the young man's castle of Mountferrant near Birdsall, and had the timber removed to Meaux.

At his death at the age of about 64, William le Gros was buried in the sister foundation of Thornton Abbey, just south of the Humber.

Statue to a Moneylender

William de la Pole, merchant of Ravenser and Hull, lent vast sums to Edward III for his French wars, and in turn received many titles and honours. Following a royal charter (1331) giving the burgesses of Hull the right to elect a mayor and four bailiffs, de la Pole held mayoral office for the next four years. He also became Baron of the Exchequer, Lord of Myton and Holderness and gained a knighthood: at a price.

A less agreeable task was negotiating with the royal creditors, like the Bardi and Peruzzi of Florence. When the king lost

Sir William de la Pole, Corporation Pier, Hull *(H. Peach)*

face, de la Pole was consigned to the Tower for 18 months, and his assets temporarily seized. Twelve years later (1354), as a result of another tiff, he spent three months in the Fleet prison. Eventual pardon and release restored him to his estates, wealth and prestige.

Thus, William de la Pole was possibly the earliest example of a merchant becoming a peer of the realm. In national and international affairs his was a persuasive voice. He died in 1366 at about 74 years of age, his reputed resting place being the Carthusian Priory of Hull.

Best Farming Practice

Henry Best (c1590-1645) was that rare combination – a practical farmer who pioneered new ideas which he then outlined for posterity in "Farming and Memorandum Books" – a prime source for students of agrarian life of the 17th century.

Not for him the open fields; enclosed land allowed experiment and could be let at a profit. Apart from his estate at Elmswell, where the Old Hall dates from about 1634, he rented pastures at Sledmere, Thixendale, Huggate and Cottam. He worked for specialisation with diversity, which amounted to trial approaches with sheep and cereals. Sheep were worth persisting with, although at Pocklington he had known four lambs sold for 11d... and then the seller handed the buyer a penny back!

Sheep husbandry, markets, corn, barley, thatching, bee keeping – Henry Best's advice covered them all. His practical tips included a prescription of scummed urine, with aniseeds and butter beaten in, given lukewarm for a horse to drink in order to dry up mouth sores and swellings.

Success in housekeeping depended on the unremitting efforts of shrewdly hired labour. Farm workers should be encouraged to live in so as to maximise their toil. Employers should never be too trusting, and valuables should be kept under lock and key. In that politically incorrect era there were no qualms about paying and feeding women less well. Vision, detail and supervision might well have been his watchwords. No wonder his pronouncements have impressed subsequent generations of hard-headed Yorkshiremen!

Marvell by Name

Born in Winestead Rectory in 1621, Andrew Marvell was a pupil at Hull Grammar School before entering Trinity College, Cambridge at the age of 12. As a poet he was an immortal phrase-maker. One thinks immediately of "Time's wingèd chariot" in 'To his coy mistress'; and the courage and dignity of King Charles I at his execution –

> "He nothing common did or mean
> Upon that memorable scene".

His private pupils included Mary Fairfax, daughter of the Parliamentary commander in the Civil War, and William Dutton, a ward of Oliver Cromwell. A short spell in the diplomatic service as Latin Secretary prepared him for a distinguished career as MP for Hull from 1659 until his death on 16th August

Andrew Marvell

1678. Conscientious and incorruptible in that Restoration period of political cynicism and licentiousness, Marvell's moral stance never wavered. He made it clear that he was no time server or tool of government. He was there to serve his constituents.

His statue (by W.D. Keyworth) has stood in five different sites in Hull; and in 1999 was appropriately installed in front of his old Grammar School. He is portrayed as steadfastly refusing a bribe at a time of considerable personal difficulty.

Premier so Nearly

Seven times elected MP for Hedon, William Pulteney (1684-1764) was well placed in opposition to Sir Robert Walpole when that first Whig prime minister resigned in 1742. And it was to Pulteney that George II turned, so that for a few days (8th-11th March) he was technically chief minister. Not for the last time in the making of premiers, however, there were intrigues, manoeuvrings and sub-plots, so that initial support fell away, and the poor man was unable to form an administration. Members rallied instead around Carteret, but the final choice was Spencer Compton, Earl of Wilmington.

Pulteney was left with such titular consolations as Baron Hedon, Earl of Bath and Viscount Pulteney. Burial in Westminster Abbey acknowledged his eminence. And there are reminders in Pulteney Bridge at Bath, and Great Pulteney Street in London.

Generals from America

It is curious that two senior officers who had fought in North America during the second half of the 18th century should in retirement have come to the East Riding. Ralph Burton was, indeed, a Cottingham man, born in 1725, who became a hardened campaigner, serving as a major-general and Wolfe's second-in-command at the siege of Quebec in 1759. Returning to his roots, he lived at Hull Bank House (now Haworth Hall), serving as MP for Wareham and dying at Scarborough, where he is buried, at the early age of 43.

By contrast, Brigadier-General Oliver de Lancey, though born in New York, nevertheless fought for Britain in the War of Independence (1776-83), raising three regiments. Seeking asylum, he bought 25, Highgate, Beverley but unfortunately died within the year (1785), aged 69. A plaque to his achievements may be found in the north transept of the Minster where he is buried.

The Yorkshire Giant

At birth, on 10th February 1787, William Bradley weighed 14lb. His parents,

William Bradley

John and Ann, were but of average size, as were their first three children and their later nine. And William continued to grow. Aged 11, he was a six footer weighing 11 stone. At 19 he had grown to 27 stone and a height of 7 feet 9 inches, thereby becoming England's tallest man.

In his native Market Weighton, Will was a popular and amiable young man who readily attracted attention. From appearing at local fairs and exhibitions he moved on to the October Hull Fair, to Sheffield, Leeds and in due course London, where King George III presented him with a gold chain. A fine bow-tied shirt, colourful waistcoat, long black frock coat and a tall top hat made him an awesome spectacle. His shoes, finely made, were 15 inches long and over 5 inches behind the toes.

But by the age of 30 he was weary of travel and adulation, and returned to his roots. As walking became difficult he resorted to a stick; and his retirement proved all too brief, for he died on 30th May 1820. At first his enormous coffin was laid to rest in the churchyard, but fears of body snatching prompted second thoughts, and he was speedily re-interred inside the parish church.

Beloved Physician

Granted that medical fathers and sons are not uncommon: but was any town ever so fortunate as to be served by the Aldersons? John Alderson (1757-1829) was honorary physician at the Royal Infirmary, then on King Edward Street, from 1792 until his death. He was specially remembered for vaccinating the poor against small pox for nothing. Sadly, five of his own children died very young. James, however, prospered and became a national celebrity (See Chapter 13 – the Moby Dick dissection).

A Clerical Oddity

Perpetual curate at St Oswald's, Filey from 1809 until 1833, the Rev. Evan Williams was an eccentric. He allowed no female across his threshold. He himself often preferred to enter via an open window. His relationship with the milkman must have been unique. Instead of greeting him at the door, Evan lowered a rope from his bedroom window, allowed a vessel to be filled, then hauled it painstakingly up the wall.

Freedom Fighter's Wife

Daughter of a Market Weighton innkeeper, Sarah Andrews (1774-1847) set her mind on wider horizons. During her travels she met and married Francesco de Miranda, the Venezuelan freedom fighter who died in a Spanish prison in 1816. Although she found the excitements that she could never have dreamed of around the Yorkshire Wolds, she wound up as a pauper in London. In 1981 a polished slate plaque to her memory was unveiled by the Venezuelan ambassador in All Saints Church, Market Weighton where Sarah had been baptised on 24ᵗʰ July 1774.

A Yorkshire Wonder

Dressed characteristically in his frilled shirt, breeches, high boots and frock coat, Sir Tatton Sykes (1772-1863), fourth baronet of Sledmere, was described by a contemporary as one of the three sights of Yorkshire, the other two being York Minster and Fountains Abbey.

Rising daily at 5.30, and after a cold water wash and shave, Sir Tatton walked up and down his former library for a while before breakfasting on apple pie and milk. Most of his father's considerable library he had sold off. Books played no significant part in his life. He was an outdoors man, a tremendous walker. On one occasion he conducted a flock of Leicester ewes, bought at Lincoln, up to Barton ferry. He was also a renowned pugilist, capable of putting to flight two drovers who mocked him in a pub. Even as an 80-year-old he turned out of a Doncaster theatre box a man who insisted on smoking in the presence of ladies.

But above all he was a horseman. One of his rare boasts was that he had seen 74 consecutive St Legers. In 1817 he rode to Aberdeen to act as jockey for Lord Huntley in the Welter Stakes which he won. He hated carriages and was unenthusiastic about railways, even proceeding on horseback to London to have his portrait painted.

Sir Tatton also loved his dogs. Noticing that the grass grew better where they had buried their bones led him to propagate the benefits of bonemeal fertiliser.

Most aspects of farming drew his active attention. He liked to indulge in spells of hedge cutting, ditch clearing or stone breaking. In recognition of the immense pioneering contribution to the fertility of the Wolds made by his father, Sir Christopher Sykes, Sir Tatton built the Rotunda Well, an open circular temple, by the roadside in the middle of the village.

Lees happy were his family relationships. His six daughters and two sons were required to live spartan domestic routines, including cold baths and simple food. Once he beat young Tatton for having acquired a tooth brush. Amongst his immediate kin Sir Tatton seemed to inspire little warmth or emotion.

But the rest of Yorkshire venerated him. After his death a huge monument was raised to his memory on Garton Hill, with ready contributions from his

Sledmere tenants who, it was said, "loved him as a friend and honoured him as a landlord".

Tatton II

Sir Tatton the younger (1826-1913) re-acted strongly against his overbearing father. Indeed, the fifth baronet re-acted against a good deal. He hated flowers, urging his tenants to grow cauliflowers instead. He detested neighbourly gossip; tenants were instructed to keep their front doors bolted.

He destroyed his mother's orangery. A hypochondriac, he wore in winter layers of overcoats, which he gradually shed, rewarding local children who returned them. Excessively fond of milk puddings, on hearing of the catastrophic fire that reduced Sledmere House on 23rd May 1911, his first words were to his cook in York, "First let me finish my pudding".

Whereas his father had held London society in some contempt, young Tatton spent much time there. So did his wife, Jessica – though increasingly they travelled apart.

Yet in two important respects the second Sir Tatton built on his father's interests. Racehorses, curiously, were one, except that he sold the original stud, apart from one mare, Wensleydale. He invested in quality rather than quantity, producing many classic winners, "Doncaster" winning the Derby in 1873; 'Mimi' the Oaks, 1891; "Disraeli" the Two Thousand Guineas, 1898; and "Spearmint" the Derby, 1906.

The second inherited passion was for restoring local churches. Seventeen, including Sledmere, were either restored or rebuilt, and these, together with the elegant Eleanor Monument (see Chapter 3) are his permanent memorials.

The Gull's Friend

Christopher Sykes (1831-98), younger brother of Tatton II, also sought London high society, enabled so to do through successive periods as MP for Beverley (1865-68), for the East Riding (1868-85), and for Buckrose (1885-92). Long service, but hardly distinguished: Hansard credits him with three questions and six speeches. But he generated some enthusiasm on the plundering of sea birds and supported a Bill for their protection.

As the squire of Brantinghamthorpe Hall, Christopher was visited, and increasingly exploited, by Edward, Prince of Wales, especially during Doncaster Race Week. HRH repaid obsequiousness with gross personal insults, like pouring brandy over his head, or burning him with a cigar. But always the

Christopher Sykes *(Courtesy of Hull Central Library, Local Studies)*

reply was "As your Royal Highness pleases" ... so the bully laughingly came back for more. Crippled by debts, Christopher was forced to sell his home, obliging his tormentor to look elsewhere for diversions. Fortunately, his sister-in-law Jessica intervened with the Prince, and some modest restoration was made.

The Railway King

The story of George Hudson is the meteoric rise – and fall – of an unusually determined, self-made, self-ruined Yorkshireman. Born into a farming family at Howsham in 1800, he was apprenticed to a York draper; and like many a young man on the make, thoughtfully wed the boss's daughter, Elizabeth Nicholson. Soon afterwards in 1827 the death of an uncle brought him the tidy windfall of thirty thousand pounds.

As their business prospered, George and Elizabeth moved into a large house in Monkgate. Drive and resolve made him a dominant Tory, and in 1837 he became Lord Mayor of York. A network of business contacts helped him confidently to launch the Yorkshire Union Bank.

With the dawning of the Railway Age, Hudson began to visualise the city as the communications capital of the north, with himself at the operational centre. Exploratory talks were held with the celebrated engineer, George Stephenson – and in May 1839 the York and North Midland Railway was opened. By 1844 Hudson's was the controlling voice north of the Trent, presiding over a thousand miles of track and related rolling stock.

The following year he notched up another considerable asset – Londesborough, from the Duke of Devonshire for the sum of £470,000, a location crucial to his plans for the Market Weighton – Beverley link with York. He had his own private station leading down to Shiptonthorpe. Becoming MP for Sunderland bestowed yet another cachet and business stepping stone.

George Hudson was now at the height of his powers. He felt able to speculate and juggle with the enormous funds at his disposal, like £40,000 diverted from the York and North Midland to assist the early days of the Malton and Driffield line. Unfortunately he failed to confide in his fellow directors. Rumours circulated and doubts grew. Leading journals ran articles. He was lampooned in "Punch".

Creditors clamoured and Hudson's health faltered. In April 1848 angina was diagnosed. He fled to Paris, a ruined man. His portrait was withdrawn from the Mansion House, and his statue was dismantled.

The support of some old friends enabled him to make periodic visits to Yorkshire, especially Whitby. When he died in 1871 his coffin was brought back to York on the Midland line. He was buried in the family grave at Scrayingham, only a mile or two from his birthplace. On the centenary of his death "George Hudson Street" was renamed in the city of York. Whether he can be further rehabilitated remains uncertain.

The Clod Crusher

Born in 1799 to a shopkeeping family in Butcher Row, Beverley, William Crosskill had an early incentive to get on; his father died when this eldest of seven was but 12 years old. His talent lay in manufacturing iron artefacts. A few of his lamp standards, c1827 remain in the area of the Minster.

Diversifying his approach to public utilities, Crosskill by 1844 was helping to provide Hamburg with gas street lighting. Four years later he had become Mayor of Beverley. His iron foundry off Mill Lane prospered in the production of a variety of agricultural machines. Threshing equipment was exported to Germany. Experiments with a clod crusher – a disc harrow with side teeth – in a field at Eppleworth caught the imagination of the farming world, earning the inventor the Gold Medal of the Royal Agricultural Society, followed by a place at the Great Exhibition in 1851. A steam cultivator also did well; but less popular was the "farm railway" with movable rails and a turntable, intended as an adjunct to wagons and rullies.

Crosskill's Clod Crusher *(Courtesy of Rural History Centre, University of Reading)*

By the late fifties the enterprise was experiencing cash flow problems. Crosskill had too many serious competitors. Retiring to Walkergate House, he left the business to his sons, Alfred and Edmund. He died at Putney in 1888.

Our sub-title is not intended as a fair judgement of William Crosskill. Here was a talented and imaginative entrepreneur who at his peak provided local employment for 800 people. His was an honoured and nationally respected name. He well deserves to be remembered as the Father of the East Riding's Mechanised Farming.

A Bankrupted Philanthropist

Here was yet another local business man whose fall was dramatic. Hull owes Pearson Park to the philanthropy of Zachariah Pearson (1821-1891), a once prosperous ship-owner. His People's Park was opened on 27th August 1860 with colourful ceremony and thousands of spectators. As a Methodist he insisted that the Lord's Day should always be observed, and the bowling greens remain closed on Sundays.

External affairs were the ruin of Pearson. During the American Civil War (1861-65) he tried to run his fleet through President Lincoln's federal blockade. But his vessels were captured and he was forced into bankruptcy, resigning as mayor in October 1862. Thereafter he was driven to obtain a modest income as a ship's surveyor, and living on the edge of the fine park that he had so recently created.

Snatcher Jackson

Living in Market Weighton in Victorian times, Snatcher had exceedingly long arms. He could touch his toes without bending, and reputedly could reach sacks placed at the front of carts by simply leaning forward.

Fast Hitter

John Thomas Brown, son of a Driffield licensee, born on 20th August, 1869 was probably East Yorkshire's most successful cricketer. It is said that as a boy he practised for hours with a pile of tins for a wicket and a length of wood for a bat. Between 1889 and 1904, the year of his death, he played in 346 county matches, scoring 16,380 runs at an average of 29.3. His 25 hundreds included 311 against Sussex in 1897, followed the next season by an opening partnership with John Tunnicliffe of 554 against Essex. Appearing in eight test matches he scored 470 runs. In 1894/5 he enjoyed an especially gratifying Australian tour, scoring four centuries and topping the averages. At Melbourne he hit 140, the first 50 in 28 minutes, a rare record. His performance materially helped to ensure the Ashes returned to England. Back in Driffield hundreds of supporters subscribed to mark his international triumphs by presenting him with a silver tea service.

Jack was a small. thick-set man, flamboyant and often outspoken. He was blessed with a practical sense of humour, combined with an above-average thirst. During one minor game, keen to visit the refreshment tent, he persuaded a spectator to take his place in the field, but the sub missed an easy catch. Later, however, Jack turned teetotal, publicly emptying his beer supply down the sink.

His benefit at Headingly in 1901 made £2,282, a record at the time. His last game, like his first, was played against Leicestershire. Just three months later he died through a heart condition, despite treatment from the royal physician.

Pygmies at Brandesburton

During his travels in the Iturii Forest (now in Zaire) Colonel James Harrison decided to bring six native pygmies back to Brandesburton Hall. But before reaching their destination in July 1905 they had been inspected by the Foreign Office, Westminster MPs and members of the Royal Family at a Buckingham Palace garden party. They were soon to be exhibited at the Hull

Pygmy visitors, 1906
(Courtesy of Dr J.E.S. Walker)

Palace and Tivoli theatres, and a continental tour followed in the spring of 1906.

None of the four men and two women stood taller than 53 inches. Living in the grounds at Brandesburton they were well looked after but needed careful supervision. They liked shooting rabbits, using their own arrows tipped with nail clinchings provided by the local blacksmith. They aroused a high degree of curiosity and were great favourites wherever they went. Their tribal dances were greatly enjoyed.

This compact little group stayed longer than the two years agreed by the colonel with King Leopold, partly due to Harrison's embarrassment in funding the return trip. What they made of European civilisation is uncertain, but re-adjustments had to be made immediately on the return to the Forest. Bokane's brother, thinking him dead, had assumed the chieftainship – as well as Bokane's wife, positions which were, fortunately, soon amicably reversed.

She turned down Winston

A noteworthy feature of the 1900 "Khaki Election" was the support given to the Tory winner of Holderness by that young man of destiny, Winston Churchill. Arthur Stanley Wilson, (generally known as Jack), the well-favoured son of Arthur and Mary Wilson of Tranby Croft was also brother of the society beauty, Muriel. .. so Winston's interest was not narrowly political. In 1906 he proposed to her, and although she refused they kept in platonic touch for some years. When Churchill eventually married Clementine Hozier, Muriel wrote him a letter of congratulation.

Not Lord Warter

Charles Henry Wilson (1833-1907), eighth son of Thomas Wilson of Hull was born to worldly advantage; and towards the end of his life he had built up a fleet of 99 vessels – the largest privately owned shipping company in the world – the Wilson line.

On becoming Liberal MP for Hull in 1874 he had the largest majority in England. A popular representative, he held office for thirty years. The reward of a peerage came in 1906. What was to be his title? As owner of Warter Priory "Lord Warter" might have been the obvious choice, except for the awkwardness of that family business on the high seas. But the delightful Wolds village of Nunburnholme was just down the road, and "Lord Nunburnholme" had a dignified unambiguous gravitas.

Rose Carr

Here was a redoubtable character, born at North Frodingham in 1843 and remaining a legendary figure long after her death in 1913. She earned a living as a carrier based in Newbegin, Hornsea. In her younger days Rose was partial to a drink or two and at times drove recklessly. As an occasional horse dealer she knew every trick and dodge. She was immensely strong, and it was said that she could carry a sixteen stone sack of grain under either arm. Few people attempted to argue with Rose. A Hull City footballer discovered this truth when he spoke out of turn and she held him down in a horse trough. Profane persons risked having their heads banged together. A soldier who insulted her suffered a crushed hand.

Yet Rose became a passionate Primitive Methodist preacher, illiterate though she was. Listening to her extempore delivery, while cowed by her challenging gaze, must have been a singular religious experience. She weighed, and looked, 19 stone. The left side of her face was paralysed, possibly due to a kick from a horse. Neither doctor nor undertaker disclosed whether she was really a man.

Rose with her carrier's cart somewhere in Holderness *(Courtesy of Hull Central Library, Local Studies)*

Lord A-leaping

The ninth baronet of Boynton, Sir Walter Strickland (1851-1938) practised most of his eccentricities in distant lands, like Czechoslovakia, of which he became a citizen in the 1920s. But he returned to the ancestral Hall in 1909 for the funeral of his father, Charles. At the end of the service he lined up all the servants and leapfrogged agilely over the row of backs. After thanking them all he dusted himself down and departed. He died, without offspring, in Java.

Horse Whip

Thomas David Fenby never forgot his first trade, that of blacksmith. From serving also as a county magistrate and several times as mayor of Bridlington, he became Liberal MP for East Bradford in 1924, and was promoted to party whip two years later. But whenever his duties allowed, he liked to return to the firm of G.W. Fenby & Sons at 40 St John's Street in order to shoe horses or repair farm machinery.

Aircraftsman Shaw T. E.

A few years later there were still stranger doings in Bridlington. A/C Shaw was older than his comrades. No-one seemed to censure him for not saying "Sir". He dealt easily with officers who regularly visited him at 1104 Marine Craft Unit, Gummers Landing during those weeks between November 1934 and February 1935 when he was entrusted with designing special naval craft. In his spare time he often hared down the coast road on his Brough Superior motor bike to call on his friend Wing Commander Simms at the White Cottage, Hornsea.

In this case, truth really was stranger than fiction. This airman with the piercing blue eyes and scholarly attitude was the fabled Lawrence of Arabia, ex-British Army colonel who now sought a kind of anonymity as an extraordinary lowest ranker. Classical scholar, linguist, Middle East specialist, soldier, desert fighter, mystic, writer – here, arguably, was one of the most versatile and gifted men of the century. This was his second spell in Bridlington. He had spent a few weeks there during the summer of 1932. Alderman Harker, later recalled that as mayor he had been ferried across the harbour without realising the identity of his illustrious guide.

Only a few months after leaving Gummers Wharf and the RAF, Lawrence was killed in a motor cycle accident near his home in Dorset. The little church of St Nicholas at Moreton was crowded with many celebrities from the political, military and artistic worlds. Winston Churchill wept at the graveside.

The Walking Parson

After a brief curacy at Chester-le-Street, Arthur Neville Cooper moved to Filey where he served as Vicar of St Oswald's for 55 years (1880-1935). He was an immensely industrious and accessible priest, raising money for bereaved fishing families, other widows, the renovation of schools and myriad good causes. But he was also an indefatigable walker, often averaging 30 miles a day. His books, like "With Knapsack and Notebook" teemed with anecdotes,

Canon Cooper *(Courtesy of Filey Town Council Archives Service)*

customs, people, a breezy cheerfulness and a sometimes surprising frankness.

On one occasion in Hamelin he got soaked during a storm, and back in his lodgings had to borrow a skirt from his landlady.

On this occasion he could be forgiven for dispensing with his customary cold evening bath. His remedy for keeping his boots dry and his feet free from sores was to smear them with whisky – or so he said. If so, like faith it worked!

The memorial plaque in the Church sanctuary seems most apt – "They that wait upon the Lord shall renew their strength. They shall walk and not faint". Canon Cooper died on 20th August 1943 at the age of 93.

Wonderful Amy

Amy Johnson, airwoman magnificent and subject of the musical "Amy" (by Gilbert and Nicholls) was born at 154 St George's Street, Hull on 1st July 1903. After schooling at Boulevard and Sheffield University she moved south, joining the London Flying Club, and quickly gaining both her pilot's licence and an engineer's ticket. Supported by Lord Wakefield she planned carefully her epic solo flight to Australia, setting off on 5th May 1930 and touching down at Darwin 19 days later. Her primitive Gypsy Moth, fitted with long range tanks, had been bought for £600 only a fortnight previously. She flew without the benefit of radio navigation, and was assisted en route only by basic ground services.

Other record-breaking flights were later undertaken, including to the Cape, South Africa, 1936. Amy died on 5th January 1941 when her RAF Airspeed Oxford ditched into the Thames estuary. An informative collection of memorabilia is on permanent display at Sewerby Hall.

Amy Johnson at Hedon Airfield, 1930 *(Courtesy of E. Winkler)*

Madame Clapham

Emily Clapham (nee McVitie) was born in Cheltenham in 1856, and after setting up a salon in Hull's fashionable Kingston Square in 1887, soon prospered as a society dressmaker. Her designs based on London and Paris attracted the patronage of the daughters of Charles Henry Wilson of the famous shipping line, and of Queen Maud of Norway. From 1901 the title of "Court Dressmaker" appeared in her promotional literature.

Madame Clapham *(Courtesy of Hull Museums)*

Madame Clapham, a dominant lady, enjoyed the high life, regularly visiting York, Harrogate and London. An exacting and meticulous showperson, she displayed every concern for social etiquette. Bills, for example, sordid necessities, were always sent to husbands!

But behind the scenes there were a few surprises. Floorboards were clean, walls were regularly whitewashed and conditions for the workforce were spartan. No overtime was paid to compensate for peremptory demands. Under-age employees were sometimes tucked away in wardrobes in order to avoid spot checks by visiting inspectors.

These circumstances brought much merry irreverence from the girls. Stout ladies were later ridiculed with the chanting of phrases like "Once around the waist, twice around the Hyde Park ..."

During the 1920s a slow decline began, though many older clients remained loyal. After Madame Clapham died in 1952, her niece kept a reduced business going until 1967. For an older generation of East Yorkshire ladies, certain glamorous memories linger; and who can say what sartorial elegances their great-grand-daughters may one day shake out from dusty attic boxes?

Chapter 3

Buildings and Artefacts

Decorative Blackbirds

A first-floor ante-room of Beverley's 13th century Dominican Friary revealed in 1992 some unusual murals that may pre-date the Reformation. Set among tree branches are blackbirds, doubtless meant to represent the Black Friars. While the fruit-bearing tri-lobed twigs suggest the harvest of the Trinity, some branches appear to be decked with devils' tails.

Hull Citadel

A small Bartizan watchtower on the Victoria Dock Estate is all that remains of a huge triangular fortification built immediately to the east of the confluence of the Rivers Hull and Humber. The origins lay in two blockhouses and a castle built in 1542 on the orders of Henry VIII. A new citadel, with moat, was

completed in 1685, designed by Martin Beckman, the Swedish Master of Artillery to Charles II. In the preceding 20 years there had been intermittent war with the Dutch; but, most ironically, within three years of the Citadel's re-building, William of Orange had become King of England.

The Citadel was used as a barracks and arsenal and in Napoleonic times accommodated French prisoners of war. They seem to have been comparatively well treated, being allowed to carve ships from cookhouse bones. This was in contrast to the fate of Elizabethan prisoners, especially religious recusants, who suffered appalling cruelties, including neglect at springtime floods.

The military interest was withdrawn in 1848, and the site was cleared for the building of a timber yard and ship-building docks.

Bartizan watchtower, Victoria Dock Estate, Hull
(H. Peach)

King Billy

This equestrian statue of King William III was created by the Dutch sculptor, Peter Scheemaker and funded by public subscription, originally £893. Costumed as a Roman emperor, William was given neither spurs nor stirrups. A myth long since dispelled was that Scheemaker had been so ashamed of forgetting these details that he had drowned himself in the Humber. In fact he made 90 years, dying in 1781. Interestingly, though, the king himself died as a result of falling from his horse while preparing to do battle with the French. Mounted in the old market place behind Holy Trinity Church, the statue was unveiled on 4th December 1734, the 46th anniversary of Town Taking Day (See Chapter 1).

So "King Billy" was "Our Great Deliverer" from Roman Catholic ambitions. Successive generations have continued to esteem him, even if to some farmers in the market place he was sometimes "nobbut Gowden 'Oss".

Another myth has claimed that when the church bells ring at noon, Billy dismounts and proceeds to a very adjacent hostelry – or to the toilets built just below – something of a Hull tradition with regal statues. In Victorian times these subterranean premises were sumptuously maintained, with uniformed attendants distributing soap and towels, as if rehearsing for a first royal visitor.

A Memorable Guy

Not every Member of Parliament bequeaths a building to his constituents. At Hedon, however, the town hall, built in 1692 was presented to the borough by Henry Guy (1631-1710) whose coat-of-arms is set above the doorway. He served as MP eight times between 1669 and 1705, although he did time in the Tower of London for some financial irregularities. The Great Mace (1669) was also his gift; and the original weather vane bearing his initials "HG 1692" is displayed on the staircase wall.

Hedon Town Hall *(H. Peach)*

A Barbarous Relic

Cemented into the surrounding wall at the eastern end of Kilham Church is an iron ring that was once used for bullbaiting. Setting dogs onto a tethered bull was once considered a sport, and centuries ago it was illegal not to bait bulls for their meat whose taste was thought to be enhanced. At Hornsea contests took place after the December fair – and here again, right outside the church. Bull-baiting was not formally abolished until 1835.

Look-Out, Look-Out!

Near the Holderness coast are two unusual buildings erected to serve as look-out posts. Based on the Temple of the Four Winds at Athens, the exposed Carnaby Temple was built c1770 by John Carr for the fifth baronet of Boynton Hall, Sir George Strickland who enjoyed looking towards Bridlington. During the Second World War it was brought back into use as a military observation post.

Further down the coast at Hilston, retired admiral, John Storr, son of a Hedon magistrate had this brick tower built on a mound (c1750) so that he could watch passing ships. As a prominent landmark, it has been a useful aid to navigation.

Lighthouse Country

Flamborough has two. Built by Sir John Clayton in 1674, the old Beacon Tower, now surrounded by a golf course, is an octagonal limestone structure. It was intended that coal fires should be lit at the top – but it is uncertain whether this ever happened. During the 19th century it was in use as a marine telegraph station.

By the cliff top stands its replacement, constructed without scaffolding and in only nine months of 1806 by John Matson, an enterprising local man who in earlier days had been press-ganged, seen military service in India, and survived a shipwreck on the way home. Its original white flares were later superseded by a powerful light that carried for over 20 miles.

Withernsea has a street lighthouse, England's tallest at 127 feet, and with 144 steps leading to the lamp room. It was the work of Robert Drewery in 1894, last coxswain of the offshore lifeboat, and grandfather of Kay Campbell, the famous actress. An exhibition of her life is permanently displayed

Matson's lighthouse *(H. Peach)*

in the lighthouse which, since closure in 1976, has been converted into a museum.

Near Spurn Head the 120 foot High Lighthouse, designed by Thomas Matthews, dates from 1895, replacing John Smeaton's tower of 1776. Oil-lit until 1941, it stayed in service up to 1985. The older stump (1852) of the Low Lighthouse lies opposite on the western shore. Over the centuries many temporary lights have been swept away by sea and storm, generally to be replaced by others on the less exposed western side. At Paull, on the Humber estuary, a lighthouse built in 1836 for Hull Trinity House is now a private dwelling.

Gothic Gatehouse

Set off in woodland near Garton, this turreted embattled grey-bricked gatehouse comes as a surprise to many visitors. It was designed by the Hull architect John Earle in 1812, no doubt as an eyecatcher for Grimston Garth, a most unusual triangular residence created (1781-86) by John Carr for Thomas Grimston of Kilnwick on the Wolds. The gatehouse stands on the western edge of landscaped parkland, inspired by Thomas White. Thus, in this quiet corner of Holderness, some of the great names around the turn of the 18th century combined to produce distinctive Gothic architecture as permanent innovative features.

A Two-Castle Village

Cottingham may well be unique in claiming two castles: though the term "castle" needs some inspection. In the usual historical sense of fortress, Baynard's Castle, located between Northgate and Hallgate, approximated to the medieval type, built during the second half of the 12th century by William de Stuteville, and later occupied by the Bigods and de Wakes. Although there was a moated mound, and presumably a fortified superstructure, it seems not to have lasted long. It was important enough to receive royal visitors. In 1298 Edward I spent Christmas as guest of Lord John de Wake. A gatehouse was rebuilt about 1500. So there was waxing and waning in the castle's fortunes. John Leland in 1538 dismissed it as ruined – "dobell diked and moted ... of which nothing now remaynith". One mysterious aspect has remained: who was Baynard?

"Cottingham Castle", so called, was different. Built by a Hull banker, Thomas Thompson, it was an ostentatious, castellated mansion, sporting white-bricked towers, situated at the west end of the village from 1815. Here was Thompson's principal residence until his death in 1828. The building was destroyed by fire in May 1861. The only surviving part is a tower folly near the Beverley Road roundabout. Since 1916 the site has been used for the progressive development of Castle Hill Hospital.

Sundial Village

Celebrated for its sundials is the village of Seaton Ross. Two have 12-foot diameters: the first, on Sundial Cottage in the middle of the village; the other is the centrepiece on Dial Hall Farm once the home of the sundial specialist, William Watson (1784-1857). They were constructed about 1840. Watson wanted to convey to his young workers that punctuality mattered hugely, especially first thing in the morning when reporting for work. A small sundial, signed by Watson and dated 1825 is above the door of St Edmund's Church. His epitaph near the church-yard gates reads –

> "At this church I so often with pleasure did call
> That I made a sundial upon the church wall".

Watson was also a professional surveyor who drew up detailed street plans of Market Weighton (1848) and Pocklington (1855), indicating occupants and occupations.

Sundial Cottage, Seaton Ross *(H. Peach)*

Rotunda Well

Opposite the Lodge gates where Sledmere's Main Street dips into a hollow, this roadside open temple, with eight supporting Tuscan columns, was erected in 1840 by the fourth baronet, Sir Tatton Sykes (1772-1863). As a memorial to the patron's father, Sir Christopher Sykes (1749-1801) it was designed by Joseph Buckley of York. An inscribed frieze recalls this pioneer's astonishing achievements in physically re-locating the village, enclosing, landscaping, building and tree-planting, thereby changing "a bleak and barren tract of country to become one of the most productive and best cultivated districts in the County of York".

Perhaps Sir Tatton's contempt for his heirs, Tatton and Christopher (see Chapter 2) whose interests lay elsewhere, can be better understood when set against the love of the outdoors, farming and sport which he had shared with his own father.

Sledmere's Rotunda Well *(H. Peach)*

Bettison's Folly

William Bettison, – a Hull brewer and newspaper proprietor, was an exacting employer of predictable habits. One of these was his fondness for dining immediately he stepped out of his carriage and into Newbegin House, Hornsea. Accordingly, he had this tower erected in his garden so that a servant could vigilantly keep his eyes trained on Southorpe Hill, above the Mere, and duly warn the well-trained kitchen staff of the master's approach.

Bettison was not universally popular. A neighbour's sailor son, home on leave, one night mounted a placard inscribed "Bettison's Folly", an apt description retained by posterity.

An unusual feature is the "treacle bricks', locally over-baked. Apparently the tower, costing £500 in 1844, was not fully paid for, as Bettison ran into embarrassing cash-flow problems. The folly is maintained by the Hornsea Civic Society which raises the flag of St George on 23rd April and on New Year's Day.

Spurn Cobbles

A characteristic feature of many Holderness churches (Skeffling, Long Riston, Tunstall) these rounded boulders have been put to considerable building use and road repair. In 1735 the Court of Sewers, fearing additional erosion at Spurn, expressed concern at the theft of cobbles sent as far away as Gainsborough and even Boston in Lincolnshire. There were, of course, many legal purchases. Fifteen years later the Constable family (Lords of Holderness) received the sum of £12 for 240 tons used in the construction of Westminster Bridge.

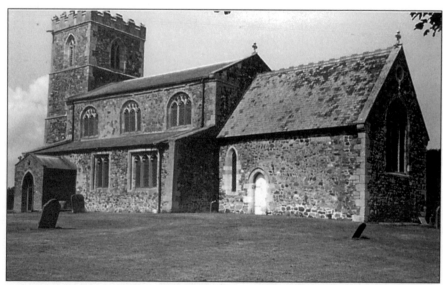

Tunstall Church *(H. Peach)*

On a more modest scale the pleasant little bungalow called Warren Cottage, near the information centre and approach gate to Spurn, repays inspection. The front wall is agreeably patterned with thin sea cobbles, while the other walls are faced with a more rounded variety. Used nowadays by the Spurn Bird Observatory, the cottage was built in 1845 for the bailiff who collected royalties for every ton of stones taken from the beach for ships' ballast.

City Windmill

Rank's Mill, Holderness Road, Hull *(H. Peach)*

What is a windmill still doing here, only a sail's length from the constant traffic of Hull's Holderness Road? It is an early 19th century five-storey tower mill, converted into a pub and restaurant. The adjacent mill-house was the birthplace of Joseph Rank (1854-1943), grandson of John, the mill owner, and destined to guide the family to still greater commercial and civic glories, philanthropy and Methodist connections.

Two hundred years ago this part of Hull was still largely rural, and mills were a familiar sight. Some were still flourishing in Victorian times. Joseph, having grown up at his father's mill on Sculcoates Lane, set up in business at several others, including Waddingham's (1875) and West's (1880).

Whalebone Tusks

Once a common feature across Holderness, whalebone tusks were constructed as novelty gateways, sometimes meeting as a pointed arch, sometimes leaning outwards where the entrance was wide. They were brought back as souvenirs or given to friends by whaling captains like William Barron (1835-1913) of "Truelove". Few are left, though one or two are treasured as garden ornaments, as at Mere House, South Dalton. The pair outside Crow Grange on the eastern fringe of Beeford date from about 1865 and may have originated with a whale that became stranded at Skipsea.

Fish-Scale House

Dating from the early 1870s, 31 New Road, Hornsea has a thoroughly comprehensive covering of Wade's patent acorn tiles made at the Brick and Tile Works started by Joseph Armytage Wade in the 1860s. This arresting feature is the more curious because in the late 19th century it was occupied by Alfred Maw, one of Wade's vocal critics.

A few streets away is "Farrago" (6 Wilton Road), c1908, designed as his retirement home by David Reynard Robinson, a Hull builder. This eccentric specialised in ubiquitous coloured tiles, somewhat to the embarrassment of his son-in-law next door who put a high wall between them. Maddeningly, his daughter contrived to burn all his records.

Moving Masonry

The East Riding seems to have so many interesting bits of masonry that have been moved from their original site. And it has been happening for centuries. Colonel Anthony Gilby, Deputy Governor of Hull, was accused of illegally removing stone from the town's blockhouse in order to build a house on Sunk Island. Not only was he unable to provide documents of the sale: pleading that he was too ill to travel, he requested the inquiry to come to him. But in 1682 he died before properly answering the charges.

Cupola from Brodrick's town hall, now in Pearson Park *(H. Peach)*

Since 1827 the historic Kilnsea Cross has stood in the garden of Holyrood House at Hedon. It is thought to have been erected to mark the landing at Ravenspur in 1399 of Henry Bolingbroke (see Chapter 1). Washed up at Kilnsea in 1818 it was claimed by Sir Thomas Hugh Clifford of Burton Constable Hall, but moved to Hedon after representations by the influential town clerk, James Iveson.

Iveson amassed a motley collection of ecclesiastical masonry, including samples from Hull's Holy Trinity Church, and put them together as a kind of "chapel garden" in the grounds of Ivy House, Hedon. Something of the resulting "Albina's Tomb" (Albina being the poisoned wife of Drogo de la Beuvriere – see Chapter 10) may be seen from Ivy Lane.

After its demolition in 1912, Cuthbert Brodrick's Hull town hall reappeared elsewhere. The cupola is in Pearson Park. More controversially, miscellaneous oddments were utilised to fashion the war memorial at Brantingham.

In Hornsea's Memorial Gardens sit together two stone lions brought from the Criterion Cinema, Hull. They seem to be guarding a 20-yard wood-and-metal fragment of the former pier which was badly damaged by storms on the night of 28th October 1880, only months after its completion.

Clamped into the garden wall of the old vicarage and opening onto lower Eastgate in Beverley is a 16th-century Friars' Gateway. It had to be moved in 1964 when a development of Armstrong Patents Ltd. threatened to encroach on the ancient Dominican Friary which now functions as a youth hostel.

Moreover, the 15th century stone gateway in the Friary grounds used to be sited at the Guildhall.

Norman doorway retained in Hilston's third church (1957). In 1862 it was incorporated into the second church – which was hit by a German bomb in 1941 *(H. Peach)*

Royal Dog and Duck

"Dog and Duck" is a common enough name for a pub, and East Yorkshire has several e.g. at Walkington, Patrington and Beverley. Few patrons or landlords will remember the days when ducks were bound so they could not fly, and were then set upon by dogs. As a country sport it had its nastier side.

More proudly adopted was "Royal". This historic Flamborough pub, dating from the 18th century, recalls the visit in 1900 of Prince and Princess Louis of Battenberg, parents of Lord Louis Mountbatten of Burma.

Nellie's

Ale has been served here since 1666. An emissary of Charles II here combined business with pleasure. The pub values its antiquity. Regulars and visitors thrive in an old-time atmosphere. The furniture is clean, functional and unashamedly old. Outdoor prints adorn the walls. Many dark corners are ill-lit by gaslamp. There are iron ranges and open fires. There are cupboards galore. The floors are uneven. All of which contribute to its charm, for Nellie's must be one of the most popular pubs in all East Yorkshire.

For centuries the hostelry was owned by the Church until Francis Collinson bought it, as a sitting tenant, in 1927. And it stayed as a family concern until taken over by Samuel Smith's Old Brewery in 1976. Nellie

Collinson was one of five daughters, eventually becoming licensee, and resistant to change. Prior to 1976 there was no organised bar; drinks were served from a kitchen table. Electricity was spurned until Nellie could be persuaded of the merits of powered lager dispensers. Dedicated though she was to her trade, Nellie had a man, intermittently, in her life – a lodger nicknamed "Suitcase Johnnie", with whom she quarrelled frequently.

Nellie is remembered as a cantankerous strong-minded old stick who had her own ways of selling ale. Her legend lives on. Ask in Beverley for the White Horse Inn, and there may be a doubt; ask for Nellie's and anyone will tell you!

Eleanor Memorial, Sledmere
(H. Peach)

Eleanor and the Waggoners

As Edward's Queen, Eleanor of Castile died at Harby near Lincoln in 1290, Yorkshire was too far north to be on the route to London to mark a resting place for the cortege. Nevertheless, Sir Tatton Sykes II commissioned Temple Moore to create one at Sledmere in 1895, based on that at Hardingstone in Northamptonshire. Sir Tatton was moved by the old story. He admired the loyalty of the long-dead queen, whose conduct compared rather favourably with that of his own bride, Jessica.

In due course, the cross was adapted as a World War One monument, with the names of officers and men added to the lower panels. It stands as a twin focus to the splendid Waggoners' Memorial nearby. This was commissioned by Sir Mark Sykes in honour of the 1200 men from the adjacent Wolds villages who were specially "volunteered" to take their wagons and horse teams to France in 1914. Scenes crisply sculpted in Portland stone show various stages of the campaign from embarkation to military action, some of it brutal. There is little here of the cosy or sentimental – and for that reason it makes a strong impact.

Kilnsea Mirror

This 16 feet high half-hexagon of concrete, with a concave face looking east, is situated in a field about a quarter of a mile from the shore, and was built c1916. A microphone was mounted near the centre to pick up the sounds of incoming enemy aircraft and zeppelins. It was part of a chain of such "mirrors" stretched around the coast from Northumberland round to Hampshire, reminiscent of the ancient defensive Anglo-Saxon forts.

A 17th-century Saker against a background of a World War II D-Day training unit. In 1642 the fort had 32 Sakers. *(H. Peach)*

Fort Paull

On the Humber bank to the east of Hull stands this Scheduled Ancient Monument, occupying 10 acres and lying within a brick and stone pentagon. Instigated by Henry VIII as a gun battery in 1542, it was attacked by Parliamentary ships during the Civil War. The fortress was rebuilt in the 1860s after a brief revival during the wars against Napoleon. World War One was comparatively quiet although the fort was primed for possible action.

During the Second World War, however, Fort Paull was the focus of a number of initiatives. Its site made it a natural bastion for anti-aircraft activity. It served as an ordnance depot, also undertaking secret laboratory work. A WRNS unit was actively concerned with anti-magnetic mine tactics. In 1944 it became a D-day training area for the invasion of Normandy.

But in the summer of 1940 the fort had a very different role. After the fall of France, and on the direct orders of Winston Churchill, it became a collecting centre for the nation's bullion. Its subterranean chambers were a repository for gold ingots each worth £5 000 and weighing 27lb 6oz. From Fort Paull and other highly secret depots, some £637 million were sent to Canada for the duration of the war; and despite intense German submarine interference with Allied shipping in the Atlantic, nothing was lost.

Alpha and Omega

At the Cliff Road entrance to Hornsea's Hall Garth Park is a pair of highly unusual wrought iron gates. They were commissioned by John Hollis, a timber merchant in 1929, and fashioned by a local blacksmith, Chris Burton. A legend reads:

"Enter Hall Garth with title free,
You'll find your name is wrought on me".

In short, you can pick out your name from the letters of the alphabet. That done, the park offers a satisfying stroll.

Chapter 4

Churches and Religious Life

Cleopatra's Needle of the Wolds

This remarkable monolith stands only a few feet from the east end of Rudston church, rising to a height of 25 feet and buried to the same depth.

The Rudston monolith *(H. Peach)*

Exposed and weather-beaten for many centuries this rough-hewn gritstone is geologically different from any local rocks, and was brought, somehow, from Cayton Bay, 10 miles away.

While little credence can still be given to an ancient tale that the Devil threw the rock at the church and missed, archaeologists continue to speculate on its origins. Could it have been a Celtic tribute to the Sun-god? A focus for tribal worship? A monument to a famous chieftain? Whatever its remote beginnings it was at some point adapted by the Christian community who crowned it with a cross, long lost, making it "rood-stone", from which the village very likely derives its name, and giving rise to the expression "as seear (sure) as Rudston steean".

In her 'Folk Lore' (1912) Mrs Gutch tells of Archdeacon Wilberforce asking one or two local folk what they thought the stone commemorated. Most pleaded ignorance, but one forthright response was "It were put up to remember a great victory between the Danes and the Roman Catholics".

The Wart Stone

A much smaller stone, the height of an average man, situated just to the left of the footpath and a few paces from the porch of Barmby Moor church, is also much weathered. It is claimed that rainwater collected from its numerous crevices will cure warts. Interestingly, one or two sceptics making the experiment have been surprised at the results!

The Fridstool

In medieval times a fugitive from the law would have been well pleased to espy the distant towers of Beverley Minster. Here lay sanctuary; and the nearer he approached, the harder it became for pursuers to apprehend him without themselves incurring penalties. Fines for breach of sanctuary became progressively heavier as the Minster was neared, and violations within the building could result in death for law officials.

Most fugitives were on the run for either debt or murder. Many of their homes were outside Yorkshire. Their ultimate goal was the Fridstool (Peace Stool) by the Minster's high altar, which had survived from a Saxon church. By tradition King Athelstan in the year 937 had granted the privilege of sanctuary in honour of St John of Beverley. Fugitives were sheltered for 30 days during which time they bore no weapons, agreed to obey church officers and made themselves available for dutiful employment. Meantime the canons sought to reach a settlement. If this was not forthcoming, a choice was offered between trial and banishment; or the refugee could become a "frithman", a lifelong servant of the church, surrendering his possessions but as far as possible following his former trade.

Abuse of the system was such that murderers escaped justice. Sometimes the evidence seemed overwhelming, as in 1331 when broken sanctuary led to the arrest of frithman John Acreman of Bruges, accused of a murder in Norwich. Felons lay low for a time before returning to their hidden loot. Defaulters on repaying loans subsequently shared the money with accomplices.

As a follow-up to his suppression of the monasteries, privileges of sanctuary were swept away in 1540 by Henry VIII.

Origins of Kirkham Priory

The foundation of this establishment in a spectacular riverside setting was due to a bereavement. Lord of the manor Walter Espec and his lady Adeline had but the one son who fell from his horse and broke his neck. In 1122 Walter decided to invest his wealth in two monastic houses, Rievaulx and Kirkham. On his death he was buried at Rievaulx.

Amongst the most curious gifts later bequeathed to the priory were those willed in the fifteenth century

The gatehouse at Kirkham *(H. Peach)*

by George Foster – his best black cow, eleven sheep and the sum of 3s 4d.

Kirkham is the only East Yorkshire monastic foundation with any substantial ruins, notably the gatehouse.

Three St Johns

Beverley

According to ancient belief John was born at Harpham, near Driffield about 640 AD. His parents were Christian and sent him to several monastery schools culminating in Whitby, where he was influenced by the Abbess Hilda. After some time in a northern hermitage on the River Tyne, where Bede became a pupil, John was consecrated Bishop of Hexham by Archbishop Theodore in 687. Some 18 years later he moved on to York.

From about the year 690 John had been visiting a new Christian community amid the swamps some twelve miles north of the River Humber. This became "Beverlac" – Beaver Lake – the nucleus of the later Beverley. In 718 he left York, installing Wilfrid as bishop, spending his last years in his developing township. And there he died in 72I. He was canonised in 1037.

A number of miracles have been attributed to John of Beverley. He raised the paralysed son of an earl; he restored speech to a dumb boy; in 1321 a 10 year old boy from Ferriby Priory received back his sight and hearing after a visit to St John's shrine. Over many centuries St John's Well, near the medieval church of St Nicholas, had serious claims to healing properties, especially for eyes and body sores. According to the account books of Burton Constable, on 23rd June 1742 Will Stafford visited the Beverley well and was cured of his sores. During the 19th century Hodgson's tannery workers and other townsfolk found the waters beneficial. St John's memory remains green.

Howden

It is believed that John of Howden was born in London about 1215 to a family of means. After showing prowess as a scholar, writing religious and lyrical poetry, he became a clerk in the service of Henry III's queen, Eleanor of Provence. About the year 1270 he was elected as prebendary of Howden, beginning the building of a new quire, a scheme interrupted by his death in 1275. Many pilgrims were drawn to his tomb, including kings Edward I, Edward II and Henry V, and various miracles were claimed by the medieval church. The fact that he was never officially canonised did not inhibit worshippers from acclaiming him locally, and his special day within the York diocese is 2nd May.

Bridlington

A spiritual headstart over other East Yorkshire coastal communities enabled Bridlington to turn its claim to having a saint to commercial advantage. Prior John, born at Thwing manor in 1320 had been an inspirational leader and was canonised in 1401, a mere 22 years after his death. For centuries pilgrims made their way to the Old Town centring on the priory, as well as the developing Quay. The two remained as distinct communities until the strategic positioning of the railway from Hull provided the incentive for a fuller street network. The priory church has remained a considerable tourist attraction.

Boy Bishops

This was once a widespread medieval church ceremonial. Senior choristers elected one of their number to act as a miniature cleric from St Nicholas Day (6th December) to the Epiphany (6th January). They were particularly prominent in the seasonal festivities in York, where Edward I once attended Vespers conducted by the boy bishop who was congratulated on his deportment and given 40 shillings. During their visits to other churches the boys were well respected and regaled. But the pomp and ceremony were too much for Henry VIII who in 1541 abolished this popular custom.

Reminders in the East Riding include a stone effigy of about 1275 in the south wall of Filey St Oswald's and an image of the same period of a child with crossed legs is situated in the north aisle of Nafferton church. These memorials may suggest that the youngsters died during their time of office.

A Bishop Beheaded

In Reformation times beliefs changed to please new monarchs, and even bishops stood firm at their peril. One deemed to be insufficiently flexible was

John Fisher

John Fisher, son of a Beverley mercer who became Bishop of Rochester and chancellor of Cambridge University. As Catholic confessor to Catherine of Aragon, Henry VIII's first queen, his support for the king's ambitions wavered. But Henry was not prepared to tolerate any opposition to his divorce; and when Fisher failed to recognise him as Supreme Head of the Church of England, martyrdom became a matter of time. The bishop was beheaded on Tower Hill on 22nd June 1535. Canonised in 1936 he is remembered also as the founder of St John's College, Cambridge.

Cloistral Hospitality

The monastic reputation for good living is encapsulated in the following ditty:

> *If you go to Nunkeeling*
> *You shall find your body filling*
> *Of whig or of whay.*
> *But go to Swine and come betime*
> *Or else you go empty away.*
> *But the Abbot of Meaux ("Mews")*
> *Does keep a good house*
> *By night and by day.*

Double House

Watton Priory, founded about 1150 by an Anglo-Norman baron, Eustace Fitz-John belonged to the Order of Gilbert of Sempringham, and was unusual in that it accommodated, albeit separately, both monks and nuns. A dividing wall separated the cloisters, and another in the church permitted corporate mass. There were but two official concessions – administration of the last rites, and the exchange of any essential objects via a revolving hatch.

Washing presented another kind of double standard. Hoods were cleansed seven times a year but baths in the nude were forbidden.

Nevertheless, human nature will out, and stories once circulated of a nun called Ethelfrida who became pregnant by a lay man who then deserted her, but was lured back by the sisters and tortured. Another account says that Ethelfrida, having brought shame to the community, was beheaded. Intermit-

Prior's Lodge, Watton (H. Peach)

tent ghostly activity, featuring a distraught nun, may or may not confirm the legend.

Such tales of immorality strengthened the case of Henry VIII for dissolving the nation's religious houses, and the priory was handed over by Robert Holgate on 9th December 1539. The Prior's Lodge survives still, Holgate being allowed to linger for a few months before taking up his appointment as Archbishop of York.

During the Civil War a Royalist lady hiding in the ruins with an infant was discovered by soldiers and beheaded. So there could be at least two headless women haunting this field of bumps and hollows, once the site of the biggest "double house" – 600 feet – in England.

Policing Compulsory Attendance

The Elizabethan Act of Uniformity of 1559 required all parishioners to attend church worship, with penalties of one shilling for absentees. Such fines were collected by the churchwardens and in general were re-distributed to the poor. Backslidings were noted from unexpected quarters. At Roos in 1686 the Rev John Shore felt compelled to warn churchwardens and overseers of the poor failing to appear in church on Easter Monday morning that they would incur fines of 6d.

Two centuries later the East Riding's chief constables were still taking a strong line on church attendance. Lt. Col. Bernard Granville-Layard expected his officers to attend Divine Worship except for calls of duty. His successor from 1872, Major H.J. Bower insisted that constables should somehow spend a few minutes at prayer, and the times of these withdrawals from the beat were to be recorded in their notebooks.

Although many Sunday inebriates sobered up to find themselves in the stocks, this was rarely, if ever, the fate of uniformed constables. Noteworthy, however, was the fact that the first two years of professional constabulary (1857-8) saw 29 dismissals for drunkenness. Others were fined and posted elsewhere. For gross inebriation, neglect and absconding from the force, Superintendent Jacob Gibson of the North Hunsley Beacon was reduced to sergeant. It is a fair bet that he did not seek sanctuary in any church.

Archbishop Grindal's Visitations, 1575

Parishioners were named and shamed for irregular attendance, for failing to contribute to the poor and in particular for sexual sins. Here is a flavour:

Burythorpe: "Bartholomew Wightman presented to be an often swearer, a dronkarde, a ribalde, contentyouse, an uncharitable person, a common slanderer of his neighbours, a railer and sower of discord".

Bubwith: "Avise Butler is with childe but who got it they can not tell".

Desecration

During the Civil War and afterwards the tomb of Anthony St Quintin, rector of

Hornsea church from 1397 to 1423 was vandalised by Puritans carving the soles of shoes. Roundhead soldiers, horses and all, were encamped briefly in Howden Minster, during which time they dismantled the organ and tried to blow the pipes like giant recorders.

Holy Trinity, Hull

Many historical curiosities are associated with this, the largest parish church in England. The considerable expanses of exterior brick are possibly the earliest in this Riding since Roman times. Towards the end of the 13th century Holy Trinity was begun as a daughter church of All Saints, Hessle four miles up river, gaining independent status only in 1661. During this time many of Hull's dead were brought by boat for burial at Hessle – the so-called "river requiem".

During the siege of the Civil War the church was used as a gunpowder store; and some years later a wall was built across the transepts so that a Presbyterian assembly could meet in the nave, while an Independent congregation worshipped in the chancel. With the restoration of the monarchy in 1660 the wall was removed and the Anglican tradition revived.

Many of the town's famous people have had links here. At the 14th century font of coralloid marble William Wilberforce was baptised in 1759 and this was his regular place of worship. He even married the vicar's daughter.

When Napoleon threatened our peace, the Hull militia drilled in the nave. And during the Nazi blitz of the city the folk of the Old Town sought refuge in the crypt.

Burn-roast

An hour-glass, working like an egg timer, and mounted by the pulpit was supposed to regulate the length of a sermon. But some priests ignored them or turned them over again. "Let us take another glass", as some determined preachers wryly observed. At Cherry Burton, for example, the Rev. Thomas Micklethwaite, incumbent from 1613 until 1662, was nicknamed "Burn-roast" because his notoriously long addresses ruined many a Sunday dinner. Deprived of his living after nearly half a century, under the Act of Uniformity enforcing the strict use of the Prayer Book, he turned to farming and helping his wife to run the village school.

Recusant Burials

In later Tudor and Stuart times recusants – mainly Roman Catholics refusing to accept Church of England authority – were often denied a Christian burial. Thus, Thomas Cletheray was lowered into his grave in Drypool churchyard on 7th March 1602 by Henry Garrub without the order of burial according to law. At All Saints, Low Catton the church register records that Everill Byrd of Stamford Bridge, having died in childbirth, was buried at night on 5th December 1689. The reason is unclear, but the presumption was that, as a Catholic, the woman was denied the Established Church's last sacrament. It is just possible, however, that the family wished to be spared the daylight burden of further public grief.

Clerical Opinion

In 1720 the parish clerk of St Mary's, Lowgate, Hull wrote with regard to a proposed gallery – "Customs officers want a whole loft. It will be as nigh Heaven as they'll ever come".

Archbishop Herring's Returns, 1743.

Thomas Herring, Archbishop of York from 1743 to 1747 sought to follow the tradition of St Paul and St Barnabas by re-visiting as many diocesan churches as possible. Most incumbents were content to volunteer little beyond the facts and figures requested in connection with their parishes. But from time to time some additional human foibles are revealed, as the following examples may show: –

At Beeford the Rev. Samuel Dennis noted his church wardens' reluctance to present local delinquents in church, as officially stipulated. Malefactors hereabouts were quick to take revenge on bumptious vestrymen ... "and was I to do it myself, nothing would be safe about me".

At Cottingham the Rev. Thomas Mease had refused the Sacrament to the wife of a man with an earlier bride living at Paull; and his churchwardens had been slow in making inquiries. There had been further trouble over Sunday drinking in local pubs. Mease had been reduced to asking questions himself, outside church service hours, of course, but had been confronted by tipplers from Hull who "did but engage me in disputes, wasting my spirits after the fatigue of the day, and consequently tended to impair my health". .

Another thing: he had not received all "churching fees" owed by the wives of Dissenters following child-bearing, notwithstanding the fact that the ceremony had been performed in their meeting house.

Fortified by such spiritual insights in Yorkshire, Herring became Archbishop of Canterbury in 1747.

Visitation Celebrations

There is evidence to support the view that periodic visitations by bishops and archdeacons were by no means cheerless affairs. When Archbishop Sharp investigated St Mary's, Beverley in 1657 there may well have been more than moderate supping, for the churchwardens' account read -"Vs for two quarts of Canary for the Archbishop".

At Long Riston in the mid-19th-century Richard Fewson, eccentric school-master and churchwarden admitted to a colleague:

"Sally won't believe I've been to the visitation. I've been going for thirty years and it's the first time I've come home sober".

(see also Chapter 8)

Thespian Tip

Each summer during the years 1750 to 1753 David Garrick, one of the stage's immortals, was a visitor to Lord Burlington at Londesborough. One day he was nobbled by the rector, Bryan Allett for advice on improving his reading of the Bible in church. The great man called a halt to the cleric in mid-flow.

"Yes, yes, that's all right – but the start is everything. Don't open the Bible as if it were a tiresome thing, like a day book or ledger. Open it carefully, respectfully, as if it really is the Word of God. From the first moment you've got to mean business".

Wesleyan Wanderings

John Wesley visited the East Riding on many occasions. An entry in the Sancton parish register dated Monday, 23rd June 1788 confirmed an exacting schedule:

"The Rev. John Wesley preached here at nine o'clock in the morning, at the age of 85 after having preached twice in the High Church at Hull the preceding day; and went from hence to preach at (Market) Weighton at eleven, at Pocklington at two; and at York in the evening of this day".

Back in 1752 the Hull crowd had given him a hard time. After a service in Holy Trinity church, he had proceeded the short distance to Myton Carr where clods and stones were thrown with such violence that the poor man was grateful to be allowed to escape in a lady's crowded carriage. The unruly mob followed hurling missiles and abuse. Wesley's embarrassment must have been acute, screened as he was by a large gentlewoman sitting on his knee. At a friend's house, there were a few hours of respite, but not before a hostile crowd had registered further disapproval with oaths and bricks. On the following day Beverley Minster must have seemed like a foretaste of Heaven.

Ecumenical Bust

It is odd to find a bust of John Wesley prominently displayed in an Anglican church. On Bishop Burton green he had once preached a sermon under a wych elm which was struck by lightning in 1826. The accomplished wood sculptor, James Elwell was commissioned by the squire, Richard Hall-Watt to create a bust of Wesley from the stricken tree, and a place of honour was readily found in the nearby Puddingate chapel. But after developing woodworm it was brought outside and eventually (1898) was bought for two pounds by the vicar of All Saints Church, the Rev. William Pearman. It is claimed that the workman's timesheet was worded thus:

" . . . to rebaptising John Wesley (with paraffin) and curing him of worms – 25s".

In 1966 the bust was re-dedicated and mounted on the wall of the nave in the parish church.

Public Penance

During the 18th century there were many instances of parishioners brought into churches to do public acts of penance, notably for immorality. In his Archbishop Drummond's Visitation Returns, 1764, for example, the Rev. Robert Hewett reported, "Hannah Andrews performed public penance in the church of Fangfoss 8th January", Similarly, for the sin of fornication, Elizabeth Stephenson was led, barefoot, clad in a white sheet and holding a white wand, into Driffield church on 4th July 1779. There in front of the congregation she admitted the sin, received admonition and a grudging pardon. Sometimes, but not always, the man involved was likewise paraded. At Pocklington in 1708 Thomas Sixton and his wife Joan did penance for ante-nuptial fornication.

There were other sins that brought humiliation. In 1534 the Rev. Richard Browne, vicar of North Cave had been arraigned in Holy Trinity Church, Hull on a heresy charge. Perhaps he was thankful to escape by recanting. Walking barefoot and in the customary white sheet, while carrying a sizeable faggot, this was a public sign that a burning issue had narrowly been avoided.

Cheating Churchwardens

"I suspect a fraud committed by the churchwardens in 1756, who borrowed fifty pounds for the repairs of the church for which interest is still paid by the present churchwardens at the rate of 41/2per cent, while fifty pounds was never brought to account by the then churchwardens". – Rev. Samuel Johnston reporting in Archbishop Drummond's Visitation Returns, 1764, St Mary's, Beverley.

"Knawper"

This was the local name for the dog whipper, a church official appointed to control and eject dogs which became a nuisance during divine service, While dogs were tolerated within the building, their masters were supposed to look after them – but problems arose when masters dozed in sermon time. The vicar of Kirk Ella noted in 1596, "Nicholas Gallaway – a sleeper in sermons". So we read in churchwardens' accounts typical items like – "Whipping dogs out of church – 5s." (Kirby Underdale, 1790). "Whipping ye dogs – 5s" (Robert Marshall, South Cave, 1765). The knawper also woke up slumbering worshippers as necessary.

Often he headed a funeral procession, his rod of office decorated with a black crepe bow.

Lofty Calling

A 26 year old bricklayer, John Burdas was commissioned in 1766 to fix a weather-vane on top of Patrington church steeple. When he reached the pinnacle the holes and joints did not fit. For some hours he had to stand with one foot on the top stone and the other on a ladder raised from the scaffolding while he made the adjustments. Meantime, the vicar, Nicholas Nicholls and many bemused parishioners successfully prayed for his safe return.

Charities

Many of our churches still display charity boards which convey something of the basic needs of past generations of poorer families. In 1800 at Market Weighton Mrs Dorothy Barker arranged "For 30 4d loaves to be given to the poor immediately after morning service. Every alternate Sunday the remainder to be given in dole to the poor." She left also the sum of £600 at nearby Shiptonthorpe for 10 4d loaves to be distributed at the discretion of the minister and churchwardens fortnightly after Divine Service.

At Newbald even in 1914 there were 30 applicants for the 20 doles of William Gill's Charity dating from 1723.

Pluralism

During the 18th and 19th centuries especially, some privileged parsons held several simultaneous appointments, treating their parishes almost as absentee landlords. For a brief period, 1816-18, Dr William Page combined the rectorship of Nunburnholme with being headmaster of Westminster School, Prebendary of Westminster, Vicar of Willen and Steventon (Hampshire) and Rector of Quainton (Buckinghamshire). It is doubtful whether he ever lived in Nunburnholme, and may have visited the village only for his induction. Presumably his conscience was untroubled by the fees and tithes to which his East Yorkshire ministry entitled him.

Skin Pennies

Another well-known pluralist was Dr Richard Osbaldeston, who at various times during his ministry at Hunmanby (1715-1762) held office as rector of Hinderwell and Folkton, curate of Muston and Dean of York. At first his customary fees included one "skin penny" for each burial performed by a colleague at Reighton. A new incumbent, John Sumpton, however, challenged this anomaly, and the payment stopped forthwith.

Scoresby of Bessingby

William Scoresby (1789-1857), son of an equally renowned father, was a man of many distinguished parts – scientist, whaling captain, Arctic explorer and scholar. In 1806 Scoresby senior took him to within 510 miles of the north pole; and his own "Account of the Arctic Regions" (1820) remained a standard work for a century, earning him his Fellowship of the Royal Society. He was also a founder member of the British Association at York in 1831. The story is told of him lecturing the BA into the late evening, the chairman intervening at 11pm but allowing him to resume the following morning.

Less well known is his career as a parson. After a training in Theology at Cambridge, Scoresby was ordained at York in 1825, becoming a curate at

William Scoresby Jr *(Courtesy of Hull Museums)*

Bessingby for two years. Here he was surely under-employed, Bridlington and the sea doubtless offering some compensation. We know that he went to preach at a memorial service at St. Mary's Church, Whitby, following the loss of two trawlers. By the spring of 1827 he had had enough and moved to Liverpool in order to become chaplain to the Floating Church for Seamen. In May 1839 he received the degree of Doctor of Divinity at Cambridge and became vicar of Bradford; but after 10 years he gave up his ministry and returned to science, researching into magnetism in Australia.

Churchyard Antics

An old story about a Cottingham sexton asserted that his feet were so big that they covered a young child's open grave, and he had to step aside for mourners to see. Hence the ultimate in outsize shoes – "Cottingham feet".

Down the ages there have been complaints about the misuse of churchyards. In 1596 the vicar of Kirk Ella named names:

"The churche yards is undecentlie used with
geese and swyne in defalte of Mr John Harrison".

Nafferton's church register noted that in 1837 the new iron gate was to be kept locked "to prevent indecencies and depredations". It was necessary for three dung heaps to be removed. This latter injunction is understandable - but we can only speculate on the "indecencies".

Pilgrim Rabbit

On the arch to the right of the sacristy in St Mary's church, Beverley is an unusual and distinctive carving of a rabbit with a pilgrim's staff. There is a strong probability that it provided the inspiration for the White Rabbit in Lewis Carroll's "Alice in Wonderland". As a boy Carroll stayed with his grandfather, Major Charles Lutwidge, a customs officer in Hull; and a visit to his uncle, the Rev. Charles Henry Lutwidge, rector of Burton Agnes would very likely take him through the streets of Beverley.

Contrasting clerics

Connop Thirlwall (1797-1875) who became rector at Kirby Underdale in 1834 was a considerable classical scholar, weaned as a toddler on Greek and Latin. He was an earnest and conscientious priest, though some of his flock may have thought him a bit aloof. His mind was probably on his books: cartloads of them brought frequently to the rectory during his six year incumbency amazed local residents. But in this delightful rural setting Connop had the leisure to compose his monumental "History of Greece" which became a standard work. Such was his application and adaptability that within six months of becoming bishop of St David's in 1840 he was able to deliver his first sermon in Welsh.

An eventual successor at Kirby Underdale was Thomas John Monson (1825-1887) whose output was of a different order. He had married well: his wife was the Hon. Caroline Isabella Monckton, so that a country parson's stipend was not a limitation on good breeding. They produced a family of 15 children, eight being born at Kirby Underdale during his incumbency (1859-1887).

Telling Inhospitality

Etiquette nearly always required that visiting Methodist preachers should be entertained to a meal by a chapel elder. On one occasion in Victorian Lund this courtesy was somehow forgotten, though not by the visitor thus slighted. The next time Bradley Johnson faced this congregation he announced how delightful it was always to be called to this pretty village – and this time, because he did not want to go hungry, he had brought his own sandwiches. And he held the package aloft.

So Be It

During the last part of the 19th century a cottage near Ellerker Church was occupied by a verger who delighted in intoning the Amens during Divine Worship. So his house came to be called Amen Cottage, as it still is.

At Sutton on Derwent there was once a priest who became so hen-pecked at home that he acquired a separate house, at the far end of the village. And as Peace Cottage it remains.

Weddings

As with Romeo and Juliet some spouses were caught very young. And well-to-do families arranged marriages. When Rachel, daughter of Sir Thomas Parker of Willingdean, Sussex came to Bishop Burton in 1645 to marry William Gee of a similar knightly family, she was just fourteen.

Pass the Ward

More than a century earlier the village had witnessed a considerable furore over competition for a young lady's hand. Anne Cresacre-Rokeby was an infant carefully watched by her stepfather, Ralph Rokeby of Bishop Burton manor. Her inheritance deserved no less! Accordingly, he betrothed her to his own son, John. In April 1524 Sir Robert Constable, well aware of Anne's financial attractions, besieged the house, kidnapped the girl and wed her to his son Thomas, aged 11. Constable at this time asserted guardian rights from the Crown. Unfortunately, for his part in the Pilgrimage of Grace he was executed. (See Chapter 1). Anne subsequently passed into the custody of Sir Thomas More, Henry VIII's Chancellor who betrothed her to his own son Peter.

More Weddings

During the period of Oliver Cromwell's Commonwealth (1653-1657) the introduction of civil marriages meant that banns were often called at the market cross. On 11th February 1657 Thomas Cowlam of Spaldington and Jane Millington of Willitoft were married in an alehouse, Robert Browne, vicar of Eastrington performing the ceremony, with Richard Clarke JP as witness. With the restoration of the monarchy in 1660 civil marriages disappeared and the clergy took full control.

At Lowthorpe in the 18th century the best man mislaying the ring was not the embarrassment that might have been elsewhere. The parish registers recall that in 1711 Mrs Francis Rokeby gave a gold ring cryptically inscribed "Obey and Rule" for the use of those coming to be wed and unprovided with a ring.

Penmanship in those illiterate days was often minimal. At Yapham, for example, between 1780 and 1835, of the 60 marriages solemnised, on 25 occasions either bride or groom or both was unable to sign a name, and accordingly made a mark. At Sigglesthorne John West, parish clerk for many years in the mid 18th-century added his own mark to the registers, serious record keeping being done by the rector.

A particularly firm clerical hand was required at Barmby Moor in early Victorian times. At the completion of the ceremony the custom had grown to throw hassocks and prayer books at the vestry door while the register was being completed. But from mid-century the practice ceased.

Up to the first quarter of the 20th century, guns were sometimes fired over the heads of the newly married couple as they emerged from church. The only danger was from falling feathers that had been loaded into the barrels.

Local society weddings have been major occasions in East Yorkshire village life. Even the return from the honeymoon has involved a dutiful turn-out in estate villages, as in 1923 when Alvery Digby Hall-Watt, sportsman and master of the Holderness Hunt returned to Bishop Burton High Hall with his bride, Angela (nee Leyland) of Haggerston Castle, Northumberland.

The Squire's Pew

Although church worshippers may all have been equal in the sight of God, there has been a good deal of inequality amongst pew holders. Until later Victorian times pews were allocated by the purse; after a death there were sometimes unseemly quarrels amongst ambitious members of the congregation. It has even been rumoured that small boys armed with hatpins were recruited to "incommode" perceived usurpers. As numbers of worshippers gradually fell there was reduced competition for prestigious places, and pew rents were gradually abolished. Kelly's Directory for 1897 noted that at North Cave 348 seats out of 370 were free.

Above and aloof from these squalid jostlings were the squire and his family, often accommodated in very special quarters. At Boynton the Strickland Pew on the first floor of the tower was reached by a delightful curving staircase. At Hotham the old Clitherow family pew, complete with fireplace, balcony and private stairs is built into the north chapel. From such vantage points the village's main employer could form judgements on attendance and deportment, as well as on the virtues of parson and sermon.

Nearer to God in a Garden

Between 1921 and 1945 Sutton on Derwent found that rare earthy quality in its rector – a passion for gardening. The estate of the Rev. Michael Hallett Pimm was regularly featured on the front covers of country magazines. He produced also wonderful calendars, with contributions from famous authors, whose sales raised thousands of pounds for church repairs. Church fetes made an unusual challenge to children – a prize for every weed they could find. This effective spade work also contributed to the building of a fine village hall in 1929.

Ecclesiastical Imps

Medieval architects may have included Imps as a tacit recognition of evil which could become tolerable, simply mischievous or even benign if incorporated as a church artefact. The Beverley Imp, located over the door to the priests' room staircase in St Mary's Church, has welcomed visitors for the past 500 years. Other notables are in the north aisle at Patrington and at Easington on the north side of the tower arch. That in Holy Trinity Church, Hall is carved in wood and is harder, perhaps, to find, situated as it is amongst all the "poppyheads" in the pews in the north-west corner. These were the work of George Peck, c1845.

Treadwheel

Although the technology of the great cathedral builders still holds many mysteries, one compelling clue remains in the 15 foot high treadwheel still in situ at the top of the central tower of Beverley Minster. It was used for raising and lowering wood or masonry, and, of course, the wheel was turned by a

The turkey lectern at Boynton *(H. Peach)*

workman walking with measured pace inside it. Such survivals are rare, and others are to be found at Canterbury, Salisbury and Peterborough.

Turkey Lectern

It is a view widely held that turkeys were introduced to East Yorkshire – and England – by William Strickland who brought a few of the birds back from the New World after sailing with Cabot. The turkey motif is incorporated into the family coat-of-arms, shown above. In St Andrew's Church, Boynton the lectern has been most beautifully carved in the shape of a turkey by local craftsman Harry Scott, after a design by F.F. Johnson.

1300 Years On

About the year 731 Bede recorded the story of Coifi, pagan chieftain, who was so affected by the words of the missionary Paulinas that he dramatically changed his allegiance. Riding from a council at Londesborough he returned to Goodmanham, scattering his acolytes, knocking down all the images and setting the place ablaze. A new Christian church was built on the site, a predecessor of the present All Saints. Here was a cradle of Christendom.

On 21st July 1927 these events were remembered at a special service held at Goodmanham to celebrate the conversion of Edwin of Northumbria and the 1,300th anniversary of the founding of St Peter's Church (a forerunner of the Minster) in York. A distinguished gathering of clergy included the Archbishop of York, Dr Cosmo Gordon Lang.

Better Before Lunch

George Nellist, North Wolds man, farm lad, author, preacher has seen a thing or two in a long and varied life. Sunday afternoons were hardest; you were preaching "next to Yorkshire pudding".

Epitaphs

In Memory of
SAMUEL BUTLER,
"A poor Player, that struts and
frets his hour upon the Stage,
and then is heard no more—"
Ob: 15: June 1812,
Æ: 62.

Samuel Butler, a renowned actor-manager, is buried in St Mary's
Church, Beverley. This plaque carries an apt quotation from
Macbeth Act V, Scene 5. *(H. Peach)*

According to legend Thomas Newman of Bridlington lived to the age of 153. In the south aisle of the priory church an inscribed board, copying the fact from an ancient stone, bears testimony to "this remarkable prolongation of human life".

Another Grand Old Man was Valentine Cateby of Preston, near Hedon who died in 1782 at the age of 116. He had two equally long careers of 36 years, first as a sailor, then as a farmer. Clear-minded to the end, he favoured a diet of milk and biscuits in his latter years.

By the east end of Welton church a stone commemorates the life and marital achievements of Jeremiah Simpson who died in 1719, aged 84 and who was married eight times. "May he rest in peace" is surely in his case a sentiment thoroughly deserved. A few speculations here may be warranted. Were all his wives buried in wool, as by law commanded? How many children did he have? What would be his place in a league table of, say, Yorkshire marriages?

Although William Tate of Spaldington achieved only seven weddings, he died at Bubwith in 1800 a widower and a centenarian.

A churchyard stone in Hedon claimed this astonishing record:

> "Here lies the body of William Shutton of Patrington, buried 18th May 1744 aged 97 years, who had by his first wife 28 children, by his second 17. He was own father to 45, grandfather to 86, great-grandfather to 97 and great-great-grandfather to 23, in all 251".

Another long-lost headstone, this time at South Cave, remembered the fortunate Thomas Scratcherd:

> "That Ann lov'd Tom was very true.
> Perhaps you'll say, 'What's that to you?'
> Who 'ere you are, remember this –
> Tom lov'd Ann, 'tis that made bliss".

At Barmby Moor a memorial close to the Wart Stone laments the passing of a young musician on 9th December 1789:

"Stephenson and time

Are both now even.

Stephenson beat time

But now Time beats John Stephenson".

Amongst the examples of epitaphs more fully reflecting the trade or business once followed are these:

William Clark of Skeffling who died at 56 in 1865 and was buried in Keyingham churchyard:

"He laboured in the fields his bread to gain.

He ploughed, be sowed, he reaped the yellow grain.

And now by Death from future service driven

Is gone to keep his harvest home in Heaven".

Robert Adams, blacksmith of Leven, died at 82 in 1827 and was laid to rest in the far left corner of the old St Faith's churchyard:

"My anvil and hammer lie declined,

My bellows too have lost their wind.

My fire's extinct, my forge decayed

And in the dust my vice is laid.

My coals are spent, my iron's gone,

My last nail's drove, my work is done".

Not all epitaphs are complimentary. Take Jane Alcock whose grave is situated to the left of the lychgate in the churchyard of Holme on Spalding Moor. Dying at 69 in 1810 she had been married to George Alcock of Howden; but George – or posterity? – decided

"She was a virtuous but not a loving wife".

And lastly ...

For over 40 years (1880-1921) Canon Henry Edward Nolloth was a much loved vicar of Beverley Minster. His contributions included manifold acts of generosity, financing new statues for empty niches, vestments, bells, the organ case and many Minster projects. Although his cassock was, towards the end, somewhat green with age, he was an inspirational preacher whose sermons drew up to 800 worshippers. Some of them were perhaps amusedly counting the times he used the phrase "And lastly", which punctuated the last quarter of many an address.

Chapter 5

What A Way To Go!

Celtic Chariot Burials

So far these seem to be unique to East Yorkshire, J.R. Mortimer making one of the earliest finds at Danes' Graves near Driffield in 1897. At Garton Slack in the same area T.C.M. Brewster in 1971 uncovered another burial (c200 BC) complete with harness fittings and two iron tyres with 12 spokes reduced to soil stains. A further three burials were excavated at Wetwang Slack in 1984. The corpse was arranged centrally, lying on its side, head to the north. A common extra was the forequarters of a pig, presumably for sustenance in the after-life.

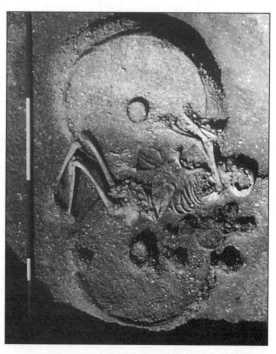

Excavations at Wetwang Slack, 1984 *(Courtesy of Kingston upon Hull Museums)*

Grave Situation

Grave 49, uncovered during the excavation of the Anglo-Saxon cemetery at Sewerby in 1959 revealed a woman of about 40 whose position was so unusual that she may have been buried alive. Beneath her was a younger woman. Archaeologists could but speculate on the circumstances – an odd ritual? a sacrifice? a punishment? a defaulting slave?

Mass Murder

Reputed to have been responsible for many brawls, woundings, raids, even murder, John Dring made enemies enough around Driffield. Patrick Langdale hired a gang to kill him as he came for Mass on the Friday before Michaelmas, 1367. What happened to the avengers is unknown.

Drumming Well

Seeing the archer fumble with his bow, lord of the manor St Quintin stepped forward impatiently. He brushed against the drummer boy, Tom Hewson, who stumbled, lost his balance and fell into the well where he drowned.

His mother, Molly, for once could draw on no magic to retrieve her son. But her abiding curse was fulsome and terrifying. In future whenever a member of the St Quintin family was about to die, Tom's drumming would be heard from the bottom of this Harpham well.

Shiner

Whilst a new pulpit was being prepared in Pocklington Church in Victorian times, the removal of part of the floor revealed a skeleton with an abbey token, believed to be 500 years old, in an eye socket.

These did take it with them!

Excavations of the Augustinian Friary in Hull revealed that monks buried in the middle of the 14th century had sticks of hazel and willow interred with them – whether in anticipation of flagellation, giving or receiving, we shall never know.

Unlucky Percies

It is astonishing that so many Earls of Northumberland, strong in their East Riding connections through their manor houses at Wressle and Leconfield, should have suffered long periods of imprisonment and violent deaths. All too often they were the focus of political intrigue, or they were allied to a weaker cause.

The first earl, after a dispute with Henry IV, mounted an insurrection, was routed at Bramham Moor (1407) and his estates confiscated. His severed head was stuck on London Bridge, and his quartered torso was dispersed to the walls of London, Lincoln, Newcastle and Berwick.

The second earl fell at St Albans (1455) fighting for the Lancastrians.

The third earl, also on the Lancastrian side, fell at Towton (1461) when the Yorkists gained control in these Wars of the Roses.

The fourth earl was murdered by a Topcliffe mob while trying to collect taxes in 1489. His mangled corpse was buried in Beverley Minster. In an interesting aside Celia Fiennes, who kept a diary of her travels in 1697 reported –

> "... his tomb was a little fallen in and a hole so big as many put their hands in and touched the body which was much of it entire – of the bones the skull was whole and the teeth firm though of so many years standing".

The sixth earl, rumoured to be a lover of Anne Boleyn, Henry VIII's eventual second queen, was warned off by Chancellor Thomas Wolsey, whom he later had the satisfaction of arresting. Having made a sad and mutually disdainful marriage with Mary Talbot, the earl was duly directed by the king to sit at Anne's trial. He died of grief at her execution in 1537.

Unwise enough to lead the Rising in the North for Mary, Queen of Scots, the seventh earl was beheaded at York Pavement in 1572, declaring with his last breath, "I am a Percy, in life and death". His head was spiked on Micklegate Bar.

The eighth earl plotted to free Mary, Queen of Scots, suffering three periods of imprisonment in the Tower of London. There on the 21st June 1585 he was found dead in his cell, shot through the heart, apparently by his own hand.

Accused of complicity in the Gunpowder Plot, in which his kinsman Thomas Percy was directly involved, the ninth earl was forced to pay a heavy fine, and was a political prisoner in the Tower for 16 years. But he survived, dying at Petworth in 1635 after 14 years of comparatively tranquil retirement.

Meantime the house at Leconfield, having long fallen into decay, was demolished c1608; and at the end of the Civil War Wressle Castle was seriously "slighted".

The fifth earl? A favourite of Henry VIII, he died through natural causes in 1527 at the age of 70. It was during his time that the later renowned House-hold Book was written (See Chapter 11).

Hard to Swallow

Some final moments are inherently improbable. Sir Marmaduke Constable, having fought in France and against the Scots at Flodden (1513), somehow managed to swallow a toad – in his drinking water, perhaps – and the creature is said to have eaten his heart. On his tomb on the north side of the sanctuary in Flamborough Church is an image of a chest cut open to reveal the heart.

Buried with her Favourite Doctor

Dr John Dolman, founder of Pocklington School (1514) was much loved by Margaret Easingwold; but as a priest he was unable to marry. Heartbroken, Margaret retired to found an institution herself, a nunnery at Wilberfoss. There she grieved away the rest of her life. Her ghost haunted her successors, and at last her body was brought back to Pocklington to be buried near Dr John. She is commemorated by a memorial near the pulpit.

This Mortal Coil

In the registers of Beverley St Mary's is this entry for 1610:

> "There was buried of ye plague this month of July thirty-two, besides forty that was shuffled into graves without any reading over them at all".

Into the 18th century some of the poor of Hull were not buried but stacked up against the east wall of Holy Trinity Church until they rotted.

Winestead Woes

The parish records tell a depressing tale of George Tummond, butcher of Patrington, who had imbibed perhaps too freely in an Ottringham alehouse. Next morning, 10th March 1623 in this marshland of ditches he was discovered "in the bottomes, about sunne rising"; and was more ceremoniously laid to rest two days later.

An unlikelier demise was that of Robert Allington who on 26th September 1631 was fatally struck by lightning as he "did sit in a haycock". He was buried at Patrington.

Persistent Suicide

Then there was the Kirk Ella parishioner who was bent on self-destruction.

"William Swindale who stabbed himself in two places in his left side after yt drowned himself in ye dale well ye 4th day of November was buryed in ye field ye 5th day of November 1664".

Parish Coffin

Few burials have been done on the cheap, though as we have seen, delays have bought time. An arrangement once widely used was the parish coffin, which conveyed the enshrouded corpse to the graveside, and was afterwards returned to the back of the church. Few of these coffins have survived, but one example dated 1664 rests in the Saltmarshe Chantry, Howden Minster. Another is in Easingwold Parish Church, North Yorkshire.

The Howden Parish Coffin, 1664 *(H. Peach)*

Buried in Wool

In 1678 at a time when the woollen industry was in the doldrums, a law was passed requiring that all shrouds should be made of wool; and an affidavit to this effect had to be sworn before a magistrate. Parish records offer some interesting details. Thus at Cherry Burton:

"Will the son of John Dickinson was buryed in Wool by ye oath of Isabell Baker given before Mr L. Delgarnoe, March 11th 1700.

Infringements resulted in a fine of five pounds, and of course many mourners preferred to pay the fine rather than obey the miserable law. At Hunmanby on 3rd August 1746 Matthew Buck was "Buried in linen by which means ye poor people got £2 10s to be distributed among them".

Gradually the practice fell away, and the requirement was repealed in 1814.

Gloves and Garlands

A custom pre-dating the Reformation is the retention in some churches of mementoes of young girls who died prematurely. At the funeral of Ophelia in *Hamlet* (Act V, Scene i) Shakespeare talked of "virgin rites" and "maiden strewments". In Beverley St Mary's is such a garland inscribed "Elizabeth Ellinor died 14th August 1680 aged 21". It consists of strips of bent wood painted with red flowers and green foliage.

In the vestry of St Oswald's Church, Flamborough is displayed a pair of white paper gloves used at the funeral of a Miss Major in 1761. These gloves and garlands were carried by friends of the deceased at the head of the procession, and afterwards hung up in the church, on a wall, perhaps, or the rood screen or commonly above the pew hitherto associated with the young lady. It was thought unlucky to move them, so they often stayed until they disintegrated.

Forking Accident

The North Ferriby registers describe a horrific accident to the blacksmith Daniel Roxby in 1698. He was slain by a fork "thrown from a bean stack by his brother, a child, when it was almost dark which pitching in one of his ears pierced almost quite through his head which threw him into convulsions of which he died in twenty-four hours".

Same Day Deaths

Sir Matthew Peirson and his brother John died on the same day, 11th February 1712, Matthew at 3am, John at 3pm. They were buried three days later in the chancel of Lowthorpe Church.

Scaffold Confession

The Rev Enoch Sinclair, vicar of Owthorne, was unlucky enough to be murdered in June 1708 by two nieces and a servant called Adam Alvin. After burying him in his own garden the conspirators spread stories of finding his hat and wig on the beach. But suspicions were aroused, especially when Alvin and the elder sister, Mary fled to London. Four years later, the other sister, Catherine, on her death-bed confessed all. Alvin was arrested, tried at York and condemned. Mary was acquitted. At a last service prior to the execution, the congregation was startled when the preacher, Mr Mace fell dead in the pulpit. The opportunist arose in the prisoner. This is the Hand of God coming to my aid, he cried. He was not believed, however, and the following day went to meet his Maker ... but on the scaffold he admitted to the murder.

Long-term Warning

Notorious pirate, smuggler and murderer, Edward Pennell was captured in 1732 and executed in London. His body was returned to Hornsea where it was gibbeted as a warning to others of his ilk. There it remained until it fell with the crumbling cliffs c1845.

Nimrod of the North

William Draper, squire of Beswick, was a good family man, raising 11 children, and passionate about foxhounds. He lived most of his waking hours in the saddle, and he died there, too, on his way home from appraising a pack at Market Weighton. He was buried in the churchyard there in August 1746 at the age of 75.

Hemingbrough Parish Registers

24th May 1753: "Thomas son of John Acomb of Hemingbrough who died suddenly by his going hot into the river".

28th January 1768: "Mrs Sarah wife of Mr Faulkener of Bowthorpe. Her death was occasioned by the bite of a mad dog".

Worth it?

Francis Consitt was reputed to have lived at Burythorpe for 150 years i.e. 1618 to 1768. He attributed his long life to temperance, chastity and sucking raw eggs.

A Clutch of Dalton Goners

"The following dreadful instances of sudden death have happened within a few days of each other in the neighbourhood of South Dalton. A gardener belonging to the Rev Francis Best, after having been to receive his wages was seized on his return home with a violent bleeding of the nose, and died almost instantly. A gentleman who was riding on the road near that town was seized with an apoplectic fit and immediately expired; and a woman sitting at her spinning wheel, apparently in good health, fell from her chair and survived only a few minutes.

Two labourers belonging to Beverley having last week received a bottle of rum as a present from a gentleman, drank the whole of it almost immediately in course of which one of them died a few hours after, and the other was extremely ill for several days".
– *Hull Advertiser, 3rd January 1795.*

Some Stroke

The parish registers of Ellerker Church mention Christopher Coates, aged 17, buried at Brantingham "in consequence of a Stroke from a horse" in 1810.

Dick Turpin

Following his capture at the Green Dragon Inn, Welton, Dick Turpin spent his last days in the condemned cell at York Castle. One of his last purchases was a new fustian frock coat which he donned for his cart journey to the Knavesmire. Arriving there he stood and bowed to the thousands of spectators before climbing the ladder, resolutely stamping down his trembling right leg. There followed a long conversation with the executioner, and when all was ready, the noose tight at his throat, he deliberately threw himself off, his limbs jerking for several minutes.

On the same day, 7th April 1739 he was buried in St George's churchyard, but his body was "snatched" and later found in a surgeon's garden. His re-burial, this time in unslaked lime, took place after an unintended public parade.

Not for the Queasy

Soon after a French prisoner of war had died in 1746 a male torso was found in the moat near Hull's Salthouse Lane. Its legs were missing and a huge abdominal cavity contained the head. Dissecting doctors, presumably, had been at it again. There was no inquiry and no prosecutions.

In 1830 a Drypool father, sadly burying one of his children, was appalled to find that an earlier child's body had vanished from the grave. New corpses were in steady demand by medical students prepared to pay four guineas per cadaver. Parishioners took to erecting spring guns, patenting iron coffins or reinforcing them with metal bars. Fortunately the Anatomy Act of 1832 decreed that anyone could "direct that his/her body after death could be examined anatomically", and thus body snatching became superfluous.

"Like stones in a quarry"

On a visit to East Yorkshire in 1835 Sir George Head described the ruins of Kilnsea Church as successive tides eroded the surrounds. Hideously strewn about were the contents of the graveyard – bones, skulls, coffin fragments, garments. Eventually the bodies were re-buried at Rimswell.

George Poulson, historian of Holderness, reported that things were no better at nearby Owthorpe in 1841:

"....old persons tottering on the verge of life have been recognising on the shore the remains of those whom in early life they had known and revered."

This helps to explain churchwardens' accounts in 1800:

"To 15 days attendance at old churchyard when leading bones to new churchyard – £1 10s".

1822: "For burying bones from sands – 3s 0d".

A century later (1923) the situation in Aldbrough churchyard was investigated by the Ministry of Health who declared the site should be closed, being injurious to health ... "many human bones were lying about exposed to view". As this was the high point of the village there were fears of rainwater percolating into local wells; and already there was a high incidence of infectious disease ....

Rabbit Nannie

Nannie was known in the streets of Hull for stridently announcing her wares – rabbits. Before she died a certain Dr Hay gave her £5 for permission to dissect her body when life was extinct. Her skeleton disappeared from the Hull medical school, seemingly to soldiers at Fort Paull. It became the subject of many pranks, frightening many recruits. A disenchanted officer ordered its burial, so her bones lie beneath the fort.

Toddler Deaths

A capricious windmill sail is a potential accident. And it happened at Gilberdyke Mill in October 1827 when Thomas and Robert Bell were struck. They were buried at Blacktoft.

Pelling's Downfall

A stunt man well-known on both sides of the Humber, Thomas Pelling, was an accomplished tightrope artiste, and drew a large crowd when he appeared at Pocklington in 1833. Alas! while he was crossing on a rope suspended between the church tower and the Old Star Inn, he lost his balance and broke his skull against the church wall. He was buried where he fell.

Death-Bed Achievement

The abolition of the slave trade was William Wilberforce's life's work; and he applied himself to this cause with unswerving purpose. As a schoolboy at Pocklington and later at St John's College, Cambridge where he met William Pitt the Younger, he gathered the facts and marshalled his arguments. Becoming MP for his native Hull at the age of 21 he and his supporters detailed the circumstances of the kidnapping of African negroes, the inhuman conditions of the Atlantic crossing and the subsequent ill-treatment in the plantations of the West Indies.

Year after year he introduced parliamentary bills aimed at stopping this

Statue of William Wilberforce in the garden of Wilberforce House, Hull *(H. Peach)*

nauseous trade. At last in 1806 a Bill was passed to end it in the British Empire – but this was no more than a first step towards dismantling the system. At the General Election following, the Hon. Henry Lascelles was third in the triple contest for two seats, as his father owned West Indian slaves; and a powerful slogan that moved the electors' hearts and minds was "No Yorkshire votes purchased with African blood". Wilberforce held this seat for a further five years before becoming a member for Sussex.

Many practical difficulties remained, particularly the changed situations that would ultimately confront owners and former slaves. But at last the Emancipation Bill was ready, and Wilberforce, having retired from public life since 1825, learned of its triumph in the Commons as he lay dying.

"Thank God I have lived to witness a day in which England is willing to give twenty millions sterling for the abolition of slavery", he said.

This was the compensation sum to be given to the slave owners. Three days later, on 29th July 1833 Wilberforce died at the age of 73, his life's mission completed. He was given a public funeral and was buried in Westminster Abbey. His vast memorial column towers over Queens Gardens in the middle of Hull.

That Portly Priest

It is regrettable that sometimes a man's human qualities seem to be diminished by his physical exterior. Born into a wealthy Hull family in 1775, Joseph Coltman served Beverley Minster and the townsfolk very faithfully for 24 years until his death in 1837. He was a cheerful compassionate priest, a gifted scholar and a valued part-time classics tutor at several schools; he was a public benefactor, a patron of the arts and a local magistrate. Eloquent when the occasion demanded, he rarely lost the common touch. Once on a cold day he advised a group from the Minster Moorgate workhouse to adjourn with him to a Hallgarth hostelry for glasses of mulled ale – which would warm them more than his prayers.

One physical factor separated him from his fellows: at around 40 stone he was thought to be one of the biggest men in England. When he was still youthful his legs had become uncertain, and he needed help to move. About town he used a velocipede, or "dandy-horse", pulled by a boy with a rope. In the minster a ramp was erected so that three vergers could draw him to the pulpit.

He died tragically, suffocating in bed after rolling onto his stomach. On the day of his funeral Beverley shut its shops and dutifully processed behind the immense lead coffin measuring 7ft by 3ft 2 inches, and 1ft 8 inches deep. He was buried close to the south wall of the minster.

Just in Case

When Tom Spofford was married to Maria Watson at Roos on 25th July 1842 he felt he was taking one or two chances. This was his third marriage and he was 76 years old. But in one crucial respect he wanted to feel secure; so he brought the coffin into the bridal bedroom. He had made it himself and painted it blue, decorating it with love knots and entwined hearts. A number of earlier ones had been fashioned, but they had been vandalised by local lads, and a recent example of his craftsmanship had been used to bury his second wife. So this blue one was immediately available, should circumstances so require. That was a comfort.

Maria's inner thoughts can only be guessed. But Tom's premonitions were not far out. He died on 18th August and two days later was laid to rest at Halsham – in his own blue coffin.

Train Strike

Born at Reighton Hall in 1811, and a grandson of Edmund Cartwright, inventor of the power loom (1785), Hugh Edwin Strickland was fascinated as a boy by the cliffs near his home. An expert on molluscs and the Dodo, he became Reader in Geology at Oxford in 1850. Unfortunately, he was killed by a train near the Charborough Tunnel on the Sheffield and Lincolnshire line whilst examining geological strata.

Nancy's Nemesis

After the death of her father, the Rev John Jackson, master of Drax Grammar School, just over the River Ouse, Nancy married his successor, John Nicholson in 1811 when she was 26. She treated the boys extraordinarily badly, feeding them with scraps, beating them but encouraging them to steal eggs which she sold in the neighbourhood.

Despairing of his bride's unprofessional style, dirty attire, bad language and expanding girth, the Rev John took to the bottle and striking at her with a horsewhip. In 1844 they separated, she taking to a farm at Asselby. John took up residence exactly opposite, on the other side of the river, playing his accordion just to annoy her. She responded with bursts on the organ. She wrote to the Archbishop, succeeding in getting John suspended from preaching for two years. She attended his funeral in 1850. But the locality was outraged when Nancy turned out her niece and husband, auctioning off their stock. Her effigy was pointedly fired outside her farm. Partial amends were made in her will.

In 1854 this remarkable termagant fell ill. Sensing her days were numbered Nancy ordered a five gallon barrel of ale and drank the lot just before she died on 6th August at the age of 69. She had paid for it, she argued, and she was going to drink it. There was no-one to argue.

Flamborough Failings

There was significant tippling elsewhere in the Riding. In July 1857 there was an opening for a doctor in Flamborough. The last two had drunk themselves to death.

Drowned Sorrows

In May 1866 Richard Chadwick, a farm servant at Leven Hall Garth, rebuked by his foreman in the fields, left his horse team and went straight to the public house at Wilfholme. On his return he asked for his wages which were refused. After spending more time in a Leven pub, Chadwick proceeded to walk along the Leven Canal bank, followed by two men who were alarmed at his conduct. Suddenly he jumped into the water. The two others were unable to rescue him and called for help. The body was later pulled to the surface with a rake. Coroner's verdict – temporary insanity.

The Glasgow Poisoner

Before moving to Hunmanby and Filey as a general practitioner in 1849 Dr E.W. Pritchard had served as a naval surgeon. And long before he moved on to Glasgow twelve years later, tongues were wagging. He was a famous attention seeker, even arranging to get himself called out of church services. Suspicions arose over some of his prescriptions, particularly over the death of a certain Betty Chandler and his efforts to remove pills or potions from her house. His departure was generally welcomed.

In Glasgow he soon made his mark. His maidservant died in a house fire. Mysteriously a fellow surgeon he was treating also passed on. Then he was accused of murdering his wife, Mary Jane Taylor, an Edinburgh lady whom he had wed in his Hunmanby days. After due trial and condemnation Pritchard was hanged on 27th May

Dr E.W. Pritchard *(Courtesy of Glasgow City Council Cultural and Leisure Services)*

1865 in Glasgow, the last man to meet that fate, before a crowd estimated at 50,000. No wonder that East Riding folk treat off-comed-uns warily until they have proved themselves!

Gravill of the Diana

Whaling ships leaving Hull in February or March aimed to return for October and Hull Fair. But the Arctic ice claimed many victims, and it nearly claimed the *Diana*, caught for four months in the straits west of Greenland, despite the efforts of a 40hp steam engine. The Truelove was sent as a relief but was unable to make contact. Thirteen men died from exposure, too little food and no fuel. They included the captain, John Gravill who succumbed on Boxing Day, 1866. Thereafter the ship's surgeon, Charles Smith took charge, bringing back Gravill's body. As the *Diana* reached Hull the coffin was mounted on the ship's bridge.

Further to this dramatic and emotional return, a huge wave of mourners almost swamped the funeral proceedings at the Western Cemetery on 29th April 1867.

From "Diana fast in the ice" by R.D. Widdas *(Courtesy of Kingston upon Hull Museums)*

Choked in Chimney

Workmen at Wilberforce House, Hull on 3rd June 1870 found a skeleton in a chimney. Presumably it had been someone in hiding, most likely a thief who had got stuck and suffocated.

A Wrangler's Misjudgement

To transfer one's self from the presidency of St John's College, Cambridge to a rural East Riding rectorship, and to stay there for 35 years does not look like an obvious career move. But this was the chosen path of Dr John Hymers, brilliant mathematician (second wrangler, 1826) and author of many learned treatises. At Brandesburton from 1852 he was not particularly successful. His sermons were well above the heads of his congregation, and he was an indifferent social mixer. Yet here was a maverick and therefore an interesting man.

Despite considerable investments, notably in the railways, John Hymers acquired a reputation for "nearness". His house became as neglected as his church, and his servants rarely stayed for log. He kept a wary eye on his fees. More at home in his garden, he kept bees and pigs, sold fruit and vegetables to his parishioners and through his rhubarb sales became known as "Three Sticks a Penny".

Yet there were quiet and benign sides to his nature. He was genuinely sorry for poorer folk; and as a magistrate he sometimes privately paid the fines which he had helped to impose.

Like most of us, the rector enjoyed looking for bargains, and took his horse and trap regularly into Beverley. He must have brought back a noggin or two, for at his death 145 dozen bottles of excellent wine were discovered in his cellars.

A characteristic independence of spirit and a lifetime's way with words induced him to draw up his own will leaving the greater part of an estate of £200,000 to "found and endow" a school in Hull "for the training of intelligence in whatever social rank of life it may be found". Sadly the wording was held to be contrary to the Statute of Mortmain; and this considerable inheritance went instead to his brother Robert and other relatives. Finally Robert diverted £50,000 to the Mayor and Corporation towards Hymers College which opened in 1893, six years after John Hymers' death.

Sculptor's Suicide

William Day Keyworth was a sculptor talented enough to receive commissions for the statues of Andrew Marvell, Wilberforce and William de la Pole in Hull, plus another of Sir Rowland Hill, of Penny Post fame, for Westminster Abbey. But his business worries drove him to shoot himself, the bullet shattering his skull, on 9th August 1902. He was only 59. His body was found by his daughter Martha in his workshop at 244 Spring Bank, Hull.

Stiff Ti-morn

On 31st May 1905 Abraham Featherby, a Goodmanham farmer, died after being kicked by a horse. At the time he had tried to make light of it. When his foreman inquired whether he was much hurt he replied, "No – but I shall be stiff in the morning". And, sadly, he was.

Boyle's Lore

Born to an illiterate mother on the wrong aide of the Pennines (Accrington) in 1853 , Robert Boyle became a distinguished antiquarian, expert in Latin and Norman-French documents. As a parson he eked out a living as a records clerk in Hull. It was money worries, no doubt, that persuaded him foolishly to sell for £15 a bundle of priceless letters penned by the poet Andrew Marvell to the Mayor and Corporation. The dealer thoughtfully passed them on to Sotheby's ... and inevitably news of the sale reached the town clerk of Hull. Boyle was peremptorily sacked and arrested on 17th May 1905. Pleading guilty at the resulting court appearance, he was sentenced to 12 months hard labour at the Hedon Road jail.

Ill, impoverished and now deserted by his friends he emerged a broken man and died in the workhouse on 3rd September 1907. Several of his works, like the Early History of the Town and Port of Hedon (1895) and Lost Towns of the Humber (1889) are still valuable for scholars.

Death of Local Sportsman

Ernest Richard Bradley Hall-Watt JP, Deputy Lieutenant, High Sheriff of Yorkshire (1896), Lord of the Manor of Bishop Burton and generous benefactor was also a motor racing pioneer. At the age of 43 he was killed when his car hit a tree after a back tyre burst during the International Grand Prix near Dieppe in 1908.

Ernest Richard Bradley Hall-Watt in his family vehicle at Bishop Burton, c1904 *(Courtesey of John Dunning)*

Promise Cut Short

Prime mover in the recruitment of local waggoners in 1914 , and designer of the graphic memorial at Sledmere (see Chapter 3), Sir Mark Sykes was a man of many distinguished parts. Scholar, explorer, MP for Hull and international diplomat, he represented his country at the Paris Peace Conference, where he died quite suddenly at the early age of 40, an immense loss in so many social spheres.

Old Mother Riley

On 17th May 1954 while waiting in the wings at Hull's Tivoli Theatre to appear as Old Mother Riley in Paris, Arthur Lucan, born at Boston in 1887, collapsed and died. He was buried in the Eastern Cemetery. An epitaph by his estranged wife, Kitty McShane reads: "Arthur Lucan, better known and beloved by all as Old Mother Riley. Don't cry as you pass by, just say a little prayer".

In 1986 a bust of Arthur was unveiled by Danny la Rue in Skelton's Bakery, Paragon Street. The shop stands on the site of the former Tivoli, demolished in 1957.

Chapter 6

Superstitions and Sayings

Beware Strangers

Suspicion of strangers used to be deeply entrenched in this Riding. Local interests came first, as a Hessle by-law of 1669 made clear:

"...the master of any ship or vessel which comes into Hessle Haven do cry their coals in the town 24 hours before they cry them in the countryside".

The pains set out by the Driffield manorial court a century later were meant to discourage and exclude:

"...no foreign strangers to make ways over the common, 10s; none to lodge strangers for more than one night, 3s 4d; no strangers to wash sheep, fowl or fish, 10s".

Dated 9th October 1826 a manorial requirement still displayed in Huggate Parish Church instructed its Jury to impose fines on anyone harbouring vagrants.

Such legal and social barriers, reinforcing the area's geographical isolation, help to explain much resistance to change and the lingering of so many outdated beliefs and superstitions.

Witchcraft

Until the 19th century belief in witches was a fact of village life. Imagination, rumour, supposition, belief – dark ideas readily multiplied and hardened. Ill-founded gossip perpetuated much untested nonsense, like the amphibious beast that was thought to be on constant prowl at a pool near Atwick Church. Contradictions abounded. Too much was made of the Biblical injunction "Thou shalt not suffer a witch to live "(Exodus XXII, v 18); yet exorcist incantations were rehearsed as animal organs were stuck with heated pins for dubious ends.

In 1654 John Greencliffe of Beverley swore that he had seen Elizabeth Roberts change into a cat which proceeded to pelt him with stones. Then she became a bee. But reason prevailed and the accused lady was acquitted. Given our hindsight, the perplexing aspect is that she was ever arrested.

Village Wise

In "A Victorian Boyhood on the Wolds", J. R. Mortimer recalled that at Fimber, Rachel Kirby occupied the last thatched house on the Fridaythorpe Road. Her evil eye was blamed for many local ills, especially when animals became diseased or died. Many villagers truly accepted that she could change at will into a hare, thereby occasioning many a dog chase.

Some individuals were credited with unspecified but harmless insights. During the 1730s the crypt of St Nicholas Church, Hornsea was occupied by a strange old lady, Nancy Cankerneedle, so-called because she had once succumbed to a test of innocence by holding hot needles, presumably in a late imitation of certain medieval church practices.

Against a background of slender claims and fewer facts, some reputations achieved cult status, as with Susannah Gore (1728-1826), Wise Woman of Driffield. Her fortune telling may have been uncommonly remunerative, for she managed to buy several local houses. Rumour asserted that she had sold her soul to the Devil, Incredulity might have set in when she was supposed to have flown over the church on a blazing besom to flit to Barrow on Humber.

Esteemed with fewer reservations was George Wales (1786-1860) of Barmby Moor. Apart from his distinctive physical appearance – tall, dark costume, chimney-pot hat – he brought an unusual intellectual background to his work, being both a Christian exorcist and a student of the occult. Yet some of his recommendations hardly separated him from the general run of charlatans. To cure a fever, an animal's still warm heart was to be hung on the afflicted person. Memory could be improved by eating the heart of a lapwing, swallow, weasel or mole. One memorable success attributed to his arts was at Greenlands Farm where a number of horses had died. After they were buried in a deep pit, a horseshoe hung over the stable door, and incantations intoned by George, sure enough the survivors prospered.

At Holme on Spalding Moor, Sally Mountain was reputed to exercise such a hypnotic spell on horses that they stopped by her cottage near the Star Inn until rider or driver had paid an adequate toll.

It is likely that many local sages , like Peggy Farrow at Elloughton, made unspectacular claims, contenting themselves with advising on herbal potions for a variety of ailments.

Primitive Cures

Village Wise and conventional medical practitioners were by no means alone in dispensing advice. Nicholas Nicholls, Vicar of Patrington (1734-1772) scribbled random titbits in his parish register. Cattle distemper, for example, could be treated by tying a bunch of onions around the animal's neck. The beast's nose would run, carrying away the sickness. The onions, swollen with contagion, had to be buried.

Strother's Journal (1785) told of John Archbutt and family successfully drinking a neighbour's mixture of soot and water to dispel a fever prevalent in Cottingham. In another family, where one child had died, despite doctor's medicines, this simple remedy removed all symptoms.

It is instructive and entertaining to consider some of the measures resorted to in times past. For instance:

✧ **to clear spots:** smear with blood from a white hen and leave to dry. Thereafter brimstone and treacle helped to purify the patient's blood.

✧ **hair restorer:** rub with mice droppings or ashes of burnt wasps or vinegar of roses; or pigeon dung.

✧ **sty:** rub with a gold wedding rig.

✧ **rheumatism:** comfort with hot potato in a sock. Gout might be relieved by solutions of burdock root.

✧ **toothache:** plug of tobacco in the ear; or a clove held against the tooth; sniff lighted brown paper; dabbings of dock root boiled up with olive oil.

✧ **headache:** apply brown paper soaked in vinegar.

✧ **cuts:** plaster of cow dung with goat hair and lime.

✧ **lumbago:** put a flannel on the back and rub with a hottish iron.

✧ **earache:** lodge in the ear a small snip of muslin filled with black pepper.

✧ **warts:** rub with dandelion milk – or pebbles, peas, or elder twig, then bury these.

✧ **cough:** rub chest with goose grease. Drink elderberry syrup.

✧ **aching joints:** apply horse liniment.

✧ **seasickness:** chew a straw held firm by the teeth (i.e. concentrate on something else).

✧ **whooping cough:** visit a gasworks and inhale strongly. Place the child on a donkey's back, facing the tail.[1]

✧ **burns and scalds:** cow dung poultices.

✧ **bleeding:** tap a handful of spider's web across the wound.

✧ **boils, carbuncles:** hot bread poultice.

There was a strong belief in the efficacy of onions. Bunches hung by the kitchen door attracted and neutralised harmful germs. Shredded in socks they eased chilblains and helped to counter heavy colds. A warmed centre soothed earache.

Iodine lockets worn on a neck string were recommended by some as a precaution against scarlet fever. Adornments of camphor tablets perhaps offered a mere general protection. Intakes of raw egg and milk could be expected to act as a tonic.

We may smile. It is plain that many of these remedies were palliatives, offering a degree of temporary comfort, yet a number of modern alternative medicines favour herbal nostrums: preparations of St John's Wort, for example, never seem to have lost support.

Passion Killer

Hemlock (or Kex or Fool's Parsley), growing profusely by our roadsides throughout the summer was thought to dampen down lustful thoughts. But who would knowingly drink it? Rosemary, however (the herb, not necessarily the girl) was a turn-on.

---

[1] We have the considerable authority of M.F.C. Morris's *Yorkshire Reminiscences* (1927) – see page 106 – that this actually happened.

Taboos

Superstition depends on taboo and restriction. It invites prejudice which is rarely inspected, let alone tested. The passing on from one generation to another of unchallenged customs and beliefs was particularly evident in the fishing communities on the east coast. To many otherwise hardened mariners some names, even, were distressing, especially on board ship, or en route thereto – names of animals like hare, rat, fox, pig, cat, dog, rabbit, egg. The colour green was out of favour. Church and chapel were best left behind. All these things were terrestrial, lingering thoughts of which might divert a man doing a dangerous job.

It was a bad omen for a fisherman walking to his ship to meet a man of the cloth. No boat sailed on a Sunday. No mattress was to be turned on a Sunday. There was to be no whistling which might call up the wind and endanger the vessel.

Prejudices against women were plain. They were not to walk on the nets or fishing tackle. They were not always welcome visitors, especially on Christmas Day. After childbirth they needed "churching", or bad luck would follow. When the boat left the jetty, wives should not wave or call out. Yet in whaling times the women had thrown old shoes after ships leaving Hull. There were other inconsistencies. In Victorian times at Flamborough a good herring season might be encouraged by a cheerful younger woman calling to extend good wishes – a custom whose passing many a fisherman may have regretted.

Good luck was sought also at Filey by inserting coins into cracks discovered in the corking on the nets.

Other interesting prohibitions that appear in East Riding literature include:

✧ Don't drop a ring or your partner may fall ill.

✧ Don't cut a baby's fingernails until s/he is one year old, or you may be rearing a thief. Young nails should be bitten.

✧ Don't wind wool by lamplight. There could be a fire risk, and an imperfect skein might not be noticed in poorer light. There was rarely any shortage of bad omens; almost any change might be frowned on. A curious one concerned hedgehogs, regarded as vermin and suspected of sucking milk from cows. An entry in the Market Weighton churchwardens' accounts for 1682 reads: "To Matthew Clarke for 2 hedgehogs – 4d".

Simple domestic tasks needed great care if omens were to be avoided. Children and young servants would need instruction when folding cloths or sheets so as not to create a "death's diamond".

Beggar's Litany

Here, truly, was an old prayer incorporating fears – "From Hell, Hull and Halifax, good Lord deliver us!" For our forefathers Hell was almost an astronomical location. Halifax had been dreaded for its public guillotine. And Hull – well, Hull had had its vagrants whipped and stocked, and some of its prisoners drowned on gibbets in the flood tide, or lost and tortured in the Tudor blockhouse ... then came the press gang. There was plenty in Hull to promote anxiety.

More of a smile was raised during the 1920s when citizens in Bond Street wittily pointed out the juxtaposition of a church, a pub and a building society, predictably translated as "Heaven, Hell and Halifax".

Intimations of Mortality

Some omens were too direct and graphic to be ignored. One wonders how many people frightened themselves to death by the sight of three birds in a line along a house top; or the yapping of a dog outside as they lay sick in bed; or the stopping of a usually reliable clock; or the falling onto the hearth of a coffin-shaped lump of soot. In Holderness any nocturnal growling could be interpreted as the "bargest" or "Boggle-bo", a sure harbinger of the Grim Reaper.

In the Filey area an expression used of the near-dying was "He'll soon be i' North Riding!"

When bees were kept, and the master lay dying, it used to be urged "Tell the bees". They too would want to mourn, and might be consoled by portions of the funeral fare.

Welcome

A verse well known across these Broad Acres is worth quoting. Obviously in line three any village will do.

"Ah dreamed Ah were dead and ti Heaven did go.
Ah tolled on big bell and bowed very low.
Ah says "Ah's frev——" Lor! how they did stare.
"Come thi ways in", Peter says. "Thoo's fost yan fra theer!"

Suicides

While the subject often arouses a morbid curiosity, a lighter touch is lent by a Flamborough legend. After Jenny Gallow committed suicide in a round hollow just outside the village, children running around it, especially at dusk, might expect to raise her ghost. But they had to be ready for Jenny coming back at them with –

"Ah'll put on me bonnet,
Ah'll tie on me shoe;
An' if thoo's not off
Ah'll be efther thoo!"

Spooky

Some accounts relate to the remote past. At Willy Howe, a Neolithic barrow near Thwing, there have been sightings of a funeral procession . And Hedon has been the site of a phantom twosome. After being stabbed by a monk called John Coomber, the abbess of the Hospital of the Holy Sepulchre was thrown into the Fleet; but this same Ruth soon re-appeared to frighten him and reveal the wicked plot of Sister Alice who had usurped her place. Coomber hanged himself and took to unquiet ghostly maraudings. Alice was imprisoned.

Stately homes are supposed to shelter ghosts. Burton Constable Hall seems to have experienced at least three: a 17th-century nun sweeping down the long gallery; William Constable (1721-91) – he of the gun collection and fascinating scientific apparatus – has been seen by later members of the family in the Gold Bedroom; and a wanderer, Nurse Dowdall, a 19th-century children's nanny.

Burton Agnes Hall *(H. Peach)*

During a visit to Harpham from Burton Agnes Hall in 1620 Lady Anne Griffiths was attacked, robbed and left for dead. Back home she begged her family to bury her head in the beloved house. Instead she was laid to rest in the churchyard, but soon returned and with spectral wailings rebuked her mourners. Finally, her last wishes were respected, since when things quietened down. Except that in 1915 Mrs Wickham Boynton saw this small thin woman, in a light fawn dress, on the front door steps. On closer inspection it vanished, but turned up later on the east side of the house.

Hostelry hauntings appear to be another fact of the East Yorkshire afterlife. Since the murder of a serving maid at the Feathers Inn, Pocklington in 1870 there have been several reports of heavy breathing and scrapings as of objects being dragged across the floor. Ye Olde Black Boy in Hull's old High Street, parts of which may be 14th century, has given rise to a Civil War cavalier figure near the cellar hatch door. A Victorian lady has, out of licensing hours, patronised the Black Swan at North Cave; whilst at the Nancy Inn, Burton

Pidsea poltergeists have played occasional havoc, like pushing an ornamental lounge anvil right into the middle of the room.

A strongly authenticated apparition manifested itself in the 1980s at the King's Head, Beverley where the manager saw a labourer in 1930s costume standing by the fireplace. Later a waitress approaching a table with an order pad at the ready was startled to find the gentleman absent.

When the Rev. Percival Ryder Frost was at Patrington (1928-49) a lady guest was hurled from her bed and furniture was moved. A later guest heard heavy patterings which stopped when he switched the light on, and resumed when the light went out.

In Hull's New Theatre there have been a number of unscheduled off-stage appearances by "Charlie", a cheerful sprite given to white pantaloons and a top hat.

The ghost of "Old Tin Boots" is said to haunt the raised walkway by the pond at North Dalton – or is this a Mere Fantasy?

Awd Goggie

Spectral proliferations should not be unduly wondered at when one considers the credulities once put before children. In the Withernsea hinterland youngsters were apt to be chastened by Awd Goggie, a usually benign rural spirit who could be summoned to frighten and admonish.

"Be good, else Awd Goggie'll git thee"

Rowan-Reliant Raywell

Despite a rapidly developing scientific outlook at the national level, much uncritical superstition still held sway in late Victorian East Yorkshire. Rowan trees were often planted near kitchen and stable doors to counter evil forces. Farmers gained confidence at haunted bridges and crossroads by tightening their grip on their whip stock –

"Rowan tree and good red thread

Put the witches to their bed".

Highly polished horse brasses gave further protection. Local historian Dr Arthur Wilson-Barkworth noted in the 1880s that parishioners walking to Kirk Ella Church from Raywell and Riplingham wore cross-shaped sprigs of elderberry, oak, hawthorn or ash. Even for many non-worshippers the cross was a potent image for good. Cross-plaited hazel sticks were hung about the necks of cattle.

At Leavening, St Helen's Eve (14th May) was Witch Wood Night when sprigs of rowan were cut and brought home, there to mount spiritual guard until they withered away.

For fishermen, hares night be bad news, but inland a hare's foot was well regarded as a traveller's talisman. Limmel or hag stones (with holes), common on Holderness beaches, were hung on farm buildings to prevent witches riding horses or milking the cows.

Lucky Charms

It used to be customary to take a new baby an egg, a silver spoon and a pinch of salt, hopefully ensuring food, wealth and health. Sometimes a match was added to light the infant through the world.

In more distant tines a less savoury charm was the caul, or membrane left on the baby's face at birth. Set aside between the pages of a book, it would prevent drowning and confer the gift of the gab.

Cupid's Well

Many years later at Keyingham a young man needed to beware the wiles of a girl coyly leading him towards St Philip's Well. She had but to throw in a coin, and expect her beau to do the same – and he was regarded as hooked!

Weather Lore

❖ A crow sitting on decaying wood means rain.

❖ Duck weed rising on the pond means fine.

❖ Horses standing with their backs to a hedge are a sign of bad weather.

❖ Busy spiders, better weather.

❖ Seagull, seagull, sit on the sand,
    It's never fine weather when you stay inland.

❖ Not enough wind to work Westwood windmills (at Beverley).

❖ Joe Plug's blowing strang (the wind is getting up).

❖ As cawd as Kilnsea.

❖ Onion skin thin, mild winter coming in; Onion skin hard and tough, Coming winter's cold and rough.

❖ All other months curse a fine February.

❖ On St Joseph's day throw warming pans away (19ᵗʰ March).

❖ Open chamber window to let the thunder out.

General Sayings

"High Paull and Low Paull and Old Paull Town
There is ne'er a maid married in all Paull toon".

In other words, all three places in line one were close to the Humber bank, but weddings were solemnised at the slightly more distant church of St Andrew and St Mary on an elevated site half a mile south-east of the village.

"Great Kelk, where never God dwelt,
And honest man never rode through it".

There is no church in the village; the second line is as maybe.

"Market Weighton
Robert Leighton
A brick church
And wooden steeple
A drunken priest
And a wicked people".

Leighton was a popular local name, and may have referred to a mid-18th-century innkeeper. The drunken priest could have been Henry Robinson (1736-62) who lived at Etton.

More straightforward is:

"Gilbert Gant
Left Hunby Moor
To Hunmanby poor
That they might never want".

And,

"Marriage is the same as plooin' wi' tweea hosses; yan's gorra walk id furrer."

or

"Thoo'll niver be feared o' deead if thoo kisses a corpse."

and even

"Lucky? If he tummled into Albert Dock he'd come up wi' a pocketful o' fish."

Mucky Talk

All of a muck heap, like Howden Fair.

Trouble wi' tractors is they deean' t make much muck.

Ah's muck-pluggin' ti-morn (I am spreading manure on the fields tomorrow).

Dialect Diversion

East Yorkshire dialect has many links with Denmark. The Jutland connection was energetically pursued by M.C.F. Morris in "Yorkshire Folk Talk", 1892. Intriguingly, in 1847 King Christian VIII had sent a scholar over here to record once common words which had expired in Denmark, but still used in this Riding. Here are a few juicy verbal morsels:

bellywark	stomach ache
borterin'	walking in a drunken fashion
bubblyjock	turkey
caff-arted	cowardly, shy
dowly	dull, miserable
flittermoose	bat
gallock-'anded	left handed
hanch at	grab meaning to bite
illify	to defame
juntersome	bad tempered
lanty	slowcoach
menseful	sensible, thrifty, clean
monk on	morose, disinclined
nipper-corran	miser
nunty	old fashioned

otherin' on	going on, nagging
porriwiggle	tadpole
pross	gossip
rig-welted	on back, unable to rise
rouk	snore like a pig
sackless	idiotic
scopperill	naughty child
skymin'	looking furtively sideways
spurrings	the banns
stoddy	stupid, awkward
twank	to punish by striking
upskelled	overturned
uzzel	blackbird
wemmley	wobbly
wots	oats
yat stowp	gate post

Shepherds' Count (1-10)

Yan – Tan – Tethera – Peddera – Pump – Sethera – Lethera – Overa – Dovera – Dick

Home Truths

Stoddy as a yat stowp (Daft as a gate post).

If yal (ale) were free and watther dear, there'd be neea teetotallers.

Yan o' yows is badly (One of the ewes is ill).

There are myriad versions of the tale of the new Wolds parson anxious to butter up the locals. Here's one:

Vicar: By gow, Jack, it's reeat sleeap an' fahl unnerfeeat tideea.

Jack: (Sniffing) Yes sir, it's slippery all right.

Other sayings include:

Sha's nobbut a pud-bonner (The Yorkshire pudding's burning while she's gossiping.)

She's no idea how to lay a shilling out.

Hungry as a Hornsea beach donkey.

If sandwiches were spread thinly:

Thoo spreeads butther on thin, screeaps if off ageean – an' thoo nobbut sniffs at cheease.

Complaint about sandwiches :

"Missus niver butthers 'eeadlands!" (sides)

Get thi pud etten fost (so we may save on meat).

Opening and shutting yats: falling away from posh talk back to dialect. (John Widdowson's thoughtful phrases repay study, and are collected in *his Proverbs and Sayings from Filey*, 1969).

Tweea spoons in a cup – wedding's coming up.

If you would understand someone you must

"... summer and winter them – and happen winter them again!"

And finally

Oxford for learning, London for wit,

Hull for a woman, and York for a tit (i.e. a hunting or racehorse).

Yorkshire motto
See all, hear all, say nowt;
Eat all, sup all, pay nowt.
And if thoo does owt for nowt
Allis deea it for thissen.

East Yorkshire Toast
Here's tiv us all, all on us iver:
May neean on us want nowt,
Neean on us niver.

Final Apocryphal

During off-shore storms, Kilnsea church bell still tolls beneath the billows.

The Hedon mayoral chain became progressively shorter as each mayor removed one link as a souvenir. At last it would not go over the new man's head.

Mistake in a youngster's homework – "Ah's gan an' putten putten wheer Ah thowt ti ha' putten put".

Chapter 7

Customs

Many traditional East Yorkshire customs have followed the calendar. Earliest off the mark, where it still exists, is the **Lucky Bod** (Bird). Immediately after the church bells have chimed midnight on 31st December, a window is opened to let the old year out. Then the Lucky Bod crosses the threshold armed with a silver coin as a token of wealth, a lump of coal for warmth and good cheer and a slice of bread for food. Sometimes for good luck an evergreen is added – but on this item there are two opposed schools of thought. So the Lucky Bod acts as first footer. As a rule, a dark-haired lad is preferred, but in some cases, mindful perhaps of the Viking inheritance a blonde is enlisted, intoning the old rhyme –

> *Lucky Bod, Lucky Bod,*
> *Chuck, chuck, chuck.*
> *Mesther an' misthress –*
> *Tahm ti git up.*
> *If ye deean't git up*
> *Ye'll hev neea luck.*
> *So please will ye gimme*
> *A New Year gift?*

A variation on Lucky Bods were the Early Bods, once familiar in North Wolds villages on Christmas morning. Their rhyme was –

> *A little bit of spice bread, a little bit of cheese,*
> *A cup of cold water and a penny, if you please.*

The sight of young urchins on the doorstep at an early hour must have been a serious test of seasonal goodwill. In practice there was much local variation.

At Barmby Moor in Edwardian times boys did the Christmas rounds, while girls acted as New Year Lucky Bods. But this would never do in Filey and the coastal areas: female first-footers might compromise the coming fishing season!

Scrambling

On the morning of the first working day of the New Year dozens of Driffield youngsters still scramble outside shops for coins, apples, nuts etc thrown into their midst by benevolent proprietors. The origin is uncertain, but may hark back to times when itinerant traders hoped to attract customers by offering baubles to children. Public co-operation is invited by a chorus of:

> *Here we are at oor toon end,*
> *A shoulder of mutton and a croon ti spend.*

Not that scrambling has been confined to Driffield. Hull trawler skippers often celebrated a good trip by tossing up money between the pubs along Hessle Road. In late Victorian times May Days were enlivened in Pocklington by the antics of John Lister, cab proprietor, stopping at intervals to throw coins into the air.

Time was when unscrupulous politicians threw money about to bribe electors to vote for them. Nowadays, at Hedon the scrambling is confined to children and takes place at the end of the annual mayor-making ceremony – pennies from Hedon!

An old wedding custom which still occasionally takes place at Burton Fleming church is for the lych gates to be tied together during the ceremony. Before the happy couple can leave, the groom or best man has to scatter enough small change for the children waiting outside to agree to cut the string.

Plough Stots

On Plough Monday, the first after Epiphany, young men would carry a decorated plough around the village, asking for alms at each door. Refusers were quite likely to find a furrow had been turned over, right across their lawn. In many places, like Cottingham, the practice had ceased by about 1880, unlamented for the noise and vandalism that seemed inseparable. The Stots (or Jacks or Lads) who performed a kind of mummers' play survived longer, up to 1939 around Stamford Bridge. They dressed up in old – fashioned costumes, with key figures like St George, Beelzebub, the doctor, Betty or Bosom Bet, and Blether Dick who flourished a blown-up pig's bladder tied to the end of a stick. Incidental sound effects included bells on their boots, mouth organs and spoons snapped rhythmically together. The front man knocked on a door, and if invited inside, shouted as follows –

"In comes I as niver been yit,
Wiv a greeat big heead an' varry lahtle wit.
Though me heead be big and me wit be small
It's my endeavour ti please you all".

With the table prudently drawn back, the timeless battle between Good and Evil was played out on the hearth-side, with lively struggles and panaceas applied, and Good (of course) triumphing... and a collection made. If the hostess was pleased she might pass round a plateful of chizkeeak (cheesecake).

Collop Monday

The day before Shrove Tuesday was the penultimate occasion for the eating up of meat prior to the Lenten fast: this, at any rate, was the claim for many Christians. Collops were simply pieces of meat – bacon, beef, etc – enjoyed with fried eggs. Any sizeable portions left over were salted and hung up for Easter Sunday, Good Feast Day.

Shrove Tuesday

Hip-hip-hooray! It's Pancake Day!
If you don't give us a holiday
We'll all run away.

Although the custom of pupils barring out the schoolmaster seems not to have caught on to any marked degree in the East Riding (but see Chapter 8), the tolling of the church bell at 11am, calling their elders to be shriven (confessed) was often the signal for lessons to end, and seasonal activities to begin, like pancake making, pancake racing – involving tossing it while running – and pancake eating, the last luxury before Ash Wednesday and the onset of Lent. The tradition for Hedon apprentices to ring St Augustine's tenor bell lasted until 1885.

Pancake Day heralded also a new marbles season, skipping and kepping. Keps were coloured balls, often made of leather, inked or dyed, filled with sawdust and retained from year to year. Inventive games were once well supported by parents and friends; keeping a ball in the air, bouncing it off a wall, playing tig, catching cleanly high and low, rounders, leg pelting and much more. "Kep" was a dialect word for catch, and kepping used to be a healthy outdoor communal pastime.

Kiplingcotes Derby

Kiplingcotes is a geographical oddity in that although a former railway station still bears this name, there is no identifiable community. Still, signposts east of Market Weighton and west of Middleton on the Wolds optimistically point the way. An indication that you are thereabouts is another signpost, of sorts, bearing the legend "Kiplingcotes 1519 winning post", situated about a quarter of a mile up the Warter road off the A163.

Two sides of the winning post *(H. Peach)*

This is the favoured rendezvous for hundreds of spectators who assemble from mid-morning, whatever the weather, on the third Thursday in March. They have come to see the finish of what is believed to be the oldest horse race in the kingdom, possibly going back to 1519, though Elizabethan records are stronger. In 1618 Lord Burlington and a number of aristocratic friends organised the event on a firm annual basis, and continuity has been faithfully maintained. Even in 1947 a lone farmer, Fred Stephenson completed the four mile course in 1 hour 20 minutes, braving snow drifts and atrocious conditions so that there should be no gap in the records.

Since 1933 the race has been open to women as well as men. Each jockey's weight must be exactly 10 stone, achieved by carrying flint stones if need be. Another peculiarity of the race is that the second rider past the post receives four pounds from every entrant's fee, whereas the winner has to be content with a relatively low interest from the fund, plus a cup and most of the glory.

Boon Work

Well beyond living memory, when a new tenant farmer took over, usually on Lady Day, 25th March, his neighbours would send round teams of men, horses and ploughs, just for the one day to help him to get his fields in good fettle, ready for sowing. "Boon" meant getting ready. Huge looances, including a barrel of beer, were expected of the new man. After Boon Day normal rivalries were resumed.

Carlin Sunday

This is Passion Sunday and "carlin" may derive from caring, possibly of a culinary nature. The old rhyme sets the scene:

Carlin supper we keep up
Wi' grey peas cooked for supper.
They're steeped in watter ower neeat
Then fried wi' lard and butther.

And that's about it. Another theory was that Carlin was the captain of a ship that foundered on the Holderness coast, and was unable to prevent the locals from looting his cargo of peas. More certain was the opportunism of pub landlords in placing dishes of carlins on the bar top, duly salted so as to prompt a greater thirst in customers anxious to keep up another fine tradition.

Tatie Planting

Old timers, while agreeing that timing was crucial in the setting of potatoes, were divided between the general and the particular. The former view was encapsulated in the lines:

"When thoo hears t' awd cuckoo shout
Tis tahm ti plant thi taties oot".

The more specific standpoint said that potatoes should be put into the soil on Good Friday, whatever the weather!

Throwl Egg Day

This was pace-egging i.e. throwling or trolling hard-boiled eggs down a slope, the winner being the one whose unbroken egg travelled furthest. The uneven common of the Beverley Westwood was a favoured venue. Although throwling was often done on Shrove Tuesday, Easter was the main season, recalling the rolling away of the stone from the tomb of Jesus. When an egg cracked it was peeled and eaten with crusty bread. An alternative to throwling was "jarping", or striking one egg against another until one cracked, as in conkers.

A pace-egging play, like that of the plough stots, was also performed at Easter:

> "We're tow or three jolly boys all o' yan mind,
> We've come a-pace-egging, and hope you'll be kind".

Householders taking the custom seriously might reward the youngsters with specially painted eggs.

The tradition of the Beverley Minster choir singing hymns from the top of the north-west tower was started in 1876 by the organist and choirmaster, Dr Arthur Henry Mann. An early 20th-century custom unfortunately not kept up by his successors was the distribution of hot cross buns under the town market cross by grocer George Hobson.

Kissing Day

The Tuesday after Easter week was the medieval Hocktide when rents for certain leases fell due, and special church collections were made. Impecunious ladies were sometimes allowed to offer a kiss instead. In later centuries boys could request just one chaste kiss.

St Mark's Eve

Some sensitive souls used to think that if they sat in the church porch at midnight on 25th April they would see the spirits of those villagers who would die in the coming year. An imagined coffin was likely to be – yours. Around mid-19th century at Flamborough Mrs Mikey Lawrence performed this self-appointed porch duty, subsequently spreading despondent rumours. Somewhat earlier Michael Parker (1758-1823) had more mercenary motives. As a gravedigger at Norton he took a professional interest in calculating future burial fees.

Young girls who looked into the church windows might fancy they glimpsed images of their future spouses. Few men indeed demonstrated such initiative.

Kirkham Bird Fair

More male enterprise was evident, in times past, during the early hours of Monday morning following Trinity Sunday on the Derwent's banks, close to Kirkham Abbey. This romantic setting was wonderfully appropriate for boys to meet girls, with the excuse of attending a bird fair. Jackdaws, rooks, owls and starlings were indeed traded, but for a whole day flirting and assignations were encouraged by music, feasting and dancing. This eight hundred-year-old custom, lasting until the 1830s, may have begun with the supply of poultry to the Abbey. If there are ghosts here they should have a plethora of pleasantries to tell.

Wagons Roll!

Walkington even has its own village song, with the chorus:

Happy, oh happy, oh happy are we,
Living in Walkington, you and me!
Of this pretty village we're all very fond:
Three pubs and a church and a mucky old Pond!

The hostelries (Dog and Duck, Fergie's and the Barrel) are all adjacent on the same side of the road. This is where the Hayride has assembled from late morning on the third Sunday in June every year since 1967, the brainchild of local man, Ernie Teal MBE who has done magnificent work for charity. The Hayride consists of a very motley collection of splendidly restored Victorian and Edwardian vehicles – farm carts, rullies, a tip-cart or two, carriages, phaetons, gigs, wagonettes, a donkey-drawn cart, a landau, a Clarence coach, a bread van, an ice cream cart, an Edwardian tandem. Most are horse-drawn, while a tall perky chap dodges in and about on a penny-farthing bicycle, raising a top hat and a smile. All the drivers and passengers are resplendent in

A pause during the Hayride on Beverley Westwood *(H. Peach)*

period costume, the ladies looking lovely in long dresses, shawls and flowery bonnets, the men with a liking for frock coats, boaters, blazers and well-glued whiskers.

Promptly at one o'clock the procession leads away on a roughly triangular route that includes stops at the picture postcard village, Bishop Burton and the open commons of Beverley Westwood before winding through the market town of Beverley and so back to Walkington. To various musical accompaniments in which the accordion predominates, the old favourites from bygone shows roll out – "My old man said follow the band", "Daisy, Daisy", "It's a long way to Tipperary" and dozens of like popular vintage.

When all the collecting tins have been emptied and the contents totted up, various charities will have gained thousands of pounds. It's as if the Good Old Days have returned for one memorable afternoon of undisguised nostalgia with all the colour, pride, fun, gossip, neighbourliness, clicking cameras and clinking glasses that on a sunny day, at least, make this delightful corner of the Wolds the lively focus.

Harvest Bell

Before clocks and watches were in general use the church bell was rung, often at 5am to summon workers to the fields. A further and more welcome tolling was done at 7pm to mark the end of the day's labour. Who awoke the parish clerk in good time to perform these rituals is uncertain, but he was commonly rewarded with sheaves of wheat or barley.

Bonnin' t'Awd Witch

During the nineteenth century getting in the corn harvest was still a tremendous job, with many extra hands hired, especially itinerant Irishmen. Finishing was the occasion for lively celebration. In Holderness and parts of the North Wolds a young girl, suitably beribboned, rode and waved on top of the last load. Then it was time to "burn the witch". Faces were blackened with burnt straw, a bonfire was lit amidst the stubble and there was horseplay (for those not too weary), merriment, peas and ale. In the Hornsea area "hockey" was another name for the festivities. Up went the chorus:

"We hev her up, hev her up,
All gooin' a-tether,
At oor toon end
A yow and a lamb
A pot and a pan
May we get seeaf in
Wiv oor harvest jam,
Wiv a sup of good yal
And some hapence ti spend".

Mell

Corn dollies, or kern babies, were traditionally made from a last sheaf. Some were decked out in harvester costume, or otherwise decorated with grain and flowers. Their original function was thought to be to challenge evil spirits. A "Mell baby" might be given pride of place in front of the church pulpit and kept until the following year. More immediately it provided the centrepiece, as the corn spirit, for the harvest feast, or mell.

"Mell" had various flexible connotations. Certainly it meant meal; and the mell, or mallet was formerly used to pound grain. In past centuries Lammas (Loaf Mass) was held on 1st August, an offering to God of the first loaf baked from the new corn – "First fruits". A child conceived during the Mell festivities was sometimes referred to as a "barley bairn".

Pikes

Amongst farm foremen and their waggoners there was considerable rivalry to produce functional stacks that kept the rain off the sheaves, pending threshing, but which were also architecturally pleasing. Stack sides were skilfully tapered outwards, and the crowning thatch was a veritable work of art, built to impress. The resultant pike rose to a pointed top, very occasionally sporting a weathercock.

Pikes at Bishop Burton, c1930 *(Courtesy of John Dunning)*

Tatie Scrattin'

For the October potato harvest many extra hands, including women and older children, had to be recruited. During World War Two special leave was given to twelve-year-olds and above to help with potato picking. As soon as the horse team had spun out the first few yards of a row the pickers moved in smartly with their buckets, which were soon emptied into sacks. That first

hour was gruelling. It was the first real taste of grown-up graft for the youngsters. How they welcomed their looances and mugs of tea at mid-morning!
And to be allowed to sit down was bliss indeed.

Spear Pie Day

For many years the first Sunday after 19th September was remembered in
Stamford Bridge by the baking of boat-shaped pies, fitted with a spear-like
skewer. This was an effective symbol of a turning point in the historic battle
won in 1066 by King Harold against the Northmen (see Chapter 1) just three
weeks before the Saxon downfall at Hastings. For some time the strategic
wooden bridge had been guarded by a giant Viking who easily repulsed all
comers, with deadly swings of his battle-axe. Finally a Saxon paddled a small
boat into the Derwent, and carefully positioning himself beneath the bridge,
thrust his spear upwards and brought his redoubtable foe crashing down. The
day was won. In September 1966 the occasion was re-enacted as part of a
grand pageant, and spear pies were baked, after a lapse of almost a century.
Interestingly, the alternative name of Pear Pie Feast had been used on account
of the pie fillings.

Howden Fair

Until late Victorian times the Great Horse Fair at Howden was one of the
country's largest, with roadsters and carriage horses much in demand.
Ostlers, waggoners, dealers, farmers, representatives of coal owners, footpads
and thieves jostled with agents for landed gentry and princes. During this last
week in September as many as four thousand animals were sold in a day, and
the inn stables were full every night. Many innocent buyers soon discovered
that cosmetic effects soon wore off, and there was no cheap rate for thorough-
breds.

In October 1823 Tom Ward, a fourteen-year-old stable lad at the Angel Inn
was asked to take a horse from the fair to Vienna. His new master, the Count of
Liechtenstein was soon impressed by the young man's good manners and
ready wit, and found him remunerative employment. Quickly becoming
proficient in German, French and Italian, Thomas became an administrator
and adviser to other influential noblemen. On the recommendation of the
Archduke Ferdinand, cousin to the Austrian emperor, he was given the post
of finance minister in Lucca. Moving to Parma he became Prime Minister and
a baron of the Austrian Empire. He re-visited Howden many times, generally
returning with a few prime Yorkshire hams for his diplomatic colleagues. Yet
from Howden to the Hapsburgs was a very far cry; and, oddly, the town still
has no memorial to its most famous son who died just short of his fiftieth
birthday.

Dog Whipping Day

It is part of the mythology of the city of York that a stray hound once had the
temerity to grab a wafer intended for the Mass at the Minster's high altar.

Hence, perhaps, Whip-ma-whop-ma Gate and the sanctioning of dog whipping on St Luke's Day, 18th October. In Hull, back in the middle ages, a dog was supposed to have stolen a titbit as monks prepared food for the great fair beginning on 11th October. So dog whipping was instituted on the previous day, hopefully clearing all strays before the festivities started. It was done with cruel vigour until about 1830.

Hull Fair

Under the charter of 1299 the abbot of Meaux was granted an annual market and fair to last for no longer than thirty days following St Augustine's Day, 26th May. An earlier arrangement of 1279 permitting the abbot to hold a March fair in Holy Trinity churchyard had produced complaints enough for a law to be passed forbidding the use of sacred acres as fair-grounds. It made every sense to move to the market place adjacent.

Already Hull was exporting wool to the continent and there soon developed further trade in horses, cattle and sheep. Timber and fur traders came from Scandinavia; Mediterranean products like wines, dates and almonds were available; spices were brought from Asia; and a motley array of musicians, acrobats, pedlars and vendors of religious relics enlivened the proceedings. Although by Tudor times a Pie Powder court (from the French "pieds poudreux" i.e. dusty feet) settled most disputes on the spot, the vetting of theatricals had grown lax, for in 1599 the mayor had to threaten certain actors and spectators of lewd and ungodly plays with heavy fines.

Over the centuries there have been many changes of site and alterations of date. During the Civil War there was a move to 11th October as a thanksgiving for the lifting of the Royalist siege. Some forty years later 29th September was favoured, only to be switched back, permanently, after eleven days were "lost" in 1752 with the introduction of the Gregorian calendar. "Give us back our eleven days!" howled the mob. Since 1888 the venue has remained at Walton Street.

Almost every variety of exotic excitement seems to have converged on Hull Fair. William Bradley, the Market Weighton giant was on exhibition in 1815. During the 1830s lions were paraded in Wombwell's Menagerie, and rumours were spread that some had escaped. A letter to a Hull newspaper in 1912 talked of a "struggling surging mass of people going in opposite directions", a description all visitors would surely recognise. High spirits of this period included water tube squirting and pushing handfuls of confetti down girls' blouses. Much more also was in questionable taste, like the exhibition in 1953 of a vast lady, Titania playing draughts with Anita, allegedly the world's smallest woman.

Amongst the fair's legendary showmen was Joe Barak – "Chicken Joe, the Man you all know" who for forty years until his retirement in 1962 awarded to his ticket winners a bagful of groceries topped by a chicken. Punters scrutinised eagerly the numbers arrowed when the three wheels stopped turning.

Joe was a witty, if hoarse, character, occasionally drumming up business by ceremoniously packing a large goody bag. He also raised much money for charity.

"Chicken Joe – the Man you all Know" *(Courtesy of Christopher Ketchell collection)*

Babblin' Neeat

Babbles were strips of leather, tied with whipcord, with which the youth of Holderness beat one another from time to time, especially on Mischief Night, 4th November. The following night, after further bouts, the well-worn babbles were consigned to the public bonfires. An alternative kind of babbling was to make up the leather into bags, fill them with stones and beat on the doors around Patrington and Keyingham in the confident expectation of being paid to go away.

Hiring Fairs

By the feast of St Martin, 1st November the farming year was at its slackest, so Martinmas became a convenient time for the annual hiring of farm servants. On advertised days the market places of Driffield, Pocklington, Bridlington, etc were crowded with men and women looking for new places, and farmers set on hiring the strongest and fittest for a solid year's graft. In 1863 some fifteen hundred servants thronged the streets of Howden for the largest of the hirings. When a bargain was struck at an agreed price, hands were slapped together and a "fast" agreement – a shilling or two – was given as a bond token. Any lad wanting to back out had to return the fest ("godspenny" was another name) and hope to be hired at a Runaways Fair held in December, unless, of course, he had an interim better offer.

Typical of the hiring day tales was that of the lad who had been asked by this farmer for a reference. Meeting him again after lunch the youth, sizing up his man, told him squarely:

"Ah's heeard summat o' thy character an' all – an' thoo can keeap thi job!"

Boys of about thirteen, fresh from school, might land their first job as a "Tommy Owt". More experienced youths could aspire to thoddy, or third in the hierarchy after foreman and waggoners. Teenage girls would be required to turn their hands to milking and even work in the fields, as well as helping with meals, laundry and general household chores. Farm servants lived in, receiving very basic board and lodging, and would not be paid until their year was up the following Martinmas. Loans, however, were sometimes made.

As hiring week was the only substantial holiday, with a year's wages just paid, pubs did a tremendous trade, as did the fair with its coconut shies, shooting galleries, dancing bear, wrestling, fat women exhibitions and so forth, all lit by naphtha flares each evening. One itinerant, well known in Pocklington in the 1890s, pulled out teeth with his fingers! Continuous excitement brought laughter, badinage, coarse jests, brawls and mayhem. (See Chapter 10: Smallganging).

There was no lack of middle class criticism of the hirings system, especially when school or church life was disturbed. Doctors were on full alert. Police resources sometimes were seriously challenged. Drunkenness and immorality were only too evident.

By the turn of the century hirings were on the wane. Hedon's lingered until 1913, Beverley's up to 1938. New forces were at work, like increased mechanisation, newspaper advertisements, better transport and the spread of literacy. With the advent of labour exchanges from 1909 and an Agricultural Wages Board in 1924, there was little room left for individual street bargaining.

Rahv-Kite Sunday

On the Sunday before their departure to their new jobs, farm servants were traditionally given a huge farewell family meal, a memorable one fit to bust – or rahv kites (split stomachs). Pag Rag Day was departure day: new clothes were packed into a box which was often to become the horse lad's only bit of furniture apart from his bed – and even that was apt to be shared.

Thomasing

St Thomas's Day, 21st December was once recognised as a time for generosity to the village widows who went from door to door begging for money or food. Up to 1918 the Widow Singers at Hunmanby held a torchlight procession, led by a band, to collect funds to buy seasonal groceries and flour for widows and the needy. Many communities made their own arrangements, and the well-to-do provided for widows in their wills.

Frummety

Frummety (Latin *frumentum* – wheat) could be eaten at any time, but the Christmas Eve ritual was once widely observed. Millers supplied wheat to faithful customers, and the frummety bell was rung in churches as the signal that cooking should start. Tudor revisions of the Bible had declared:

> "Ye shall eat neither bread, nor parched corne, nor frumenty of new corne, until the selfe same days that ye have brought an offering unto your God" *(Leviticus XXIII, v 14).*

Pearled wheat was soaked overnight, boiled up with milk, seasoned with nutmeg, cloves or cinnamon and sweetened with sugar or treacle. Some sophisticated tastes advocated a drop or two of sherry or brandy. When all was ready the Yule candles were lit via a last year's stub kept for continuity.

Vessel Cuppers

Still familiar up to about 1940 in a number of Wolds villages on Christmas morning were the Vessel Cuppers, or Wassail Singers. These children proceeded along the street singing carols and showing off a cup or box dressed up as a manger crib and holding oranges, apples, etc to represent the gifts made to the Infant Jesus.

Flamborough Longsword Dance

An old tradition still kept up by children on Boxing Day morning is the longsword dancing. In former times it was performed by eight Flamborough fishermen dressed in dark blue jerseys, blue caps, white trousers and black

Longsword Dancers at Flamborough, 1912 *(Courtesy of Richard Traves)*

shoes, starting outside the Rose and Crown, processing around the village and finishing up at the Royal Dog and Duck. Tunes favoured by the melodeon and tambourine accompanists were Mr Noah, Buffalo Girl and Old Johnny Walker. The set piece manoeuvres seemed to become more and more intricate, and culminated in a triumphal locking of wooden swords in a central rose. According to legend an interloping stranger used to be chosen, prior to the last dance, and held captive within the rose until a ransom was paid.

A few other non-calendar customs are worth noting:

Coastal Capers

The Flamborough area has long been known as "Little Denmark"; and significant is the Domesday name (1087) of "Flaneburg", flane in Norse meaning arrow. Medieval lords of the manor, like Sir Marmaduke Constable, paid a kind of tribute to the Scandinavian connection by standing on the cliff top once a year and firing a gold-tipped arrow in the general direction of Denmark.

Up to about 1930, at low tide on a selected day, the Lord of Filey manor rode his horse into the sea and hurled a javelin far out. This was symbolically to re-assert an ancient entitlement to be allowed to fish that distance from the shore.

Smuggling

Up to the 19th century smuggling was rife along the entire Yorkshire coast. When clergy and officials were caught up in these activities, churches might be used to hide contraband goods. Just before Christmas, 1732 the verger at Hornsea parish church was furtively occupied in the crypt when an unusually fierce thunderstorm blew up. So terrible was the lightning that the poor man believed the Devil had come for him. He had a stroke from which he never recovered.

Bears and Bulls

"Better to be at a bear-baiting than singing at a mass". This dictum arose from a disaster on Sunday, 29th April 1520 when 55 worshippers were crushed to death as the central tower collapsed in St Mary's Church, Beverley. Not very far away hundreds of bear baiters continued to flourish.

At Kilham a stone block in the church wall still retains its bull ring, to which the beast was chained. Here as elsewhere the law once compelled butchers to ensure that beef offered to the public had first been baited, allegedly to bring out the taste. Sometimes the bull was made livelier by having pepper forced up its snout, and it might well savage a mastiff or two before succumbing. For failure to meet the law's requirements there were many prosecutions. Thus, the Bridlington Court Rolls for 2nd April 1679 recorded that "Christopher Colson was fined for killing and selling one bull in this market not baited". Not until 1835 was this barbarous ritual abolished.

Marital Mullarkey

In some circles it was thought advisable for the best man to be a bachelor in case the groom failed to turn up! When a bride arrived safely back at her father's door a plateful of cut cake was flung over her from an upper window, thereby ensuring happiness and fecundity. Some families ruled that the plate had to be broken to guarantee good luck; on the other hand a prudent family might see it as a useful addition to the bottom drawer.

Next, the bride had to prepare herself for the winner of the wedding race. A number of young men ran from the church gates, the winner claiming the right to a kiss, a bridal ribbon – or even the honour of removing and keeping the lady's garter, specially made and beautifully embroidered.

The following anonymous verse, c1800, was surely penned by a man:

> *At Martha Mossop's wedding*
> *There was neither bite nor sup.*
> *She didn't wear a garter,*
> *But held a ribbon up.*
> *So lasses, take a warning:*
> *In every bride we beg*
> *To stitch a bridal hand, ye ken,*
> *And sport a bridal leg.*

It was hoped that a bucket of water poured over the doorstep as the couple departed might bring a marriage proposal to a bridesmaid before the step was dry. If the bridal pair stayed, at the end of the merrymaking they were ceremoniously escorted to their bedroom. John Day, schoolmaster-poet of Sigglesthorne, ended his verses on a village wedding (1802) thus:

> *"To bed they're now shown, the stocking is thrown,*
> *This done, all withdrew from their sight;*
> *But what was done there we cannot declare,*
> *For we left 'em and bade 'em – Good Night!"*

Riding the Stang

Alas: marital relationships sometimes soured; and when a husband was known to beat his wife, or go to another woman, a way of shaming him was to mount a stang. A mawkin (effigy) of the wrongdoer tied to a stee (ladder) was positioned on a cart and by night pushed along to the matrimonial home, all to the accompaniment of contrived noises – dustbin lids, tins, rattles, drums, mouth organs, kettles, sticks. The stang leader asked for quiet, then intoned a charge of the husband's sins, after this fashion –

> *". . . he took neither stick nor stower,*
> *But up with his fist and knocked her clean ower.*
> *Now if this coward don't mend his manners*
> *The skin of his feet shall be sent to the tanners".*

After more threats were echoed around, the leader called for the villain's repentance, then the assembly disbanded – only to re-appear on the two following nights. On the third occasion the effigy was burnt. In his autobiography about his Wolds upbringing, J.R. Mortimer, celebrated archaeologist, recalled a stang at Fimber in 1832. From time to time a stang had unintended consequences. When Henry Duggleby was the offender at Hunmanby about 1860, the liberal use of tar in burning his effigy resulted in a charring of the village stocks and a dislodgement of the head of the market cross. The reprimand publicly delivered to a Norton man in October 1873 persuaded him to sell his wife for half a crown. In general, however, we may suppose that erring men were obliged by the stang to accord their wives more respect.

Franklin Dead Brief

In 1844 a man died on Brandesburton Moor and there was no money to bury him. Accordingly the villagers contributed a few pence each until the required sum was achieved. So began this mutual benefit society, each member contributing to join and enjoying lifelong comradeship with the assurance that his eventual funeral expenses would be met. Although the welfare state has very largely removed the shortcomings of Franklin's time, an annual dinner is still held for nearly 300 members each February at the Dacre Arms.

Club Feasts

The numerous friendly societies and benefit clubs that sprang up in the 1800s generally held special days of celebration. At Kilham, for example, the Foresters' Feast was held on the last Wednesday in June. An imminent club feast was known to bring a general spring-clean. At Huggate farm cottages

Middleton on the Wolds Foresters, c1925 *(Courtesy of Mrs M. Grice)*. The three boys behind the staves on the front row were George, Harold and Billy Nendick. Noteworthy were the green sashes of the committee members.

were enthusiastically lime-washed in readiness for family re-unions. Schools were closed, and following a church parade and dinner, various sports and merry-making ensued. Most societies enjoined their members to be moderate in drinking, and exacted penalties in cases of fighting, poaching, gaming or venereal disease. Nevertheless, there were repeated lapses.

Robert Sharp, schoolmaster-diarist and secretary of the South Cave society wrote on 12th July 1827:

> "Club feast day it was at Newloves (Bear Inn) where they had a booth fixed in the yard, and the members all dined together at two tables set the whole length. There were about 120 members, a very good plain dinner and good order kept. Matthew Smith towards night got very drunk, and some boys got some soot, tallow and red and daubed his face all over, making him look wilder than an American savage".

While the Temperance movement gained later a loose foothold in the East Riding, a good many erstwhile and ribald members were to raise their glasses to various parodies of a chorus once meant to be taken seriously

"Dare to be a Daniel, dare to be alone;
Dare to pass a public house, and leave the beer alone."

Chapter 8
Children and Schools

Barring Out

How widespread this Shrove Tuesday custom ever was in the East Riding is uncertain. It may be that with the tolling of the 11 am church bell calling the faithful to confession the schoolchildren were simply given the day off. Deliberately excluding the master would probably have been a token ceremony.

Yet at Hull Grammar School in the 17th century barring out became a serious issue. The older boys virtually threatened the headmaster into granting holidays and suspending punishments. Parents and civic leaders declared this was intolerable; and in 1662 the Bench forbade repetition – though a holiday was granted as a sweetener!

Unrewarding Profession

Archbishop Herring's Visitation Returns for Garton on the Wolds explained that an unusually well educated master received meals in part payment for running the village school ... "his meat from house to house is the most he gets for his instruction, he receives very small wages."

Wool Gathering

Like other schools founded for the children of the respectable poor, the Beverley Blue Coat School taught the 3Rs, a thorough grounding in Scripture and some history and geography. But the children, a few girls as well as boys, had also to turn their hands to wool spinning. In 1725, 15 years after its opening, 2 1/2 d a day was earned for five hanks of yarn, most of the receipts being earmarked for maintenance rather than pocket money. The school probably provided a reasonable education for its time. Certainly classes were small. Total numbers were around 30 in the early days, dropping to single figures 50 years later; and there were but eight on roll when the school closed in 1890, unable to compete with the rising crop of Church and Board schools. When they left at the age of 14 most boys had taken up local apprenticeships.

Keep 'em Ignorant

In the 18th century prejudice ran deep against educating the rural poor. In his 'History of Hull', 1788, George Hadley had written of the working poor, rural or urban:

"But there is a degree of ignorance necessary to keep them in subordination, and to make them either useful to others or happy in themselves. What ploughman who could read the renowned history of Tom Hickathrift, Jack the Giant Killer or the Seven Wise Men would be content to whistle up one furrow and down another from dawn to the setting of the sun?"

Hadley went on to criticise the time mis-spent by servants on books from circulating libraries, with "mischief done to their minds by the contemplation of the monstrous and alluring improbabilities therein contained."

Ploughboys' Mentor

This was to become a view strenuously challenged by the daughter of Francis Simpson, Vicar of Boynton and Anne (nee Strickland) of the 6th baronet's family. Mary Simpson (1820-1884), though well aware of social differences had the highest hopes of educating farm boys and claiming them for the Church of England. For lads over 12, evening classes were held at Carnaby and Boynton, giving instruction in reading, writing, Bible stories and some rudimentary history and geography. She talked to the boys as they ate their mid-morning "looances." She even walked with them, reading moral homilies, as they ploughed. She also wrote to them after they had moved on to other farms. In due course her ideas were sketched out in a book entitled "Ploughing and Sowing: or Annals of an Evening School in a Yorkshire village and the Work that grew out of it" (1861). She was an ardent local supporter of moves towards compulsory elementary education.

Hers was an interesting and unusual social experiment; and the fruits of education ripen slowly and are not always harvested. But most of her young men remained stubbornly Nonconformist – when they worshipped at all.

A commemorative plaque to Mary Simpson has been placed in Fraisthorpe church.

Sancton Memories

The church of England Memorial School at Sancton was re-built in 1870 in memory of Thomas Jackson (1783-1873) and his brother Samuel, sons of a village labourer who both prospered to the extent of becoming presidents of the Wesleyan Methodist Conference. Thomas's recollections of his elementary education were critical. An unqualified master mechanically pursued a dull and narrow curriculum heavily weighed down with the 3Rs. His Church Catechism in one hand was balanced by a hefty hazel stick in the other. Beatings were given for signs of inattention, failed memory and dull apprehension. There was little of relevance for youthful minds, and many boys strongly preferred chopping weeds or bird scaring for one of the farmers. Despite these early shortcomings Thomas and Samuel became considerable scholars and preachers, and indeed, national figures.

A more recent memory: John Harrison, who attended Sancton School in the 1930s, recalled that one extra duty performed by pairs of pupils was to walk to the village pump and bring back buckets of water.

Rammalation Day

This was a form of beating the bounds. From Tudor times onwards, and especially at Ascensiontide (or Holy Thursday, as at Hornsea) youngsters were taken on a conducted tour of the village boundaries. It was a ceremony conducted once every few years – every seventh was usual at Barmby Moor. Churchwardens and other vestry officers pointed out significant features, often with good-humoured horseplay, with bottoms bumped on boundary stones or a body suspended over the beck. Liquid refreshment was provided. At Kirby Underdale in 1748 bread and ale on Ascension day cost 4s 6d; and the churchwardens' accounts for South Cave in 1769 record expenditure of £1 13s for Rammalations.

Unpaid Private Tuition

John Bielby was neither the first nor the last educator to experience difficulty in extracting agreed sums from forgetful parents. In 1816 he applied to the Driffield Manor Court claiming £1 2s for teaching two of Thomas Harrison's children to read and sew for two quarters. He won his case.

Bounties

Many village schools owed their foundation to the squirearchy. Birdsall School, for instance, was founded in 1871 by Lady Julia Middleton. And, suitably, no doubt, the squire and his lady expected and received appropriate deference. As testified by many a school log book, the lady was fond of inspecting the girls' needlework.

But there were many benefits, too. At South Cave Mrs. Elizabeth Barnard, who had established the girls' school in 1866, not only provided seasonal fare unfailingly at Christmas, but in season invited the children into the castle gardens to pick fruit.

The distribution of oranges has been a recurring and slightly curious feature of largesse to East Riding schools. It started at Spencer Council School, Beverley following the long reign (1848-87) of William Spencer as headmaster. He left £100 in his will to buy oranges, which were first given out on 13th April 1911, the year after his death. When the school closed in 1967 the tradition was carried over into its replacement, Swinemoor Primary.

Pupil-Teachers

The pupil-teacher system, based on the apprenticeship of older scholars to instruct younger ones, was started nationally in 1846. Able, lucky and assiduous girls took the Queen's Scholarship, a kind of school certificate, at the age of 18 which enabled them to enter a training college. Until centres were set up in Hull and Driffield in 1905, all tuition was in the hands of the local elementary school headteacher, and could be given only before or after normal school hours.

The regime was unsatisfactory. Youngsters of mid-teens met over-taxing disciplinary problems. Some were also browbeaten into extra duties like cleaning and lighting fires. They were given inappropriate administrative jobs. The Kirby Underdale records show that on 16th December 1867 the pupil teachers assembled in the evening to finish the third quarter of the register! Complaints were legion with regard to punctuality, appearance, and preparation. Turnover was high.

So much depended on the headteacher. There were particular temptations for a male teacher secluded in supervising the studies of unchaperoned young girls regularly of an evening. This was a contributory factor in the untimely departure of Samuel Kennard from Walkington Board School in 1892.

With the gradual extension of secondary education in the 20th century, the pupil-teacher system lapsed, and potential teachers were recruited very largely from the grammar schools.

Dicky Fewson

Dicky lived at Long Riston from about 1820 until 1875, serving as schoolmaster and churchwarden (See Chapter 4). A legendary character, he was a no-nonsense practitioner who taught the 3Rs systematically, partly via the New Testament. He seems to have been talented at imparting practical skills like penmanship and joinery, and many scholars adapted well to the world of work. A few boarded at the school house.

His reputation rests in considerable part on his approaches to punishment. A favourite device was to dump the miscreant into a large basket which was then raised by rope and pulley to the ceiling; and there he stayed, fearful of falling, until Dicky judged that a proper time for reflection had been completed. Another stratagem was to suspend a child by his arms from a beam during a flogging. The bat, freely wielded, was referred to as a "thrashing machine." Then there was the "small sieve." The pupil crawled forward between Dicky's legs which clamped him like a vice for a beating. Dicky pushed his games of bluff to considerable limits. One tale tells of him marking out the shape of a grave and threatening to bury a truant alive.

Understandably, perhaps, he was treated with every respect. Amongst the liberties he allowed himself was the sole use of a telescope bought through local contributions.

Some of his sayings have passed into folklore, As part-time sexton he carved on his axe, "Axe of the Apostles". With regard to the basket sanction used in school, he boasted, tongue in cheek, "The dullest boy has a chance to rise." As parish clerk and bass viol player in church, he officiated at over 600 funerals. Sometimes he said to his pupils, "When I'm dead, lads, jump on my grave and stamp it down."

Old Thumb Noose

A contemporary at Barmby Moor School in the 1840s and 50s was Thomas West, whose favoured punishment was to keep a scholar's hand held up high by setting the thumb in a string noose. His own professional limitations turned out to be so acute that the Rev. Robert Taylor offered to instruct him in some of the elements of fractions, decimals and land surveying. West's response was that he had as much learning in his head as he could carry.

Shouldered Punishment

An odd but probably effective sanction used in a Hessle girls' school for domestic training (1840 – c1874) was likely to be investigated further at home. The school slip had shoulder fittings with woollen balls attached. These could be removed and placed in a conspicuous position, like the classroom mantelpiece if a girl had misbehaved. Back home the child would be answerable to her parents for the telltale deficiency.

Pre-Ecumenical Days

10ᵗʰ February 1864:

"Ash Wednesday – Scholars went to Church for service – several declined going, some being Roman Catholics and others Dissenters – but made all go and punished those who omitted." – *Log Book, Pocklington National School)*

15ᵗʰ March 1871:

"I wish the boys were not allowed to use the urinal in the yard in the presence of the School girls." – *Yapham School Log Book*

Half-Timers

During their last year, subject to reaching Standard IV, or verified by Her Majesty's Inspector, some youngsters took a few months in work, especially on farms, then returned to school. At Patrington during the 1860s and 70s scholars worked as spinners either mornings or afternoons at Marshall's flax mill. But to return to their desks after a long morning session was very tiring for 10 or 11 year olds, and the scheme was not a success.

Non-Payment by Results

July 1872 – North Grimston School

"G.R. Gleadow has passed an unsatisfactory examination. If he fail to the same extent next year the Grant will have to be reduced by £10 and henceforth by £20 for every year at the end of which a similar failure is repeated." (Under Article 32c)

Headship Advertisement, 1873

"Schoolmaster wanted for Eastrington Endowed School, with or without certificate. Salary – Endowment £30; house and good garden; together with school pence etc. Apply stating full particulars and enclosing copies of testimonials." (Goole and Marshland Weekly, 5ᵗʰ September 1873)

Advance by Numbers

For the Hull School Board the virtues of Drill, on military lines, were unarguable and a direct transfer value was hoped for. Thus:

"The lessons in Drill are intended among other things to improve the discipline of the Schools. The beneficial effects physically, must of necessity be great, while the habits of prompt obedience and constant attention which are insisted upon, cannot but affect the conduct of the boys in the future, and must also facilitate the general ordinary working of the Schools." *(Hull School Board Minutes – Report, 7th January 1880)*

"In some of the Schools, the efforts of the Drill Instructor is (sic) seconded very heartily by the Teachers, who make all their changes and other concerted movements on the basis laid down by the Drill Instructor. It would be a great advantage were this practice to become general." *(Report, April 1886)*

Absences

Victorian schoolteachers were very greatly concerned at the illegal or unfortunate absences of so many scholars – though at Preston Arthur Watkinson declared 27th February, his birthday, as a school holiday. There were, after all, official holidays enough, plus Shrove Tuesday, Ash Wednesday, St George's Day, Ascension Day ... Then there were church fetes, chapel outings, club feasts (i.e. friendly society celebrations); Howden Pleasure Fair, Hull Fair and the Martinmas hirings; the St Thomas's Day devoted to the begging of corn for Christmas; and many individual variations, like following the foxhounds.

Many parents and school managers connived at children working in the fields e.g. "brassocking" – weeding out the charlock from the crops. HMI F.W. Watkins noted many such irregularities in his reports in the 1840s. At Sutton on Derwent, for example, on 27th May 1847: "half the class at present at work in the fields."

Not a few headteachers felt their hands were tied by managers and school boards. At Broomfleet, Richard Nicholls, head from 1885 until 1919, had to accept that his board did not want absentees investigated too closely. Besides, a full school might underline the case for hiring an extra teacher. Cheap labour mattered much more than schooling.

Attendances were affected by such contingencies as gathering wood from shipwrecks, as happened at Aldbrough in November 1895; collecting sea-coal at Spurn; attending a visiting circus – when Sangers visited Howden on 19th May 1904 only 45 children out of 125 attended Pinfold Street School. Brass bands, foal shows, sales of work, bush beatings, tenting animals on roadside verges, gleaning – all took their toll.

Then there was sickness, a complex situation impossible to summarise briefly. Suffice it to say that in Hull alone in the years 1881-82 nearly 700 children died of scarlet fever, the highest incidence in England. Some young-

Empire Day scene at Walkington, 1909 *(Courtesy of East Riding of Yorkshire Council Library and Information Services)*

sters were exposed to unhealthy working conditions. At Anlaby in 1901 a boy called Railton had virtually left school to work on a night soil cart with the Sculcoates Rural District Council, in open and defiant contravention of school attendance regulations and local authority by-laws.

Dirty conditions in schools alienated some children. Smokey chimneys caused many complaints. At Kirk Ella it was noted on 18th January 1893:

> "Classroom uninhabitable through the wind driving soot and smoke down the chimney" – a disincentive to the attentive new cleaner described the previous month as having "a perceptible effect on attendance."

As time went on good attendances were publicly applauded. Up to 1914 at Burton Agnes the names of maximum attenders were published in the parish magazine; and school correspondents often showed an obsessive weekly interest in attendance returns. In later Victorian times, of course, the school grant was based in part on attendance.

Few Pupils

During the 19th century some famous and ancient schools reached a low ebb. Bridlington School, a foundation of Edward VI, was reduced in 1865 to presenting the master's daughter only to the Endowed Schools Commissioners. Beverley Grammar school had but 15, and its premises were "dirty and the furniture out of repair".

Under the long headship (1807-48) of the Rev. Thomas Shield, Pocklington School, founded in 1514 reached new depths. Shield was often away for months, leaving the boys to a deaf and somewhat infirm usher; so parents transferred their sons elsewhere. Part of the premises was let off for years to a carpenter and timber merchant. In 1817 there was just one boy.

Recovery took time. As late as 1889 there were but 10 pupils. The situation was saved by the arrival of the Rev. Charles Hutton who brought with him 40 boarders from Daventry. Although for a time some regeneration followed, the new head's astonishing buffoonery, neglect of self and premises resulted in diminishing public confidence and vacillating numbers.

There was a low turnout in some East Riding village schools. In his entertaining *Yorkshire Reminiscences*, the Rev. M.C.F. Morris, as diocesan inspector, found that Routh School averaged only nine and was once reduced to one scholar. A new master arriving at Thwing on 27th February 1883 met three children in the morning and one in the afternoon. No one had told him that the premises had been closed for over a year.

Royal Oak Apple Day

The 29th May recalled the escape of the future king Charles II when in 1651 he had been obliged to shelter in an oak tree after the Battle of Worcester. Some schools took up the chant:

"Royal Oak Day, Royal Oak Day!
If you don't give us a holiday
We'll all run away."

Sometimes boys showed enough bravado to absent themselves, only to be punished on their return. In Edwardian times "Gaffer" Davis at Ellerker stood no such nonsense. There was punishment, too, for youngsters failing to sport an oak leaf. Defaulters were stung with nettles or otherwise chastised. On the Wolds it was Chalky Back Day: clothes were rubbed with chalk. Parents and teachers were no doubt relieved when these historical celebrations were over.

Web of Duties

When Albert Webb became master of Burstwick School in 1891 he received £100 salary per annum, plus £5 for cleaning the classrooms and out-offices (the nauseous "pit system"), attending the lamps and stoking the fires. Not until 1908 was a cleaner appointed. In 1930 the school turned on its new piped water – way ahead of many villages; and four years later the first issue of toilet paper was received from the local authority.

Mixed Forecast

On 15th September 1913 Seth Wilkinson, head of Barmby Moor School drew his scholars' attention to a passing aeroplane, advising them to note the date. Such an event was likely to become commonplace in their lifetime. Something that Seth did not foresee was that not long after retiring in 1915, he would be asked to return to his old job following the call-up of his successor – only to find that his former sure touch was gone, and the older lads mocked him, even showering him with snowballs.

The Picture Playhouse, 2000, is one of the oldest cinemas in the country – opening in 1911 *(H. Peach)*

High Fliers

For six privileged pupils of Beverley St John's R.C. Primary School the 5th June 1929 was a memorable day. At 11 o'clock that morning they and a teacher were taken by Sir Alan Cobham on a flight from Hedon aerodrome. The local authority granted a holiday so that all children could visit the Cobham Flying Circus.

Corruption by the Silver Screen

The Picture Palace had opened in the former Corn Exchange in Beverley in 1911; and the Marble Arch had been built in Butcher Row in 1916 – not without criticism. In May of that year a representative of the Band of Hope Union claimed that crime was increasing through children watching too many films portraying murder, stabbing, robberies, burglaries and sex!

Large Classes

Against all the circumstances of absences described earlier has to be set the fact that there were many large classes. Even in 1862 the Driffield National School was so full that some 50 applications by parents had to be postponed. Ten years later some classes had to be accommodated in an old brewery in Brewhouse Lane. At Gilberdyke in 1902 overflowing numbers meant that some pupils had to resort to kneeling on the floor in order to write on their benches – a situation that caused a number of staff changes. At Burstwick in 1904 it was calculated that each child had 16 inches of space. At Withernsea Council School in 1909 Edward Downes did well to contain, never mind teach, his 85 scholars. In 1918 a quarter of all classes in Hull numbered 60 or more. By 1959 many were still in excess of 50.

Miscellaneous Punishments

9th *December 1887 – North Grimston School*

"Punished Elizabeth Wood this morning for deliberately tearing a Standard I book. On this account she has been kept at home this afternoon. Have punished Arthur Wood for repeating to the other children an expression made by his father regarding the above."

In 1898 Hessle Cottage Homes opened for orphans up to the ages of 16 for boys, 18 for girls. While they were prepared practically against life's rigours by years of scrubbing and regimentation, nothing could atone for all the cruelties endured.

"There was never any love, just good hammerings," as one old scholar later remarked. Another told of having his thumb forced down into a cup of boiled water. The unauthorised sale to a rag man of two empty jam jars for a halfpenny each brought four lashes of the birch. One lady, looking back, would cheerfully have dynamited the place! Fortunately their memories of the day school they had attended in Hessle were much happier.

A pupil at Kilham in the early 1920s recalled that Mr. Ralph hit with a chair leg those who were not good at their work. Many a teacher who has over-reacted will sympathise with Horace Birtles, temporary headteacher at Easington who wrote in the log book on 1st November 1911:

> "I had reason to punish Alan Douglas this morning and the cane accidentally caused a wound on his face. I went and explained matters to his father and mother with the result that Alan's behaviour this afternoon has been excellent."

Standing in a corner to wear a dunce's cap was commonplace, as at Lambert Street School, Hull in the 1920s. During this period at Middleton on the Wolds School four mistakes were allowed in dictation. After that a slap was given for each error.

The Onion Remedy

Generations of children, but more especially boys, claimed that some alleviation of the cane's sting could be obtained by rubbing the hands – or buttocks – with onion skins, oil, grease or soap. Modern youngsters, educated since 1986 without fear of corporal punishment, will find it impossible to credit just how mightily the rod was wielded – and in many cases for the paltriest of reasons.

Room for Improvement

In 1912 the East Riding, less Hull, had 213 schools, served by 710 teachers. Of these only half were college trained, the rest being uncertificated, pupil-teachers or supplementaries. Until 1915 there was no overall county scale of salaries, so abler teachers gravitated to schools offering higher pay. Until 1919 when national scales appeared, most East Riding teachers received less than their "Wessie" counterparts. A good interview question, therefore, was "Why do you want to come and work in the East Riding?"

Footwear – and None

Many reminiscences (Helen Dunhill, Monty Walker) have amply confirmed that during the 1920s and 30s there were barefooted children on the streets of Hull. A small minority of such youngsters attended, for example, Holy Trinity School in Little Humber Street. "Frosted feet" was yet another reason for

Circumstances alter cases: for a winkle competition at Spurn c1910, bare feet might have been more sensible than boots *(Courtesy of East Riding of Yorkshire Council Library and Information Services)*

winter absences. When fathers were unemployed free boots were issued. Holes were clipped into the tops of the uppers as a distinguishing mark to deter parents from passing them over the pawnshop counter. On Hessle Road and Old Town schools like St George's home-made clogs were worn, with an oaken sole and sailcloth tops waterproofed with goose grease. Hob-nailed boots, almost indestructible, were sported by many boys up to 1939. In more recent years many teachers in town and country schools alike scrounged reserves of footwear for children's use on the school premises.

Combined Studies

At Muston School during the 1930s one lady teacher took her class for very regular nature walks – one afternoon per week in summer. Children were allowed considerable freedom to make their discoveries – while Miss met her young man.

Earth Closets

In 1965, 70 East Riding schools still used oil lamps and 167 had earth closets. An Aldbrough head has recalled that the slop men arrived every Thursday lunchtime to deal with the "thunder buckets". By 1967 all were on mains sewerage.

Notes

Helen Dunhill: *Old Town Childhood* – Local History Archives, Park Street, Hull.

Monty Walker: *Aspects of Hull* – Wharncliffe Publications Ltd, 1999

Chapter 9

Punishments

Roadsign off New Walk, Beverley: a reminder of a punitive past *(H. Peach)*

By Order – Beverley, 1391

Six centuries ago the town was imposing fixed penalties for specified road offences … "…no man shall have any cart shod with iron entering on the pavement of Beverley after Lammas Day next, as the penalty of forfeiting 1d to the community for each carriage, so often as shall be convicted."

Pollution Penalties

Down the centuries polluting drinking water has been discouraged, but the offence has persisted.

Beverley, 1534 – "If anyone places hides near wells or attempts to wash them there liable to fine of 40d. Nor any other tainted Thing to be washed or deposited in the vicinity of wells."

South Cave, 1664 – Thomas Burton was fined 1s for letting his wife wash "puddings" (i.e. intestines of animals) in the beck.

Hessle, 1671: The manorial court imposed a "paine" of 6s 4d for the nuisance of dead animals left in the street.

No doubt ordinary sinful mortals exchanged nudges and winks when the occasional eminent townsman was cut down to size, as in 1780 when Benjamin Blaydes, Hull shipbuilder and thrice mayor was fined £2 6s 8d for throwing rubbish into the River Hull that flowed behind his house.

Stocks

By a law of 1405 every town and village in the realm was required to provide and maintain a set of public stocks. A number have survived in the East

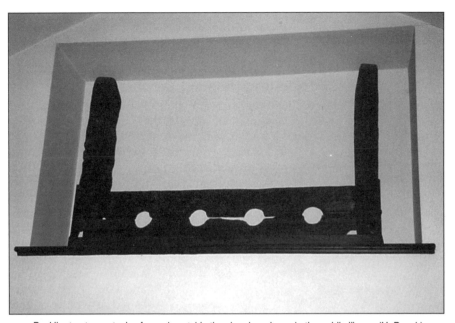

Pocklington town stocks, formerly outside the church and now in the public library *(H. Peach)*

Riding – in Beverley Guildhall and St Mary's Church; Shiptonthorpe Church; Driffield School and Pocklington public library.*

The Driffield stocks formerly stood on Moot Hill, to the north of Main Street. A regular occupant in mid-19th-century was the bellman, Tom Shepherdson, who, having drunk too freely amused passers-by by singing hymns. Nancy Crabtree, a local hawker in trouble at the same period, was mocked by onlookers chanting "By the power of war", one of her favourite expressions.

One of the last to be stocked by the Beverley market cross was Jim Brigham, put there for a few hours in 1855 for excessive Sunday drinking. On this occasion he was cheered by a lighted pipe given to him by a friend. At Kirk Ella where the stocks stood by the church gates until c1875 inebriates were confined by churchwardens and the local constable. Some remarkable stories were told of these confinements. At Kilham where the stocks had six holes for three prisoners, a one-legged man somehow worked himself free and kicked the woodwork with his timbered limb, proving the latter was stronger!

John Nicholson ("The Stocks in East Yorkshire") told another such tale. At Butterwick, known for its youth problems, it was decided to renew the stocks. Some of the lads doubted whether the new set would last long. For several nights the constable and friends kept vigil. But as soon as they relaxed the bright new frame was dug up, weighted and flung into a deep "marr". Years later, long after abolition in 1872 it was re-discovered.

Verbal offences were a common cause of women being stocked. In 1581 Jane Smythe, widow, having cursed roundly the mayor and brethren, was set in the stocks in Hull market place with a paper twisted over her head describing her uncivil behaviour. And it was for "scowldinge" that Jane Thompson was held to ridicule at North Ferriby in March 1629.

Scolds and Ducking Stools

Women certainly seem to have been discriminated against when couples had words. At Patrington Court Leet in October 1562 it was recorded – "The Jury do present Marie the wife of John Banke for a common scool".

Her punishment was not stated. It could have been the scold's bridle

which fitted over the head, and with a spikey projection to cover the tongue, discouraging its movement. One surviving example is in St Mary's Church, Beverley. Or she might have been tied to a ducking stool down at the Haven. Less likely, but just possible, was the "joug" (Latin – yoke, burden) – an iron collar fitted round the neck and chaining the victim to a building or a post. Bridlington Priory Church has the remains of one. The joug tended to be a church sanction for blasphemy, drunkenness or Sabbath breaking.

The ducking stool was used mostly against women, especially "unquiet" ones, i.e. scolds. Sexual immorality was more culpable in a woman. In 1620 Hull aldermen ruled that women "faltie for bastards" should be carted and ducked.

Scold's bridle, St Mary's Church, Beverley (H. Peach)

Not only was the sin shameful in itself; resulting children might well fall to the public purse. Up to about 1700 Ducking Stool Lane near Beverley's North Bar carried a sewer in which accused women were publicly dipped.

Sex Stooge

Set-ups for pecuniary gain are certainly not just a modern phenomenon. In 1564 the mayor and aldermen of Hull heard a convincing case made against Thomas and Isabel West. A misguided London merchant, Francis Showerd, having been lured into the matrimonial bedroom by the enticing lady, was confronted at a very critical juncture by the husband, knife in hand, springing from behind a curtain and demanding money. According to divers and honest persons, these "devilish devices" had been practised many times before. West was disfranchised as a town burgess; and the heinous and detestable pair were committed to prison; after which they were to be carted through the streets with papers on their heads declaring their offences; and banished from Hull for ever.

Nor did poor old Francis escape censure. "For consenting to so naughty a fact" he was imprisoned for two days and nights, and was fined 26s 8d, to be "distributed to ye poor people".

Unlucky Number

In 1577 the mayor and aldermen of Hull condemned 13 pirates captured in the Humber to be hanged and gibbeted (i.e. their corpses publicly displayed until the bones fell away) along the coast as examples to others of their calling.

Constabulary Duties

Over the centuries the parish constable's duties grew. Unpaid except for expenses, and elected for one year, he was required to keep watch and ward, make arrests, to provide lodging for felons and escort them to court. He was to be alert for strangers and to move on vagabonds. He was called on to record the names of religious recusants. He had to notify his JP of unsanctioned buildings like dovecotes. He needed to ensure that butts for the militia were kept in place, and that stocks, pillory, whipping post and ducking stool were in working order. He might have to help to suppress vermin, he might be called upon to collect window and land taxes.

Not too surprisingly, the job was unpopular. At the East Riding Quarter Sessions in 1782 William Hopper, miller of Patrington, who was gainfully employed in his accustomed trade, was fined 3s 4d for refusing to serve.

Especially in later Tudor times many vagrants had to be summarily dealt

The lock-up at Hunmanby *(H. Peach)*

with. At Kirby Underdale on 19th June 1578 Thomas Harrison seized James Hogson and his wife Katren as 'vagrant rogs", whipped them according to statute, and returned them to Bishop Wilton "from whence as they sayde they last came free unponissed".

Whipping Offences

For many centuries the custom had been for the parish constable or a hired

man to administer floggings, not only to vagrants, but a variety of felons. By the 18th century women were allowed to wear a vest, but in general the victim was naked from the waist upwards and roped to the back of a cart.

Jane Kay of Hunmanby was doubly unlucky. At the Beverley Spring Sessions, 1715 it emerged that the whipping she was supposed to have received the previous Saturday had been postponed because of her misfortune to break her neck. But ...

"it is now ordered that she be whipped according to her former sentence on Saturday 5th May".

A Sessions entry for 1745 records that for stealing a great-coat, waistcoat, a pair of leather breeches and a hat, William Robinson, labourer of North Dalton was to be whipped to Beverley's market cross "until his body be bloody", in the phraseol-

Whipping frame, once used in Hull *(H. Peach, courtesy of Humberside Police)*

ogy of the time.

Even relatively minor thefts brought savage punishment. In 1775 Israel Hobson, labourer of Hedon was publicly whipped for stealing two hens. And in 1819 William Randerson was flogged from Hull's Whitefriargate to Dock Bridge for the theft of a rope; he then served three months in prison.

Folk memories have brooded on still darker fancies. Near the top of Newbald Green is a circular flat stone, thought to derive from the 17th century. According to legend, a man was whipped to death here in 1624.

Branded

After appearing in the York Court of Quarter Sessions, 1640 Stephen Martin of Filey, described as a dangerous rogue, workshy, a wanderer and a burglar was branded on the left shoulder with the letter "R" for rogue.

Reputations

Dealing with Catholic recusants was a steady problem for the Elizabethan church hierarchy. Thomas Young, Archbishop of York wrote to Lord Burleigh in 1569 concerning Dr Vavasor, renowned for his pro-Catholic oratory. Let us not recommend him for York Castle, urged the archbishop, where other prisoners might hear him and be moved by his words. Far better to send him to the Hull blockhouses, where he could talk only to the walls.

Give Ear

Less fortunate was Henry Burton, a Puritan preacher born at Birdsall in 1578. When he was unwise enough regularly to criticise the Anglican establishment, he was sentenced to have his ears cut off and to stand in the pillory. For some time he was imprisoned in Carlisle Castle. Later he was freed and given £6,000 as compensation for his sufferings.

Contempt of Court

In order to finance his various schemes, including waging war, King Charles I sold honours to certain of his subjects who owned land worth at least £40 per year. A number of East Yorkshiremen declined, partly because of the expense and burdensome duties that went with knighthoods, etc. Robert Wright, a Gowthorpe yeoman was fined 14s for being absent at the 1625 coronation; presumably he had been offered a lesser title, whereas Thomas Strickland of Scampton was obliged to pay £10 for opting out. Perhaps the Royal impatience with ungracious Yorkshiremen was reflected in still higher penalties as time went on. In 1630 Robert Crompton, a prosperous Driffield man, preferred to pay £30 rather than submit to an empty honour.

Black Barmby

Barmby Moor's reputation in the 17th century was indeed infamous. And it has to be owned that some villains were natives – like William Pendleton, convicted in 1603 for the murder of John Young of Pocklington, and subsequently hanged in chains on the Moor. But much more frequently the miscreants were off-comed-uns. Charles Spooner, aged 23, for example, was a Bradford man executed at Walmgate Bar, York on 29th May 1659 for the robbery and murder of Francis Groves at Barmby Moor just before Christmas the year before. Spooner was gibbeted on the Moor for some years. Perhaps the sight of so many gibbets contributed to the village's unenviable reputation.

Pocklington Records

Some 17th-century church records make dramatic reading. For example –

✧ 1630 Old Wife Green dragged into the market place and burnt for a witch.

✧ 1649 Isabella Billington aged 32 sentenced to the stake at York Special Assizes for crucifying her mother at Pocklington on 5th January, and offering a calf and cockerel as a burnt sacrifice. Her husband was hanged for his share in these misdeeds.

✧ 1642, 4th March – Petronel Haxby, the smith's wife, was executed in the market for a witch.

Peg's Promise

Peg Fyfe seems to have operated over a wide area, ranging from Market Weighton over Holderness and down to Spurn. A mid 17th-century legend attributes a terrible fate to a lad recruited to leave open a stable door to facilitate the theft of a horse near Skeffling. Instead he told the farmer of the planned raid. Shots were fired but the gang escaped. Months later Peg's men returned to carry out the threat made if he refused to co-operate. They skinned him alive, down to his palms and soles, and naked and bloody he crawled home to die.

Various tales have been told of Peg's own demise. One says that she tried to avoid hanging by choking on a spoon. Another avers that in a wood on the York road she was hanged by soldiers who then ran her through with swords.

Doubing Take You!

There is reason to think that rolling pin attacks were not just a music hall joke. In April 1654 Emmott Daykes, wife of John, was fined 20d by the Patrington manorial court for striking Gregory Bilton with such an implement, then known as a doubing.

The Strickland Pardon

Exhibited in Flamborough Church is a replica of the pardon granted by Charles II to Walter Strickland in 1660, absolving him from high treason charges, despite his long opposition to the benighted Charles I during the Civil War. As an emissary of the Long Parliament, Strickland had gone to Holland to protest at the active help given to Queen Henrietta Maria in her bid to raise arms and supplies for her husband. Oddly, the pardon eventually turned up in the church safe. Occasional stock-taking should not be despised!

Beastly Bothers

Stray animals have always been a nuisance. Pindars were appointed to secure the wanderers, exacting a fee before the owner was allowed re-possession. Nevertheless, there were many cases of illegal "rescue". At South Cave in 1663 Richard Robinson was fined 3s 4d for attempting to rescue a cow.

Pigs, alive or dead, were often cited as annoyances. Back in 1494 Robert Smith was fined 8d for leaving a dead and decaying pig in a Beverley Street and refusing to move it when ordered by the town governors. Dangerous dogs caused much alarm to ordinary townsfolk. A by-law of 1794 empowered the mayor to give notice "by the bell" of canine perils; and penalties of 6s 8d were to be imposed on defaulting owners. A pain of the Nunburnholme manorial court stated that sheep, too, should carry bells. In 1673 the court leet fined John Smith and others the sum of 6s 8d for negligence.

Court officials were known to carry scars incurred in the line of duty. In October 1833 the Nunburnholme court bailiff was bitten by a "ferocious mastiff", the property of Francis Vause who was ordered to keep the dog muzzled, on pain of a £1 fine on any future occasion.

Another very common offence was the illicit milking of cows in the field – "milking kine on stealth" – which generally brought a fine of a few pence.

Licence Lost

The socially indulgent landlord is another stereotype. Joseph Crowder, an innkeeper of Pocklington, a "person of ill character and suffered people to tipple in his house on the Lord's Day and hath had several scandalous parties in his house" had his licence revoked at the East Riding Quarter Sessions, Beverley in 1712.

Petty Treason

This was another term for the murder of a husband. In 1776 a Flamborough woman, Elizabeth Boardman was convicted at York for poisoning her spouse. The judge recommended, as an act of leniency, that she be strangled before being burned. Thus she was drawn through the city streets on a hurdle and throttled with the executioner's rope – a customary practice, and of course, in full public view. Thirteen years later the burning of murderesses was abolished.

Hue and Cry

Over child maintenance, which might otherwise fall on the parish, officials sometimes went to considerable lengths. During the period 1792 to 1796 a certain William Chaplain was in constant arrears with the Hunmanby overseers of the poor. The Hunmanby constable spent much time making inquiries in villages as distant as Brandesburton – time lost, of course, to his own occupation. In 1793 the offender was made to pay 11s and a further £3 3s in 1796.

Slapdown for HRH

Midshipman William Henry, Duke of Clarence, the future "sailor king" got his face slapped by a chambermaid, Sally Gibson in the Ship Inn, Bridlington during a visit on 7th July 1785. What exactly he did to deserve it must now be a matter of conjecture. But for a trusted Yorkshire lass to behave like this to a visiting VIP, well – there must ha' beean summat!

Transportation

Under an Act of 1718 early transportees were sent to the American colonies such as Virginia and Maryland. So often their crimes looked to be trivial. In 1754 William Jewitson, a labourer – yet again, a labourer – of Molescroft, Beverley was sent away for seven years, the usual sentence, for stealing 4s 10d from the pocket of Elizabeth Matthews. Even more astonishing was the like fate of Dawn Richardson, spinster of Etton, convicted in 1763 at the East Riding Sessions for stealing three iron screws.

With the outbreak of the American War of Independence in 1776 a new outlet had to be found for English criminals. The coast of New South Wales, so recently named and explored by Captain James Cook became a penal colony for many Yorkshire expatriates, like George Williamson who had retrieved a quantity of soot from a field in Bishop Wilton, where presumably a local chimney sweep had dumped it as worthless. Thomas Ash, labourer of Walkington, was expelled in 1812 for the theft of nine ducks. Somewhat more culpable, perhaps, was Hull labourer John Thompson, a man of many aliases, who in 1815 was transported for the stealing of two linen sheets, two pairs of cotton stockings, one pair of silk stockings and three silver teaspoons.

Transportation was not abolished until 1868 .

Pillories

The pillory was a tall wooden frame with a cross-piece holed to secure the neck (hence "necktrap") as well as the arms, while leaving the victim standing. It was applied to a variety of cheats, liars, defamers, fortune tellers and sexual adventurers.

In 1552 a man and wife were so punished at Driffield for selling pots of strawberries with only a few bits of fruit near the top and the lower part stuffed with fern. William Hill was pilloried in Howden market place in 1796 for setting fire to a barn. In January 1808 two Garton conspirators, Paul and Escreet were convicted at the Beverley Sessions for extorting money from a Kellythorpe farmer, Francis Brown. Part of their punishment was to spend one hour in the Driffield pillory on three successive market days starting on 5th May. Two years later the last man and woman to be pilloried in the town were fortune tellers.

When, in October 1800, James Grange was convicted at the Beverley Quarter Sessions for an indecent assault on a female relative, part of his punishment was to stand in the pillory in the market place on Tuesday, 6th January 1801. Thereafter he was to languish in a solitary cell for twelve months.

A "misdemeanour" was generally a euphemism for an indecent offence; and in Regency times, as nowadays, the very occasional schoolmaster made an error of judgement. John Abbott of Sculcoates, Hull had to suffer abuse and ridicule in the Grimstone Street pillory for one hour on Tuesday, 21st January 1812 as a preliminary to twelve months imprisonment in the house of correction.

Pillorying was abolished in 1837.

Conscience Time

For keeping a disorderly house Catherine Fisher, wife of William Fisher, was consigned to Beverley's house of correction for two months in 1804. It was stipulated that the last fortnight should be spent in a solitary cell – possibly to work out at leisure some strategies for not getting caught so easily next time.

Sea or Solitary?

The Beverley magistrates in 1810 gave labourer Henry Webster two options for stealing a silver cup and one piece of silver. He could spend six months in the solitary cell at the house of correction; or he could join one of His Majesty's ships of war. The prisoner's choice was not recorded: neither was an alluring prospect.

The Dungeon Harp

A Scots staymaker by trade, Robert Peddie was sent to the Beverley house of correction for his part in Chartist conspiracies in Bradford. During his stay he penned some impassioned and caustic verses entitled The Dungeon Harp, which have passed into the national folk lore of Victorian prison conditions.

Much of his censure was on lines long familiar. The food was disgusting. Beds only 32 inches wide sometimes had to be shared. Jobs like stone breaking were very tiring and caused many accidents; or they were tedious, as with beating and dressing flax, or picking oakum. The Silent System was grievously irksome on Sundays when prisoners had to sit still for long periods without drawing even the slightest attention to their discomfort. Infringements, like trying to signal urgent lavatorial needs, could bring three days in the "black hole". Peddie railed against the hypocrisy of the chaplain, the Rev. William Hildyard and enforced attendance at Sunday chapel.

But his prime attack was on the treadmill – "the monster grievance", a rotary staircase which inmates were compelled to climb for many daily sessions of 20 minutes – three stints before breakfast, six before dinner, nine before supper – the equivalent of ascending 1100 steps; and all the time exposed to the gaze of others "like wild beasts in a managerie". It became hard to breathe, sweat soaked the shirt "and even the leathers of braces and body belt". Giddiness affected vision. Encaked in dried sweat the prisoner was left cold and stiff during the night. Within a fortnight nine out of ten needed medical attention. He went on to describe the deterioration of a young man, Creaser, who died within a few months.

To refuse the treadmill was to invite the lash and the black hole. Comparisons were made with the Negro slaves, recently freed through the efforts of Wilberforce.

After his release in 1845 Peddie continued his work for the People's Charter; and a petition to the House of Commons presented by Joseph Hume MP called for an inquiry into the use of the treadmill. Gradually its role declined as an instrument of punishment, but formal abolition had to wait until 1898.

Juvenile Offenders

In Victorian times youth was no excuse. At the Hull Sessions of 1840 William Waudby, 11 years old, was convicted of stealing Is 9½d, the property of John Brittain, and for this he was transported for the customary seven years.

At the same Sessions Carl Hebdon (11) and John Foster (13) pleaded guilty to stealing two petticoats, a handkerchief and a pint bottle of brandy, the property of William Cockerline. In consequence of their tender years the Recorder sentenced them to a mere three months hard labour, and to be well whipped before returning to freedom. It would be illuminating to know the reasoning behind this punishment, severe as it was, compared to the transportation case cited above.

Typical of punishments a generation later (1868) was the three days in prison, plus six strokes of the birch awarded to William Smith (10) by a Beverley court for stealing two pipes from a local tobacconist's.

Fishing Apprentices – the Papper Case

Notoriously ill-used were fishing "apprentices" at sea where there was no chance of redress. The Papper case became a 'cause célèbre'.

Aboard the Hull smack, 'Rising Sun' William Papper was inhumanly bullied and beaten by the skipper, Osmann Otto Brand who habitually picked on him, deprived him of food, dangled him over the side – and finally let go. Subsequent inquiries led to Brand's arrest, conviction and execution by William Marwood at Armley, Leeds on 23rd May 1882. An official Board of Trade investigation followed.

Spectral Earful

Seeing a ghost is likely to be sanction enough. But at White Cross, Leven there are tales of a female phantom who in Victorian times leaped up behind horse riders and slapped them behind the ears.

Loose Reins at Leven

At Leven Petty Sessions on Saturday, 8th September 1860 labourer Richard Harper of Hornsea denied being asleep while lying prostrate in the first of two carts being pulled by a horse team. On payment of costs the case was dismissed.

On 5th September 1867 George Medforth, a Leven agricultural labourer was fined 19s 6d for leaving his horse and cart unattended outside the Prince of Wales Inn, Beverley.

Victorian Vagrant

William McMahon, described by the Driffield Times (31st December 1869) as a "stranger to the police, to razor, to soap and water and ready for the rag bag" was sent by the Petty Sessions to the house of correction for 14 days for wandering abroad without any visible means of subsistence.

Hired Absconder

Cases of agricultural workers breaking their contract were noted by the local press. John Spencer of North Ferriby, appearing at Beverley Petty Sessions in January 1869 on a charge of absconding from the service of his master, Mr F. Johnson of Bishop Burton, was ordered to return and complete his contract, presumably until Martinmas, and to pay costs.

Speeding

An Act of 1903 permitted speeds of 14mph in built-up areas and 20 mph in the open countryside, and these remained the official limits until 1930.

On 4th July 1908 John Vernon Townsend of Hunmanby Hall drove a car through the North Bar, Beverley at 15 mph when under a local by-law the restriction was down to 5 mph. He was fined £7 10s, plus costs. And on 5th June 1909 a London physician, Mr L.H. Smith was fined £3 and costs for driving in Bridlington at a speed estimated at 20 mph.

College Reformer

Prison and an already prestigious new independent school seemingly have little in common; and probably when the Juvenile Reformatory was opened at Hull Prison in 1906 a few eyebrows were raised at the appointment as educational adviser of Mr G.H. Gore, headmaster of Hymers College. Yet suitably graded work in literacy, numeracy and physical routines, backed by a firm but humane discipline must be basic foundations to all educational ventures. More middle class support came with the provision of work and materials by a sympathetic ship owner. It was a far-sighted move away from punishment towards re-habilitation.

Naughty Nurse

According to the publicly displayed Hospital Record Book at Castle Hill, Cottingham a probationer, Joan Morton, was dismissed from the sanatorium on 14th September 1938 on disciplinary grounds, viz. – familiarity with male patients. Lucky lads!

Billy's Lang Wots

In some ways Billy Bugg, Skidby blacksmith in the 1950s, was gullible with horses. He liked a flutter at the Beverley races and suffered a certain amount of cheating when a friend failed to place a bet on an unlikely steed. What Billy afterwards said on finding out is not recorded.

More certain was his unsentimental approach to the occasional awkward horse.

"Ah'll gi' thoo some o' lang wots!" he would threaten. "Lang wots" were literally long oats, but in this case it meant a crack with a hammer across the beast's rear flanks to show who was master.

Chapter 10

Disputes

Homicide in High Places

A Flemish adventurer, Drogo de la Beuvriere, was rewarded for his support of William the Conqueror by receiving the Seignory of Holderness. His bride was the Lady Albina, the king's niece. Skipsea Castle was built for them, and at first all seemed well, but one story goes that Albina was suspected of sorcery, and her lord, having poisoned her with a pretended love potion, went directly to William, borrowed money and vanished for ever to the continent.

Over the centuries a ghostly white lady is reputed to have stalked the ramparts, and may or may not be carrying a poisoned chalice.

Other intermittent apparitions may be of two brothers who, in Civil War times, fought a duel over their inheritance in the drying moat. Both, however, died of wounds and were buried nearby.

St Mary's v Meaux

These two famous abbeys came to violent clashes during the thirteenth century. In 1230 there was rivalry over the use of Hornsea Key (harbour) for merchandise' and shipping. Some time later, about 1260, William de Lascelles, a tenant of Meaux, was denied by York monks the right to fish on Hornsea Mere. Speedily the quarrel escalated, and York justices, perhaps doubtful whether an imposed ruling could be made acceptable to both sides, ordered a "jus duellum", or trial by combat, several on each side. The contest was waged from morning to sunset, St Mary's gaining the victory. Meaux was compensated with land at Rudston.

Ravenser Odd v Grimsby

By an old tradition it was a Grimsby man who described (c1234) Ravenser Odd as "an island born in the sea", from depositions of sand and stone near Spurn Head. As fishermen began to use it to dry their nets, some entrepreneur built a hut from shipwreck timbers and began a trade in meat and drink. In 1230 the island was taken over by the Earl of Aumale. By 1251 there was enough commerce to justify a Thursday market and a September fair.

A quarter of a century on, Grimsby men were complaining that ships approaching the Humber were being escorted to Ravenser Odd, and tolls exacted. Ravenser responded that they were well positioned to cater for incoming traders; and that Grimsby had so often failed to pay fair prices, especially for herrings. An appeal to the Court of King's Bench in 1291 acquitted Ravenser Odd of trespass, and Grimsby was fined for making false claims.

More gains were to accrue to the islanders – a charter in 1299 confirming the fair and two weekly markets, in return for £300; and in 1304 two MPs – Peter at Sea and William Pailleleve.

The most serious dispute was soon to come – that with the sea. By 1346 there was serious flooding and traders left for Hull. Soon there was but one ship left, and that for defensive reasons. The future rivalry in the Humber was to be between Grimsby and Hull.

Well Springs of Conflict

While Hull's medieval wells tended to be saline, the Derringham and Julian Springs at Anlaby, four miles to the west, produced sparkling fresh water and were greatly envied. From 1293 Wyke (Hull) had indeed been supplied from Springhead, Anlaby, but this had caused great resentment, with deliberate pollution and the blocking of channels. There were fears of the supply drying up, and even of a distant effect on Hessle Haven, a developing minor port. Charge was met by counter-charge. In 1376 Hull complained to Edward III of having to transport water across the river from Lincolnshire. Haltemprice retorted that the town should use its River Hull. The king suggested that new channels should be dug, but there was no follow-up.

Further skirmishes ensued. In 1392, having let in the Humber and flooded the western approaches to the town, hundreds of Haltemprice men besieged Hull, bent on mayhem. Arrests and reprisals on both sides were the result. At length in 1413 the mayor of Hull appealed to Pope John XXII who urged Haltemprice to repent of past errors which might otherwise be held against them on Judgement Day. "By the bowels of mercy" he charged the villagers of the west not to withhold water from their townsfolk.

Still disorder continued. In 1450 Hull bought the Julian and Derringham Springs, and a new Spring Dyke was cut to link up with the municipal Bushdyke. Only gradually did tribal feelings cease to overflow.

Alternating Abbots

By August 1349 the Black Death (see chapter 1) had decimated Meaux Abbey. So much so that the sub-cellarer, William de Dringhoe, who regarded Malmsey wine as a helpful antidote, was elected as the new abbot. Robert, a colleague, grew jealous enough to report his superior for receiving a stolen horse. After the perhaps inevitable acquittal, Robert remained watchful. Embezzlement was the next accusation. This time an inquiry by the Abbot of Fountains Abbey demoted William, but allowed him to remain. And Robert became abbot.

William's next move was an appeal to high authority. He travelled to Rome and won over the Pope who ordered Robert to resign. Instead, Robert parleyed with William, conceding allowances, food, a servant, freedoms in return for keeping the Meaux mitre. So William lived the high life until, on Robert's death, he was re-elected abbot.

Mayor v Archbishop

The high-handed and quarrelsome Archbishop of York, Alexander Neville descended on Hull in 1378 to claim overdue payments of prisage – his historic rights to casks of wine (or cash equivalent) being unloaded on the staithes of the River Hull. He was confronted in the street by the mayor, Sir Thomas de Waltham, who also was stubborn, argumentative and, on occasion, short-tempered. Seizing the cleric's crosier he hit out. Neville gave a good account of himself but finally had to retreat.

News of this heavyweight action reached King Richard II, who summoned the mayor to explain his hospitality. Sir Thomas was given a rousing send-off and defended himself capably before the royal judges. Wisely, no doubt, the case was left in abeyance. Back in Hull, the mayor opened a cask or two with his civic leaders.

A Bluff Bailiff

The outrageous behaviour of John Eglesfeld, bailiff of Rise during the reign of Edward IV is a depressing example of arbitrary and selfish parochial repression. Demanding fines and making threats, he took 30 head of cattle from the villagers and impounded them. When an appeal was made to the justice, Martyn de la See, whose representatives then investigated, the bailiff refused to give way. On the contrary, the justice's men were met by "heavies" armed with "hangars, daggers and bylles". In the affray Eglesfeld was wounded; and went on to blame the justice before the landowner, Sir Robert Hildyard. Martyn de la See was obliged to call upon further witnesses to justify his own intervention. There is no record of how, if at all, the matter was resolved.

Tithes

These were tenths of farm produce surrendered annually to the church and were generally stored in the tithe barn. For centuries tithes were a prolific cause of conflict between the farming community and the parish priest. Many accounts show a mixture of astonishing clerical tenacity and pure pathos. With the North Sea waters almost swirling about his feet, John de Cottingham, charged with the cure of souls in the doomed island of Ravenser Odd, sat on a tombstone in the hope of receiving last tithes from a declining population bent on flight.

In taking St Mary's Abbey to the York Consistory Court in 1493, Hornsea vicar William Otwey felt he had a good case for an increase in tithe income. The yield had progressively fallen at times when responsibilities had increased. By custom he was still obliged to pay the pension due to his predecessor, John Wood – a considerable standing charge. Unfortunately, the Court found for St Mary's.

On Easter Sunday 1494 Otwey took his revenge – and the abbot's boat and nets to fish on the Mere. For this provocatively public act of defiance he was excommunicated. Penance and restoration followed, and Otwey survived on his diminishing income until 1499.

Yet cheating the parson was a game universally enjoyed. In her will dated 24th February 1542 Isabella Bland of Meltonby, however, showed a twinge of conscience, requesting burial in Pocklington churchyard and bequeathing 4d to the vicar "for tythes forgotten".

Seventeenth century Quakers refused to take the Oath of Allegiance or to pay tithes to the "steeple house". John Spencer of Tunstall, one such recusant, had to pay in lieu a cow valued at £3 10s.

In coastal areas tithes of fish had long been resented. Thus, at Flamborough part of the catch was supposed to be paid to Bridlington Priory, then to the Priory Church after Henry VIII's dissolution. In turn the prior had customarily exchanged flagons of ale and sixpences. In a famous case John Ogle, lord of the manor, went to London to plead for the removal of the burdensome tithe. But on 7th June 1753 he died of gaol fever, a hazard of appearing in contemporary law courts. His body was brought back by sea to Flamborough; and in view of all the dramatic publicity, this tithe was lifted soon afterwards.

Tithes were gradually modified in favour of money payments, which became official with the Commutation of Tithes Act of 1836.

Sheriff v Priory

Early in the 16th-century Prior John Nandych of Haltemprice was claiming territorial authority over parts of the adjoining countryside. A Star Chamber decision, advised by the Abbot of Meaux, rather surprisingly supported the prior.

For the Hull sheriff, Edward Mattison, this was too much. The prior had to recognise the temporal power of King's Town. So on 6th October 1515 he led a body of soldiers to line up in front of the priory. After wordy exchanges blows were struck – and the canons and tenants retreated. Just when the threat of an invasion of sacred surrounds seemed imminent, the Mayor of Hull rode up with a third force and called a halt. Brother restrained brother: for George Mattison felt that Edward was in danger of exceeding his authority.

As a consequence of further arbitration with the Star Chamber, the priory withdrew its claim on the Anlaby water springs in return for royalties from neighbouring Willerby.

Civil War Skirmish

A record in the Newbald parish registers of 1643 mentions the burial here of some 30 soldiers. The site was about halfway between Royalist York and Parliamentary Hull. It may be significant that colonel of the Royalist cavalry, Sir Marmaduke Langdale lived at nearby Sancton, and one of his captains, Sir Philip Monkton, was the owner of South Newbald Hall.

When Mercenaries Fell Out

In 1689 when the new king, William of Orange, was recruiting men to deal with the Irish problem, hundreds of Danish soldiers had been landed in Hull alone. It seems likely that two of them came to blows in Beverley, for on 16th December Daniel Straker was buried, and a week later a compatriot, Johannes Frederick Bellow was also laid to rest, having been beheaded in the market square. It was said that two cartloads of gravel were brought from Brandesburton to mop up the blood spilt around the scaffold. Had they quarrelled over a pre-Christmas celebration? or over a girl? We don't know. But an external plaque on the south wall of St Mary's Church commemorates the event.

Here two young Danish Souldiers lye,
The one in quarrell chanc'd to die;
The others Head, by their own Law
With Sword was feverd at one Blow

December the 23d

1689

Plaque on south side of St Mary's Church, Beverley *(H. Peach)*

Whose Fish?

Under a charter of 1447 the Mayor of Hull has ex officio always been elected as Admiral of the Humber. While the office has been largely honorary, original emoluments included the rights of shipwreck, flotsam and jetsam, salvage, royal fish like whales and porpoises, goods from pirate or enemy ships – subject of course to the rights of other parties.

A challenge arose in 1729 over a "large fish" caught in the Humber by a ship's master who towed it to Brough. There it was seized by a man called Hall who claimed local fishery rights. At this point William Fenwick, Mayor of Hull, Admiral of the Humber had the "fish" towed by the tail to Hull. An appeal to the courts by Hall stood no chance of success.

While the legal jurisdiction of the Admiral was abolished in 1835, the dual title has been kept. Visiting ships' captains still pay courtesy calls to the Admiral of the Humber who pays return visits, piped aboard with all ceremony with the official flag fluttering at the masthead.

Anti-Militia Riots

The Militia Act of 1757 aimed at recruiting local men at a time when thousands of regular soldiers were required overseas during this Seven Years War against the French. There was enormous opposition from young men who had no wish to wear uniforms and bear arms just to protect the property of the rich, which was their view of the situation. Particular targets were lists drawn up by chief constables and gentry, which were to be considered at a meeting at Beverley on Saturday, 17th September. In various parts of the East Riding men armed with guns, swords and pitchforks intimidated clergy and members of the gentry: on 8th September at North Frodingham; on the 9th at Winestead; the following day at Hedon and Cottingham.

On Monday, 12th September a mob reckoned at fifteen hundred broke into Kilnwick Percy Hall, bent on destroying lists of able-bodied men likely to be called up. Lady Anderson found herself in a terrifying position. Kitchens were looted and the mob took over. By the time Sir Edward returned much of the passion had been spent. He was able to pacify the leaders and eventually they all left. While no action was taken against these rioters, incidents in Howden and Bubwith brought treason charges, resulting in many prison sentences. Meantime, the Lord Lieutenant, Lord Irwin called off the meeting for 17th September.

In March 1758 at the York Assizes 80 East Riding men appeared. Forty were imprisoned, four were found guilty of high treason but their sentences were commuted. Only one, Robert Cole of Bridlington, paid the supreme penalty.

The Press Gang

Hull newspapers in 1796 carried recruiting advertisements for the Royal Navy – "a number of brave fellows to serve ... in the defence of the British Constitution against French perfidy". Inducements included "a bountiful supply of clothing, beef, grog flip and strong beer." Prize money appeared to be pushed almost within reach. "Men will be sent to capture rich Spanish galleons and in consequence will return loaded with Dollars and Honour to spend their days in Peace and Plenty".

Colourful street processions, with a boat on carriage and Jack Tars distributing ale and biscuits, were meant to enhance the call of the sea. But this time patriotism was not enough. Hull was unable to reach its quota of 731 men. From this time naval snatch squads began a reign of terror. No young man was safe from kidnap.

Specially targeted were returning whaling ships, whose skippers resorted to dropping men off further up the coast, leaving aboard only very young boys and older men. The *Blenheim* incident has become a legend. Returning from Greenland waters in 1798 it was approached in the Humber by *HMS Nonsuch* and *Redoubt* who prepared boarding parties. The *Blenheim's* captain and pilot were locked up so they could not prevent the crew's resistance. That done, the men repelled the naval parties with marlin spikes and belaying pins. In the action two ratings were killed. Another who lost three fingers afterwards stayed in Hull where he became known as Three-fingered Jack. Boarders were beaten off, and the whaling men disembarked, welcomed by hundreds of clamorous spectators. Captain Mitchinson was put on trial in York for murder, but was acquitted, returning to one of Hull's tumultuous welcomes. Sadly, the Blenheim was subsequently burned in the Davis Strait by French frigates.

One local skipper took unusual personal measures to avoid involuntary transfer to His Majesty's employment. Thomas Hawkins of the *Everthorpe* went about in female attire, accompanied by his wife and daughters. Women took a very active role in another incident c1812 at the Bull Inn on Beverley Road. Seeing a sailor seized by the Gang, a group of women haymakers rushed in from the fields, pitchforks to the fore, and scared off the marauders.

On another occasion in July 1815, seeing a young seaman about to be pressed, a gang of deck navvies intervened. When the mayor tried to read the Riot Act he was pulled down unceremoniously by his chain of office. A naval lieutenant was knocked down just when he was about to open fire. All the local men were set free.

There were many direct attacks on the Press Gang in Hull. In 1803 a hostelry, Ship Glory, a Gang rendezvous, was destroyed by a mob. The Royal Navy did not in every instance rule the tides of the Humber.

In this prolonged and bitter dispute there were some lighter ironical moments. A pottery worker called Clowes, given to practical jokes, dressed up with some pals as a press gang company and set out to terrorise the folk at Barton, just across the river. On returning to Hull to celebrate, the real Gang turned up, attracted no doubt by the high spirits. Clowes, in high panic, sought refuge in his master's china shop. Discovered, he persuaded his master and the publican to intercede with the lieutenant ... and he fled into hiding at Tunstall.

Settlement and Paternity Disputes

Arguments between different parishes over unwanted paupers often caused expensive legal wrangles. Under the Settlement Act of 1662 a poor man wanting to flit had to obtain from his native parish a certificate admitting liability to support him if he became destitute elsewhere. Overseers of the poor and churchwardens were entitled to expel strangers unable to rent a property to the value of at least £10. The ripples of this legislation were still apparent into the 19th century.

In 1815 the East Newton vestry sought advice costing £12 3s from Thomas and Charles Frost, Hull attorneys, "for the expenses of a Sessions trial with the overseers of Sunk Island to know which place Daniel Kirk belongs to". Kirk was a wanderer, unwelcome in either community; and sustained inquiries across Holderness brought a total bill of £15 15s, just for this one man.

Paternity disputes also involved much time, energy and expense. The Newbald churchwardens' accounts for 1803 record "Journey Northallerton, two men and horses after a man for bastard child, and expenses – £6 1s 9d".

The rapidly rising costs of feeding, clothing and housing the poor, including temporary vagrants and single mothers was a determining factor in the Poor Law Amendment Act of 1834, the original intention of which was to provide relief only to those reduced to entering the new harsher Union workhouses.

A Wolds Waterloo

Up to 1826 Fridaythorpe folk had always been allowed during dry summers to take their carts and buckets along the road to Fimber. But in that summer's drought supplies in Fimber were also running low and tensions grew. Words were followed by scuffles. The Fridaythorpe men came back in force, but with sticks and stones were driven back. For Fimber, that year, charity had to begin at home.

...Will be Boyes

A flamboyant and influential publican who seemed to live easily with controversy was Daniel Boyes, landlord of Beverley's Angel Inn between 1841 and 1873. As Liberal leader, skilful debater and shrewd manipulator, he had critics as well as friends. One curious miscalculation was his decision to order the lopping of overhanging trees belonging to a political opponent, Col. Thomas Marten. After a legal action (1851) which the colonel won, a special rate had to be levied to cover the corporation's costs; and thereafter the issue of Marten's trees was one to which the Tory faithful liked to raise their glasses.

A less disputatious matter was Boyes's catering ability. At New Year 1845 he prepared a 10 stone game pie to which 35 guests very agreeably sat down.

Spendthrift Wives

Sir Tatton Sykes II (1826-1913) of Sledmere was so infuriated by the extravagances of his lady, Jessica (née Cavendish Bentinck) – that he inserted a special notice in The Times of 5th December 1896 repudiating her future debts.

Sir Thomas Aston Clifford Constable (1807-70) fared even worse. His first wife, Marianne certainly spared no expense with the refurbishment of Burton Constable Hall. But his number two, Rosina Brandon, in throwing out most of the contents and buying in excellent taste, nearly ruined him. He survived but five years of this relationship.

Fairley Faithless

George Fairley of Leven failed to answer a paternity charge at the local Petty Sessions in February 1861. The complainant, Sarah Otley admitted this to be her third misfortune and her second to Fairley. In extenuation she claimed that they had thrice arranged to be married, but on each occasion Mr Fairley had failed to turn up. The magistrates made an order of 1s a week, plus expenses – but intimated that Miss Otley need never apply to them again.

Empty Threat?

Notice in the Beverley Guardian, February 1870:

"If the Party who took a PIG TROUGH out of a yard in Wood Lane does not return it, they will be prosecuted, as they are known".

Smallganging

Here is a localised East Riding term for a particular dispute – a revenge attack by two or more horse lads on a waggoner who had bullied them at work. The Martinmas hirings provided the opportunity to repay an old score up a back alley. A punishment favoured on the farm by many a waggoner was to push an offending face under a horse's tail, a sanction not always readily forgiven.

Pier Rivals

Was there ever such a keenly contested commercial rivalry to build a pier? In Elizabethan times there had been some kind of structure at Hornsea Beck, but it had gone by c1700. Joseph Armytage Wade, one of the Riding's great entrepreneurs, considered the idea for years, forming the Hornsea Pier Company in 1873, and sinking ten provisional piles into the beach near the railway station. Nothing much happened, and the piles were dubbed "the ten virgins".

Martin du Gillon, a Leeds businessman also proposed a pier only half a mile south at Hornsea Burton, and tried to negotiate a way forward with JAW. But Wade, using his position as chairman of the Local Board of Health, blocked all moves. Their wrangling spilled over into the columns of the local Gazette. In the spring of 1877 Gillon formed his own Pier Promenade and General Improvement Company; and oddly, a Parliamentary committee approved both schemes, unless one side objected. Stubbornly, neither did, and some preliminary work done by Gillon was damaged by winter storms. This could have been seen as a significant omen. During the following summer Wade's pier made useful progress, but promised financial support was not forthcoming.

Mutual recriminations continued, and at last Gillon's financial plight forced his withdrawal. It looked as if Wade had won – but his own pro-occupations with the receivers prevented the pier opening to the public during the summer of 1880.

On Thursday, 28th October stormy weather threw the vessel, the *Earl of Derby*, against the pier, causing the collapse of the last hundred yards. Further

Wreckage of the *Earl of Derby (Courtesy of Hornsea Museum)*

to repairs it was opened for a number of years from 1885, but never paid its way and was demolished in 1897.

Navigational Altercation

By their social mix, itinerant way of livelihood and working and playing hard, the navigators who dug canals and railway tunnels generated a degree of trouble, often among themselves. On 26th July 1850 four Irishmen had been drowned during a riot on an embankment on Sunk Island. But there were to be large-scale problems with the building of the Hull-Barnsley Railway between 1880 and 1885. The excavation of the Drewton Tunnel (1 mile 354 yards) near Little Weighton involved huge numbers of Irish, Scots and English navvies, ranging from 10 to 70 year olds – and their encamped families – and the resultant rivalries were bound to be explosive at times. Trouble flared in April 1882 at Springhead when some English workers, incensed by what they saw as preferential treatment of the Irish, rounded on them in a massive running brawl, driving them from the camp and refusing to let them return. Hundreds of men on both sides were sacked by the contractors.

Wold Rangers

These nomads took strange names – Mad Halifax, Mushroom Charlie, Slapface Ned, Methylated Annie, Mucky Lena, Tin Whistle Joe, Cut-Lip Jack, Soldier Tom, Cloggy Sam. Carrying their few possessions in canvas bags, happy to do a few casual farm jobs in return for the privilege of sleeping in barns or outhouses, they rarely made trouble, except when the winter was severe and one of them deliberately smashed a window to ensure a night in the police cells. But they were a breed apart, trusting few ordinary folk – though Alfred Bielby, blacksmith at North Grimston between the wars, sometimes looked after their casual earnings.

Surprisingly perhaps, there was a welcome for them at Sledmere House where Sir Tatton Sykes I had a bell fixed on the back door so that tea and sandwiches could be requested. The custom continued through to Sir Mark (1879-1919) who once had to intervene against the law. A policeman, seeing two Rangers behaving suspiciously near the House, arrested them. During the unseemly scuffle Sir Mark emerged, riding crop under his arm and remonstrated with the officer. "How dare you, constable? These gentlemen are my guests!"

The Rangers were not, however, uniformly welcome at every door. Many survived until about 1940. And they certainly added variety to the local scene.

Clerical Abattoir

A country parson's lot has not always been serene. The untoward circumstances met early in his Reighton incumbency (1901-16) by John Matthew Wynne were almost certainly unique. The challenge was immediate, direct and, so to speak, on the vicarage doorstep. John Anderson, parish clerk, found it convenient to kill his pigs in the vicar's cellar. The Rev John was entitled to order, "Get thee hence". And he did so.

The Truscott Affair

Like many another Walkington man who has completed an honest day's toil, schoolmaster James Truscott liked the occasional jar at the Dog and Duck. He was never the worse for it, and his professional work never suffered. But someone reported him to the local authority. His moral standing was called into question, and he was given notice. Since 1892 Truscott had been an effective and popular leader, and protests on his behalf were soon evident. But there was no action. Emotional scenes at his official farewell were followed by a valediction attended by hundreds.

On 7th June 1911 the family left for Kent. A supply teacher recorded, "Mr Truscott left the village for Beverley at 10.00 am and the parish and children followed him". With flags and banners flying, a trap with the Truscotts on board was enthusiastically pulled the three miles to County Hall where "For he's a jolly good fellow" was lustily sung. After waving him off at the railway station, the crowd returned to Education HQ for another defiant demonstration. It was all too late.

Cowpat Conflict

In many East Riding villages up to the 1950s cowkeepers (or tenters, or tenterers) rented the lanes from the parish, allowing the beasts to graze freely on the verges. At Garton on the Wolds in the 1930s a dispute smouldered between Butch the tenter and the Rev G. Bardett Dransfield, who objected to the cows at his home approaches. While they never came to blows it is recollected that regular confrontations produced some ripe exchanges.

Special Offer

A delightful tale recounted by W.H. Watkinson in 'A Relieving Officer Looks Back' concerned the obsequies of a pauper who had died in the Patrington workhouse. In general such burials took place in the parish of origin and at a moderate fee. But on this occasion the vicar had charged a double fee, not realising that the deceased was a native of his parish. The clerk to the Board of Guardians wrote to the vicar, challenging the fee. In returning his apologies for the misunderstanding, the vicar enclosed a lower account – and for goodwill offered to bury any or all of the guardians for a mere shilling a head.

Chapter 11

Domestic Doings

Old Rhyme

On ye Wolds we mostly barley eat,
For there they grow but very little wheat;
We live on barley bread and barley pies,
And oats and peas the want of wheat supplies.

Fire Warning

In the centuries of wood and thatch the risk of fire was acute, and warnings were frequent. Thus, in 1623 a manorial regulation at Patrington urged "that none do fetch fire from one neighbour to another but close covered". 18th-century Howden had so many fires that shifts of watchers had to be organised.

It is easier to understand cottage fires than the conflagrations that reduced so many stately homes, like Scorborough Hall (1705) which persuaded the Hotham family to move to South Dalton; Cottingham Castle, so called (1861); Cave Castle (1875); Sledmere House (1911); Buckton Hall (1919); Sunderlandwick Hall, on VJ night, 1945 when Canadian soldiers set fire to some curtains; and Settrington House (1963).

Some town fires have also been very serious. In 1691 many of Hedon's houses were burnt down.

Cassons

Up to the 18th century dried pats of cow dung called cassons were burnt with wood and coal. Apparently they produced much heat, little smoke and a pleasant aroma.

Hen Rents

In pre-enclosure times there are a number of references to hens being given to the lord of the manor at Christmas as a form of rent. It happened at Sproatley. At Ulrome six houses made annual payments of hens.

The Northumberland Household Book

Dating from 1512 but unpublished until 1770, the fifth Earl Percy's book gives a wonderfully detailed account of meals and housekeeping in the family homes of Leconfield Manor and Wressle Castle.

Breakfast must have got them off to a useful start – "first a Loaf of Brede in Trenchors, 11 Manchetts (small loaves), quart of bear or wine, half a chyne of mutton or else a chine of beef boiled".

It was not unusual for dinner to be provided for 160, plus up to 60 visitors. Particularly impressive was the variety of fowl – cranes, woodcock, bittern, dottrell, bustard, peacock and seagulls, "so be they good and in season".

Fingers were preferred to forks, and beakers and plates were of wood or pewter. Apparently it was quite customary for some plates to be shared.

Early bed was the norm. In case the earl or countess still felt peckish a bedroom table was laid with "two loaves of fine meal, a loaf of household bread, a gallon of beer and a quart of wine".

At Christmas under an "abbot of misrule" 20 plays were to be performed at 1s 8d each, and 20s were to be given to a showman of performing bears.

There was a good deal of movement between Wressle and Leconfield, involving 150 staff (which included up to a dozen priests) and much of the furnishings, too.

Change at Kilham

A local poet, Edward Anderson noted in his poem 'The Sailor' (1792) how buildings had altered since his boyhood:

> *"But when the town of Kilham first I saw*
> *Houses were built of clay and thatched in straw.*
> *What alteration in a little while!*
> *The houses now are mostly brick and tile".*

Wife Selling

During the 19th century many instances of wife selling occurred in Yorkshire, probably with varying degrees of collusion from disillusioned spouses. On 4th February 1806 George Gowthorpe of Patrington brought his wife with a halter round her neck and sold her for 20 guineas in Hull to a man called Houseman.

Three Tips

✧ To comb out lice, as with wartime evacuees: seat the victim in the back yard and slowly pass through the locks a steel comb dipped in hot vinegar.

✧ Blocked chimney? Shoot a gun up to loosen the soot.

✧ Filter water from the rain-butt by passing it through a sack. (But a Bainton elder once claimed to prefer water "with a bit of body in it").

Burn's Farm

During the 1860s Elisabeth Burn let lodgings. Then, in entrepreneurial spirit, she swilled out a redundant cowhouse, whitewashed it and had it adapted for hot medicinal showers and baths. For this purpose seawater had to be brought in carts to her farm on Newbegin. It was a brave experiment, but Hornsea never really began to compete with the more rapidly developing amenities at Bridlington.

Subsequently the premises were used as a slaughterhouse, grocer's warehouse, antique shop and a haberdashery; in more recent years, of course, it has been transformed into a superb award-winning folk museum.

Poverty Grace

O Heavenly Feyther bless us,
An' keeap us all alive;
Theer's ten of us for dinner
An' fooad for only fahve.

We may smile now – but the humour masks uncomfortable realities in many East Riding homes of times past.

Soup Kitchens

Poor harvests as in 1799 and 1800 meant malnutrition at a time when food imports were restricted by the wars with Napoleon. Large-scale poor relief became necessary. In Hull one in five families resorted to public soup kitchens. Even in Victorian Hull and Bridlington times were sparse enough for this highly visible public assistance. Over 60 families partook of soup and bread for Christmas 1868, served at a kitchen on North Street at Bridlington Quay. It was hoped that in future increased facilities would allow greater numbers to benefit from this "seasonable relief". This scale of poverty lingered into Edwardian times.

Good Awd Tahmes

Walter Turner, Vicar of Fridaythorpe from 1908 until 1916, wrote 'The Goodies', a collection of folksy East Riding tales well acclaimed by contemporaries. In the following verse from his poem, 'Good Awd Tahmes', he shows how inaccurate and foolishly sentimental the phrase was:

"Me muther she slaaved i' t' good awd tahmes,
An' scratted an' tewed[1] an' rahved[2] an' wrowt[3]
wer weeames ti trig[4],
Hoed tonnups an' wick't[5] an' gethered an' gleaned an' kep a pig
- A recklin[6] she begged – in t' good awd tahmes".

Water Supply

Youngsters are often surprised to find how recent was the provision of domestic piped water. In 1929 when Howden was short, supplies were brought from Hull and sold at 1d per bucket. The well on Huggate Green, sunk in 1760 by James Lollit for 27 guineas, is reputed to be the deepest in the country at 339 feet. It took 20 minutes to wind the bucket to the surface. At Bishop Burton water was still being drawn from the pond in the later 1940s, and springs and boreholes were used at Harpham until 1953. In general pipes and taps were enthusiastically welcomed, but some traditionally minded villagers, as at Ellerker after 1946, kept to the old ways. A number of wayside pumps remain

---

[1] toiled
[2] tore
[3] wrought
[4] our bellies to fill
[5] gathered wicks (grass roots)
[6] weakling

as reminders. Worth seeing is the unique two-handled long case "Black Jack" at Burton Fleming crossroads.

Clifford Williamson drawing water from Bishop Burton pond c1941 *(Courtesy of John Dunning)*

Great-Grandma's Chores

Monday was universal wash day. A fire had to be lit early under the copper, and water pumped up ready. Whites were boiled up with grated soap and soda before being lifted out into a tub and turned by a dolly stick – a three-to-five legged "stool" and/or pounded with a posser or plunger. Reckitt's blue, a local Hull product, was added and the clothes rinsed before being wrung out through the mangle and pegged out to dry.

Heavily soiled clothes were done separately. Stains had to be tackled first. Chalk and Fuller's Earth removed grease, and applications of juices from rhubarb, lemon or onion were efficacious for reducing other marks. A still older generation had found pig urine effective as a whitening agent ...

In wet weather or wintertime drying off clothes could take a day or two, with the windows steaming up, and complaints from the men.

But whenever possible Tuesday was ironing day. Flat irons were heated on the kitchen range and used in pairs, one always hotting up. Scorching was a fear, but great-grandma applied her own tests, like spitting on the base and listening to the hiss, or even holding the implement near her cheek.

All baking was done in the oven next to the range fire which, even in high summer, had to be stoked up. Many ranges were fitted with a reckon bar which swung inwards, and on to which cooking pans could be hooked.

Although past generations of East Riding men held that too many baths weakened the constitution, Friday night was bath night. The tin bath was hauled down from the back wall, kettles and saucepans were continuously replenished and boiled up on the hearth fire, and the various members of the family took turns, with varying degrees of privacy having to be arranged. Visiting was not encouraged.

Saturday mornings were favoured for black-leading the range and donkey-stoning the front doorstep. Tea leaves taken from the pot were scattered on the matting to lay the dust, and then were carefully swept up. Carpets were taken out and hung over the washing line to be beaten.

Great-grandma's domestic chores observed few boundaries. Patching, darning and knitting were on-going; and the old strips of material could be pushed through hessian or sacking to make another peg-rug. There were such seasonal opportunities as brambling, mushrooming and gleaning. And in those days of uncertain contraception, a very full family life was often guaranteed.

Privy Counsel

Sixteenth century privies projecting over the jetty at Hull's Horsestaithe were criticised as "very noisome to passengers in the ferry boat".

A report by Dr A.D. Home in 1871 instanced houses in Hook, near Howden, where flagstones served as floors for the privy and covers for the wells. Some residents confirmed that the first bucketful or two of drawn water were thrown away, after which the smell lingered, but the water was acceptable. Not surprisingly cholera and diarrhoea were a problem, and fifteen deaths in August and September 1868 were attributed to insanitary sources of water. In Hull the problem had been still more acute, and bad sanitation had been the prime cause of the 1849 cholera epidemic. (see Chapter 1).

For centuries great quantities of dung had had to be removed from the town's middens: 40,000 tons annually by 1871. Much of it was transported by river. The burgeoning horticulture and greenhouse industries of Cottingham owed much to the output of their urban neighbour. Up to the 1920s loads were steaming up-river to Newport and Howden, and to the Holme on Spalding Moor area via the Market Weighton Canal.

So many terraces and courtyards in Hull made collection difficult. Contractors employed night-soil men (or "wet dustmen") whose busy shift started as early as 5am – a source of much complaint. Where there was no back door, buckets, sometimes uncomfortably full, had to be carried through the house to the front. By 1920 Hull still had 41,000 privies, and a few remained down to 1960. Londesborough did not achieve mains sewerage until 1965.

The advent of easily blocked water closets meant that substitutes had to be found for sheets of newspaper hitherto suspended from a handy nail. Many families found that the chamber pot could usefully co-exist with the new amenities.

Privy now free, and old man repairing shoes: Providence Square, Providence Street, Hull *(Courtesy of Hull Central Library, Local Studies)*

Medical Matters

We forget, or perhaps never fully realised, the prevalence in former times of scarlet fever, polio, diphtheria, and tuberculosis. In 1932 in the Norton area alone 27 people died from typhoid.

In Edwardian times and after, many panaceas were advertised in local journals. Clarke's B41 Pills were "warranted to cure in either sex all acquired or constitutional discharges from the urinary organs, gravel and pains in the back." Or Mother Seigel's Syrup "to cleanse and give tone to your liver, assist digestion, brace up your nerves and invigorate your system". Curious things were done even in educated circles. At Burstwick School in 1912 a measles epidemic resulted in the fumigation of the building with 20 sulphur candles.

Children had to brace themselves for doses of brimstone and treacle, chocolate laxatives or the rightly dreaded castor oil, when a young nose had to be gripped tightly and the stuff forced down.

Jugs of elder or peppermint tea stood on many a Riding hearthside as a winter cure-all. Also in favour were Cayenne pods, Senna pods, salts, camphorated ointment, goose grease. Warm poultices offered some brief comfort. Linseed poultices were applied against pneumonia and skin eruptions. Cold poultices of tea leaves were thought to soothe burns and scalds. A widespread fear of dentists eased many a toothache.

Almost every village had its mature female factotum who could be called upon to help to deliver a baby, advise on medicaments – or recommend professional help. This was often accepted with reluctance, as it had to be paid for, prior to 1947. Many GPs requested but token payment, or even waived fees, according to their assessment of income and needs. Not infrequently a considerable journey had to be made. Thixendale patients somehow had to get a message through to Wetwang, seven miles distant. An impending visit from the doctor might mean that the entire house had to be cleaned and proudly polished, as for a commanding officer's inspection. Long-serving family doctors like John Perrin Brown at Wetwang carried immense public respect and influence.

Next to Godliness

An outbreak of scabies in Hull in the 1920s – and there were many – called for stern measures. At the Scarborough Street baths a sulphur rub-down was available, and old clothes fumigated up to three times a week. Patients went home sore, aware of stinging (and stinking) flesh.

Kitchen Table Operation

Mr John Curtis recalls that as a small boy in 1928 he had his tonsils removed on the kitchen table at home in Hornsea. The deed was performed by a surgeon from Hull Royal Infirmary. Apart from feeling a bit sick afterwards, John made a speedy recovery.

Nobbut Squeal

Pig-keeping and selling are recorded in such street names as Swinegate (e.g. Pocklington, Hessle) and Piggy Lane at Withernsea. Well within living memory many village folk kept their own pig. Provided it could be lodged in a shed or outhouse, it was fed largely on scraps, and killed to provide food, especially around Christmas time.

The killing was quite a ceremony from which children were not necessarily excluded. Only water was given to the animal on the previous day; and a great deal of hot water had to be boiled for the scalding tub. Struggling and screaming, the pig was led onto the yard, possibly with some premonition of its fate, which was very shortly confirmed when the slaughterer stunned it with a smart blow from a poleaxe, then cut its throat. Blood was deftly collected to make into black puddings. The body was heaved, with assistance, into the tub for the hairs to be scraped off. Intestines were laid in salt water to be used as sausage skins. Eventually the carcass was hung up, and refreshment and re-assurance offered to the onlookers who looked queasy.

Next day the butcher returned to cut up flitches – hams, shoulders, sides, trotters etc – which were liberally salted, covered in muslin bags and hung up to dry. Fries of "pig cheer" – liver, heart, kidneys – were given to friends and neighbours who had long contributed peelings and the like for the pig's sustenance. For good luck the plates were, sometimes, handed back unwashed.

Valued by young boys was the pig's bladder, obtainable from Hull slaughterhouses up to 1939, as well as from private killings. It was blown up and used as a football.

There was very little waste – "nobbut squeal" was a common and not unreasonable boast.

Eight-legged Pig

In May 1861 Driffield people were intrigued to see a piglet born with eight legs. Thomas Wright made a bob or two by showing it off outside the railway station.

Special Dishes

✧ Beast(l)ings was the first milk given by a cow that had calved. Whether its nutritive qualities were any greater is doubtful, but it was offered to neighbours for making puddings. As with the pig fries, the jug was supposed to be returned unwashed to ensure continuing good luck.

✧ At Barmby Moor, Easter Monday used to be "Spanish Wine Day" for the children. Unless imbibed immoderately, the concoction of liquorice and water was generally harmless.

✧ The Pocklington May Horse Fair was traditionally celebrated with crow pie.

✧ Trinity Sunday at South Cave was Cave Fair Sunday, and therefore time for "crud chissocks" or curd cheesecakes.

✧ In pre-refrigerator days poultry was hung up to ripen. If it got "high" an onion was placed inside the bird.

World War Two brought the opportunity of trying something different with reduced rations of basic foodstuffs – like 4oz of bacon and one egg per week. There was, for example, whalemeat; and Lord Woolton Pie (after the Minister of Food), which was summed up as odd vegetables with a smear of chicken grease. Despite having to use saccharine tablets instead of sugar, and travelling hopefully to Beverley or Hull to follow up rumours about extra jam for those prepared to queue, grandma's diet was, arguably, healthier. Boys and older men were exhorted to Dig for Victory and grow more vegetables.

From 1941 marginal land like Beverley Westwood was put to the spade. There was a revival of interest in oatcakes, spread like pancakes, dried and crumbled into stews.

"Hull Cheese" is a misnomer, used to mystify off-comed-uns. It is strong ale, and the term seems to be centuries old.

Sunday Special

Between the wars many worshipful families took Sunday very seriously. For some children three Church or Chapel attendances were not unusual. Newspapers, needlework and games of any kind were out – a hang-over from Victorian times.

North Ferriby owed much to the benevolence of the Turner family – Liverpool merchants and racehorse owners. In leaving allotments to the memory of her husband Charles, Anne Turner carefully stipulated that no work was to be done on Sundays.

Few East Yorkshire households, one suspects, sacrificed the ritual of Yorkshire puddings, beef, the trimmings on the altar of extreme Sabbatarian propriety. Besides, beef dripping generously smeared over toast properly done on a toasting fork held close to an open fire ensured a basic stomach lining for Sunday tea.

Parlour

To move into a house with a front room was proof of domestic ambition fulfilled. True, it might not be used much, but to light a Sunday fire in the parlour and air the three-piece suite was a considerable satisfaction. The parlour offered a modest degree of privacy for courting couples, mothers regularly popping in to see if the fire wanted mending, or if anybody was ready for a cup of tea, or to look leisurely for a lost letter or knitting.

Funerals

Before the days of funeral parlours the corpse was laid out in the front room and the open coffin was mounted on a bed or table for neighbours and relatives to pay their respects. Often curtains were drawn in neighbouring houses, too, and remained so until after the funeral. Bidder women called to issue invitations. Children were forbidden to play in the street for the duration.

To ensure the wearing of black for the occasion a family might mortgage its future. Black gloves and silk scarves were commonly given to mourners, and black-edged funeral cards were distributed. In some Wolds villages the coffin was rested on chairs outside the house and a hymn was sung. For the departure of the cortege the street would be lined with commiserating neighbours, men and boys standing with hats removed.

It was fervently hoped that the church clock would not strike during the service lest another death should too soon follow.

In contrast to the solemn wake with prayers and lit candles – though the atmosphere was lightened when drinks arrived – the post-funeral feast, "seeing 'em off with ham", was contrived to be a livelier celebration of the life of the deceased. Specially baked funerals biscuits were perhaps a salutary reminder of the dignity of the occasion.

Hoss Lads

In East Riding folklore few topics loom larger than the horse lads hired at Martinmas (see Chapter 7.). On larger farms these teenagers were placed in separate accommodation supervised by a hind and his wife. "Good meat houses" were eagerly sought. Fat bacon always seemed to be served at breakfast, followed by apple pie. Mid-day brought meat, potatoes and vegetables, with steamed or rice pudding; and supper more fat bacon and the fruit pie to

To be a farmer's boy: young Arthur Campling with his team at Newton South Wold, c1930 *(Courtesy of Miss M. Campling)*

finish off. Much looked forward to was mid-morning "looance" (allowance) – a snack of bacon cake or cheese and apple pie, and tea.

There were many curious aspects to the meals. It was common for meat to be boiled up in the copper used for clothes washing – though the lads took their washing home as and when they could. Puddings were dished up on the same plate as the savoury course; and apple pies were known to have the entire fruit intact – peel, core and all. Drinking vessels were of great variety. Some hinds[1] favoured basins rather than mugs or cups. Others saw the merits of pint mugs to be shared by pairs of lads.

In all things the waggoner took precedence. Outside he had the best choice of horses and he ploughed the exemplary furrows. His discipline was dictatorial. He had the first choice of room and any single bed. The rest doubled up. He washed his hands first, followed by Thoddy and Fowerty (third and fourth lads), while poor Tommy Owt, the youngest odd-job lad, had to make do with very dirty water.[2]

Many tales are told of leaking roofs, rats chewing boot laces and socks and unimaginable privations with working clothes. Lavatorial facilities were often of the most primitive – the fold yard or the back of the hedge.

Yet, as with many kinds of makeshift communal living, theirs bred a rough

---

[1] The hind was the man in charge of the domestic arrangements for the boy workers on the larger farms.

[2] In general the hierarchy was foreman, waggoner, third lad, fourth lad, etc.

Looance time at Woodgates Lane, North Ferriby *(Courtesy of J. Wheeler)*

camaraderie and humour. Some "revenge" accounts may be apocryphal or exaggerated – like the Thoddy who invented a grace lampooning eternal rabbit pies, and the young man who decided that the only way to stop rhubarb pies was to dig up the rhubarb patch. Being a hoss lad, with all its difficulties, was a special experience, capable of producing in some autobiographies a kind of nostalgia for a way of life whose very vocabulary is almost lost.

Hessle Road

The traditional heartland of Hull's close-knit fishing community, Hessle Road, right up to the industry's decline was the scene of much hardship, fortitude, neighbourliness and humour. Between the wars it supported eight pawnbrokers. Many a fisherman's wife, it was said, put her husband's suit in pawn, only to redeem it when he was expected home. Between trips housekeeping money was very tight. A weekly feature of the times was Fish Dock Pram Race Day when wives hurried with young children to the trawler offices to sign for their men's wages.

After a vessel had docked, there were celebrations, bets, confrontations and high jinks in the pubs, especially Rayner's, at the corner of West Dock Avenue, after a famous landlord, George Henry Rayner, incumbent from 1921 to 1940. One intriguing spectacle was the meat pie race in which competitors, kneeling and with hands tied behind their backs, each advanced on a huge meat pie and attempted to eat it by a direct frontal attack using only the mouth, teeth and head.

Chapter 12

Communications

Pre-historic Boats

It is remarkable that several ancient hulls have been unearthed in the East Riding. In 1937 C.V. and Edward Wright, amateur archaeologists even as boys, stumbled upon three huge planks in the mud below Red Cliff on the Humber foreshore at North Ferriby. Between tides over the next few months they kept detailed records. Preservation had been helped by oxygen-free conditions. The carpentry was surprisingly sophisticated. Bevelled oak planks had moss caulking between, held together by "withies" of yew branches. Carbon dating has estimated the boat's age at c1500 BC. Edward, on leave in November 1940, found a second boat; and a third in 1963.

The Hasholme Boat, discovered near Holme on Spalding Moor in 1984 had been preserved in a bed of clay and peat. The biggest ever found of this era – c300 BC – it was 41 feet long, carved from a single oak and was apparently used for carrying cattle and possibly iron ore. After treatment at the National Maritime Museum at Greenwich, where the Ferriby boats have had attention, it was returned to the Hull and East Riding Museum, permanently sprayed with a wax and water preservative.

Prayerful Pointers

According to a story about a 12th century hermitage at Welham Bridge, near Home on Spalding Moor, one monk acted as a guide for travellers while the other prayed for those exposed to all the dangers.

Water Everywhere

Time and again one is struck by accounts of floodwaters, and not always near the Humber or the sea. Admittedly, however, rivers overflowing caused endless damage and inconvenience. In 1301 Archbishop Corbridge wrote to the prior of Gisburne, patron of Hessle Church, asking for a cemetery to be established in Hull. At that time funerals had to take place at Hessle, westwards up river, as this was the mother church. As bodies and attendants had been swept off wagons crossing the marshes, it was generally easier to convey the dead, at least in winter, in "requiem boats". Thornton corteges were taken to Pocklington until 1415 when John Prophete, Dean of York conceded there were too many risks of drowning for mourners "by reason of inundations which frequently happen both in summer and winter".

In his "Itinerary" c1540 John Leland wrote "From Cottingham to Kingston upon Hull about four miles by low ground whereof two miles be causeway (raised), diked on both sides." Writing to the Leeds antiquarian and diarist, Ralph Thoresby on 29th December 1707, the Vicar of Holy Trinity, Hull, the Rev. Robert Banks commented – "The ways of Holderness at this time of year are next to impassable and some have lost their lives who have ventured through them, and for that reason it is very difficult to hold any correspondence by letters into the several parts of that division".

"Carr boats" were necessary to cross the carrs and swamps north-east of Beverley in winter and spring up to the late 18th century. At Tickton, for example in the 1730s John Woodmansey had two boats and a gun, which suggests that wild-fowling was a prevalent activity.

In the Emmotland area farmers used flat-bottomed boats to carry goods to Frodingham market – and according to the historian George Poulson they smuggled contraband covertly inland. It used to be said, half-jokingly, perhaps, that stepping stones were needed to approach some villages. Hence, no doubt, the expression, "Ah's gannin' ower steeans ti Swine".

There was little success in raising roads above the flood level until the turnpike era e.g. the Hull-Preston-Hedon turnpike of 1745.

Humber Pilotage

Sandbanks and treacherous currents still challenge the skills of Humber pilots. Whilst a piloting service has existed since 1512, organised by the Guild of Masters, Pilots and Seamen of Trinity House, Kingston upon Hull, it took the personal intervention of Henry VIII to make pilotage compulsory. During his visit in 1541 to review the town's defences, he noticed a vessel approaching, and finding it had no pilot he ordered it out until one was aboard to direct its passage. In 1906, pilotage was taken over by the Humber Conservancy Board, and in 1968 by the British Transport Docks Board.

Bonny Boat

Off the Greenland coast in 1613 an Eskimo canoe made of whalebone and sealskin was picked up by Captain Andrew Barker of Hull. Its owner was frozen and near to death. Barker brought the canoe back to Hull, where it was lodged in Trinity House, passing into legend as the Bonny Boat. This was not its only tragedy. A Dane, John Magnus, was drowned on 7th September 1794 as his craft, the Bonny Boat of Trinity House was passing the Trent mouth. Washed up near Thornton Land he was buried at Blacktoft on 26th September, following a coroner's inquest.

North-West Passage

Of the mariners who tried to find a north-west passage to China and the East Indies, several Hull-connected men are of particular interest. One was Luke Fox, so passionate about the challenge that he was nicknamed "North-West Fox", born in Hull in 1586, explored the channels west of Baffin Island in 1631, but like all others was finally beaten by the ice pack.

Two centuries later it was the turn of the scot, Sir John Ross (1777-1856).

On 15th October 1833 he was brought back to Hull by R.W. Humphreys in the whaler Isabella. There was a huge civic welcome – despite his animal skin attire! And he was invited to become an honorary brother of Trinity House and a member of the Hull Literary and Philosophical Society.

On this second attempt to find a north-west passage (1829-32) Ross's paddle steamer Victory had become frozen in the ice near the head of Baffin Bay, where Humphreys found him on 26th August 1833. That he should have been rescued by the Isabella was oddly intriguing, for it was on this former whaler that he had made his first attempt on the passage in 1818.

In 1850 Ross led a further expedition with a different mission – to find another stranded Arctic explorer, Sir John Franklin. Sadly, this too failed.

Controversial Explorer

Born in Hornsea in 1815 and third son of the Rev. Anthony Eyre, Edward John Eyre went out to Australia at 18. His experiences in working for a sheep farmer, taking flocks vast distances – like Sydney to Melbourne – turned his interest towards exploration. Having walked through South Australia and on to Perth, before covering vast terrains in the outback, he produced a series of reports which earned him the Gold Medal of the Royal Geographical Society.

Unfortunately, later events clouded this distinguished East Yorkshireman's reputation. As Governor of Jamaica in 1864 he was heavily criticised for his troops' handling of an uprising. And after his part in the arrest, trial and execution of a Baptist minister, George Gordon, he was the subject of three censorious Parliamentary debates, and his effigy was burnt in London. Nevertheless, he had much support in Jamaica and was eventually acquitted. Pensioned off, he retired to Devon where he died in 1901.

Atlantic by Prayer

Remarkably, Robert Fowler and 11 fellow Quakers, having built their own boat, the *Woodhouse* at Bridlington, and knowing little of the skills of navigation, reached New England largely by prayer and good luck in 1657 – only two miles off course.

Bligh and the *Bounty*

The story has links with Hull where the 70-foot long, 200-ton vessel was built in No. 2 Dry Dock, Drypool in 1784 by the Blaydes family, and was then called "Bethia". Three years later it was bought by the Admiralty, and was the scene of the notorious mutiny when on 28th April 1789 Captain William Bligh (1754-1817) with 18 loyal officers and men was given five days supply of food and cast adrift in the Pacific by Fletcher Christian. The mutineers took the ship to Pitcairn Island where many stayed.

After his miraculous survival, Bligh returned to Hull in 1797 on *HMS Director* to undertake a calmer cartographical survey of the River Humber.

Former Ports

From the Middle Ages Patrington vessels took corn to London, and coal was brought in from the West Riding. But gradually the approach channel from the Humber became silted up with deposits from Spurn. The progressive reclamation of Sunk Island sealed the fate of the Haven whose board of trustees was wound up in 1867. The last barge sailed two years later. Isolated amidst the fields remains one derelict 18th-century brick warehouse, the reminder of a lost economy.

Unmentioned in the Domesday of 1086, Hedon nevertheless won borough status via a charter of Henry II to William le Gros of Albemarle. In Stephen's reign it was important enough to have a mint. A further charter of 1348 made it an independent borough, entitled to a mayor and corporation. But already it was suffering from the rivalry of Ravenser Odd, off Spurn, and was soon to be overtaken by Hull. The antiquary John Leland commented c1540, "When Hull began to flourish, Hedon decayed". In 1774 an Act of Parliament set up the Hedon Haven Commission; but even after dredging, the Haven had silted up beyond redemption.

Ferries

Sanctioned by Edward II the ferry at Booth near Howden was first used in 1513. The owner, the Bishop of Durham granted his lessees not only ferry fees but salmon rights. Until the building of the Boothferry Bridge in 1929 Harold and John Robinson provided a useful public service.

At Howdendyke the ferryman was customarily alerted by hopeful passengers shouting from the Ouse's opposite bank. All manner of goods and

Booth Ferry c1926 *(Courtesy of East Riding of Yorkshire Council Library and Information Services)*

chattels were transported, sometimes precariously – furniture, sheep, cattle, farm loads, motor vehicles – which last had to be manoeuvred with perfect timing and precision.

Daniel Defoe was not enamoured of the Humber crossing from Barton to Hull. He commented in his diary of 1725 on "an open boat in which we had about fifteen horses and ten or twelve cows mingled with seventeen or eighteen passengers. We were about four hours tossed about on the Humber before we could get into Hull".

Probably the shortest ferry crossing in all Yorkshire, operating until 1948 was surely at Wawne. It crossed the River Hull, saving a roundabout road journey to Beverley or Hull. Teenagers proceeding to school in Beverley had to catch the ferry, walk a mile to the main road, then catch a bus into town – quite a variety of transport within five miles.

Spurn Lifeboats

Spurn is unique in being the only permanently manned lifeboat station in the UK. There has been a lifeboat there since 1810, thanks to the enterprise of the Brethren of Hull Trinity House. By 1854 nearly 800 people had been rescued. The Royal National Lifeboat Institution's involvement dates from 1911; and in 1924 the name was changed to the Humber Lifeboat Station. Oars and sails provided the motive power until 1919 when the motorboat *Samuel Oakes* came into service.

Spurn's continuing saga tells of unimaginable fortitude and heroism. Outstanding even in this elite company was Robert Cross, a crew member since 1905 and coxswain from 1911 until November 1943, retiring at the age

RNLB City of Bradford II *(Courtesy of the Royal National Lifeboat Institutution)*

of 67. This most decorated man in the service of the RNLI was awarded two bronze medals, three silvers and two gold medals. His acts of gallantry included the rescue of the entire crew of the Grimsby trawler *Gurth* on 12ᵗʰ February 1940, carried out in the dark and in snow blizzard conditions. Continually buffeted by heavy seas, Cross and a depleted crew had immense difficulty in nosing near enough for the nine men to be taken off, one at a time. Other problems multiplied. The port engine stopped, and severe damage including a split rudder was suffered by the lifeboat, *City of Bradford II*.

Safe in Grimsby after three and a half hours, the rescuers were more bruised and exhausted than the rescued. This epic event earned Robert Cross both a gold medal and the George Medal. His crew of five each won a silver medal. It has been calculated that this valiant coxswain took part in the rescue of 403 lives in North Sea waters.

Arthur Jarratt, doyen amongst East Riding dialect poets, has drawn attention to an older tradition of fishermen and lifeboatmen, brought up with the idea that swimming merely prolongs the death throes when the circumstances are hopeless.

In his poem, "Lifeboat Launch at Hornsea", he concludes:

> "*That lartle boat; this great storm, an' riskin' life an' limb*
> *To save men from a warthery graave – an' neean on 'em can swim*".

Smallest Window?

The George Hotel, a 17ᵗʰ-century coaching inn in Hull's oddly named street, Land of Green Ginger, has a claim to the smallest window, measuring approximately 12" x 1" Its origin is uncertain. It may have been placed there for the porter to watch for the next coach; or give warning of the press gang; or revenue men; or smugglers. There have reputedly been some unexplained creakings and crackings in an adjacent bar room by night.

Guided by Bells

During the 18ᵗʰ century it was common for night travellers to get lost in the wild open countryside between Pocklington and Stamford Bridge. One man returning from Stamford Bridge Fair late on 1ˢᵗ December regained his bearings on hearing the bells of Pocklington Church, So in gratitude he left a sum of money for the curfew bell to be rung for an hour on the anniversary, a custom maintained into the twentieth century.

Diarists

Two contemporary East Riding diarists had much to tell posterity. Richard Allen, vicar of Driffield from 1798 to 1835, comes over as a sanctimonious, narrow-minded hypochondriac who none the less was informative about weather, crops, people and parochial doings. There was nothing charitable in his comments on carpenter William Holtby, who on 15ᵗʰ May 1828 had fallen from the scaffold of the new meeting house; the very next day Allen wrote smugly, "Holtby expired this morning, a martyr to the pride of Methodism". But he accepts the limitations of his calling against secular values.

> "18th February 1830: The bazaar was numerously attended. No less than 97. Religion could not have assembled so many".

And his disillusion of 6th February 1832 had a timeless ring:

> "Reading newspaper which contains little more than crime, disaffection to rulers, and many more symptoms of disloyalty and insubordination".

More sanguine and good-humoured was Robert Sharp who, as schoolmaster at South Cave from 1826 to 1837 kept a fascinating account of village events. His annual salary of 50 guineas, reduced to £30 when numbers on roll fell in 1835, was augmented by outside work as surveyor, friendly society clerk, overseer of the poor, census taker, rates assessor, constable. He steadily involves us in characters like William Lancaster, occasional constable though himself something of a villain; and various groups and cliques, like the farmers whom he regards as self-seeking. Often Sharp goes into exquisite detail about a parishioner's plight and lifestyle, as on Monday, 15th January 1827 when Tommy Pinder died, despite 30 leeches applied the previous day, and the consolation of 10 glasses a day of liquor. (See also Chapter 7).

Balloon Goes Up

In 1824 W.W. Sadler ascended from the Hull Citadel, a fortress on the east bank of the Humber/Hull confluence, in a hydrogen balloon, rising to about 1,000 feet and watched by an estimated 10,000 excited spectators. He came down safely at Preston, six miles to the east, just north of Hedon.

Hedon, Hamel and Amy

To the west of Hedon an aerodrome was built on the site of the former racecourse (1888-1910). A memorable afternoon was Saturday, 13th July 1912 when the glamorous German pilot, Gustav Hamel made three flights around the area, rising to no more than 500 feet so as to thrill the crowds gathered to watch. Hamel had been dubbed the flying postman because he had carried the royal mail between Hendon and Windsor as part of the coronation festivities of the previous year.

Even more tumultuous was the reception given to Hull's own flying ace, Amy Johnson when she landed at Hedon on 11th August 1930, her epic flight to Australia still uppermost in the minds of her admirers. (See also Chapter 2).

The aerodrome was closed in 1939.

The R38 Disaster

During the late afternoon of 24th August 1921 the 700 foot long airship R38, on a test flight between Howden and Norfolk, split in two whilst attempting a starboard turn, caught fire and plunged into the Humber just off Hull's Corporation Pier.

Gustav Hamel, looking at camera, with the mayors of Hedon and Hull, 1912 *(Courtesy of E. Winkler)*

Out of 49 crew and passengers only five survived, including the commander, Flight-Lieutenant A.H. Wann. The city entered a period of mourning, and most of the victims were buried in the Western Cemetery.

Despite this apocalyptic catastrophe the airship station at Spaldington continued its programme, under the direction of Dr Barnes Wallis, later immortalised as the designer of the "bouncing bomb" of Dambuster fame. But in the long run airships were abandoned as too unwieldy and risky.

Hackney Backed

"On Thursday last a young man of Beverley for a considerable wager undertook to ride a common Hackney from the Bar in that Town to Walmgate Bar in this city (York) and back again (59½ miles) in Four Hours and a Half, and performed it in Four Hours and 18 Minutes". – York Courant, April 4th 1775.

Carriers

Up to the era of motorised transport carriers' carts provided a vital service in village life. They conveyed all manner of household items. They even helped people to flit. They took regular passengers like farmers' wives to market to try to sell their butter, cheese, eggs and poultry. They took orders, collected medicines, placed bets, delivered and collected parcels. Moreover, they were purveyors of local news, gossip and scandal. Some risks were undertaken. In 1823 a Skipsea carrier was gaoled until he could pay a £100 fine for the illicit conveyance to Hull of three gallons of gin he had secreted inside a firkin of butter.

Carriers made their own arrangements for stopping. Horses were trained to stop at particular hostelries. I'Anson of Little Weighton looked for a flag or handkerchief on a hedge or fence. They had to be early risers. By 3am the Welwick and Skeffling men, like Thomas Branton and John Hodgson in the 1870s and 1880s, were on their way to Hull.

En route they met up with other colleagues, and once arrived in the market place there was conviviality and refreshment. Some lasted well into the motor age. Up to about 1950 Messrs Rispin and Hodgson, long motorised, were operating in the villages to the west of Hull.

Fire Frustrations

These were but to be expected before the internal combustion engine appeared! In September 1890 a messenger was despatched to Driffield to summon the fire brigade to a stackyard blaze at Watton Carr. It was three quarters of an hour before the appliance, drawn by four horses, was on its way. Meantime the stack was utterly consumed.

At Filey a cyclist used to dash up to a field just north of the town, throw down his bike, mount the horse and ride it back to Queen Street for harnessing to the fire engine.

Between 1912 and 1919 passengers aboard Tom Fussey's omnibus commuting between Cottingham and Hull had to be prepared for delays caused by the sudden need to unharness their horse team for an unforeseen fire emergency.

Horses in Twilight

Although the coming of the railways meant the slow demise of the stage-coach, horse-drawn transport in general still had a century to run. At Howden John Bowman's carriages from the Nag's Head met every train arriving, and he also hired out gigs and carts. Up to about 1914 most vehicles had authentic horse power – the funeral hearse, the mobile shop, the snow plough, the night soil wagon, even the lifeboats were drawn into the shallow waters on the beaches of Hornsea and Bridlington. Church and chapel outings to the seaside used local drays and rulleys, beautifully decorated, brasses gleaming, to take the revellers to the station; those living near the coast were horse-drawn the whole way.

From late Victorian times Binningtons ran a service from Willerby into Hull, via Anlaby; and for many years the fare stayed at 4d. Generally the five-mile journey took about two hours. Passengers stopped the bus when they wanted a particular shop; having bought their goods they continued their journey. Upstairs the bus was open to all weathers, and when it rained umbrellas were put up.

Between Easington and Spurn there was a horse-drawn omnibus service until 1945.

The Hull and London Royal Mail *(Courtesy of Hull Central Library, Local Studies)*

Despite the popularity of the Beverley races and the annual Kiplingcotes Derby (see Chapter 7) the Hedon Racecourse referred to above was not a success, and after seven years it closed. It re-opened in 1901 for a further eight years, but support dwindled. Tradition was lacking, and the site, barely removed from industrial Hull, lacked atmosphere. Popular interest lay elsewhere.

Railway Objections

It was foreseeable that landowners would resist most plans for the development of railways across their territories. It happened in the late 1830s with the Raikes family of Welton over the Hull-Selby proposals; and in the sixties Lord Hotham diverted the Beverley-York planners from Goodmanham to Kiplingcotes, which had no community and which was to be train-free on Sundays.

In 1847 Sunday objectors to a proposed Hull-Market Weighton line found a forthright spokesman in the vicar of South Cave, Edward Stillingfleet who wrote to the company Chairman:

> "I have just cause to complain of Sunday evil at the public houses here and had we a railway I have little doubt that bad would be made worse. The scum of Hull would make it one place for their Sunday revels".

With divination the vicar could have rested with a quiet mind. There was to be no rail link for his parish until the arrival of the Hull to Barnsley Railway in 1885.

Station Names

For a variety of reasons there were in this East Riding many changes of station names. Everingham was once Harswell Gate; Londesborough was first

Shipton; in 1904 Goxhill was renamed Wassand. Nunburnholme station was actually at Burnby. Sigglesthorne had started as Hatfield – but there was another Hatfield near Doncaster. Up to 1922 Ellerby was called Burton Constable, after the nearby stately home, but there was passenger confusion with Constable Burton in North Yorkshire. In Hull, Botanic Gardens was thought more cheerful than Cemetery Gates, a destination not universally favoured.

Trade Name

Between 1875 and 1900 the stationmaster at Hornsea was William Train. On 7th January 1957 the first two-car diesel multiple unit ran the 52-minute journey from Hull to Withernsea. The driver was – Ernest Train.

The Train Now Arriving

At 1pm on 6th October 1846 three locomotives, the Aerial, Antelope and Hudson, and 66 crowded carriages steamed into the new Bridlington station from Hull, to be met by the assembled Lords Feoffees, a crowd of 2,000 and the Railway King himself, George Hudson. A banquet followed for the VIPs in a highly decorated goods shed. Thus was a tremendous boost given to the developing seaside resort. Day excursions soon came from the Midlands and the West Riding. By the early fifties crowds of 5,000 were surging onto the beaches during August bank holiday.

With the rail network expansion, hitherto remote villages found new horizons. In 1922 folk from Foggathorpe could get to Bridlington on a cheap day excursion for 4s 11d or from Fimber for 2s 11d.

Anthony Bannister (Courtesy of Hull Central Library, Local Studies)

The Hull and Holderness Railway

Less propitious was this opening day, 20th June 1854. Rain and wind caused the huge banqueting marquee at Withernsea slowly to fold. There was no special reason for the choice of Withernsea. The terminus could have been Tunstall or Easington. But at least Withernsea had a population of 109 by 1851. And Anthony Bannister, the bearded entrepreneur, had an eye to developing an east-coast Brighton. There were supporters and critics aplenty. The

Doncaster, Nottingham and Lincoln Gazette offered its good wishes (9th November 1855), but permitted itself of some doubts:

"Let not the scoffer throw ridicule upon the Hull and Holderness line by asserting 'What can we expect of a railway that runs nowhere?' Nor let him in the exuberance of his imagination declare 'Here's a railway with a sandbank for its terminus'".

Scepticism appeared to be justified. On 1st January 1860 the line was taken over by the North-Eastern Railway. Withernsea never gained mass appeal, and the Queen's Hotel, designed by Cuthbert Brodrick hopefully to attract middle-class custom, was bought in 1902 by Sir James Reckitt and turned into a convalescent home.

Inconvenienced

A disadvantage of most early local trains was that they carried no lavatories. On a journey from Bridlington to Hull in 1859 William Kime opened the doors of a third class compartment at Beverley and "committed a nuisance" on the platform. In fining him 10s the court told Mr Kime that he should have alighted at Arram station, though admittedly the stopping time there was short.

Beware Bogie

The Spurn Railway began in 1914 when the army needed to move men and supplies from Kilnsea to the fortifications near the tip of the peninsula. Steam power was the norm, but a wind bogie with a triangular sail was casually used by civilians and off-duty lifeboatmen making for the Crown and Anchor at Kilnsea. The bogie could achieve a speed of up to 40 mph. Drifting sand was a problem, and shifts in the terrain necessitated various adjustments to the lines. The railway survived until 1951 when most of the track was taken up and the rolling stock sold off.

No Overtaking

John and James Donkin ran a stage wagon from the Beverley Arms Inn, Scarborough to Hull – a valuable service, but trouble arose in 1811 when the wagon daringly overtook the Royal Mail coach near Beverley and raced it to Hull. At all times the Mail was to have precedence, and to overtake it was an offence. Accordingly Messrs Donkin were fined 20 guineas.

Locomotive Guide

Ralph Kedeley, a locomotive owner of Lund, appeared in court in Beverley for not having a man walking in front of the engine at Lockington on 18th November 1885. Police Constable Clarkson asserted that he saw no-one in front, but a witness declared he walked about 30 yards in advance between Lund and Lockington. The case was dismissed.

Dr. Christmas

For many years from 1891 William Henry Coates was an esteemed family doctor in the Patrington area. Qualified also as a chemist and a barrister, he was a man of many parts – fund raiser, theatre director, cinema builder, chairman of the parish council, county councillor.

In general he was a kindly practitioner, though he could be waspish with hypochondriacs. Once he met his match with an expectant mother who rebuked him for saying he knew how they all felt. Often the worse for drink, there was an occasion when he fell into a Hull dock but fortunately help was at hand.

His impressive gifts did not seem to extend to personal transport. On buying a motor bike he tried to rev up the engine by running with it. Soon breaking into sweat, but with no corresponding burst of life from the engine, he walked it to Ryehill, dumped it at the station and caught a train back to Patrington. En route he found the ignition key in his pocket.

When at last he invested in a motor-car, he became so fond of it that he sent photographs of himself at the wheel on his Christmas cards, a characteristically flamboyant touch. He died, widely lamented, in 1924.

Blitz Buses

In October 1940 16 Hull buses were loaned to London to replace those destroyed or disabled by German bombs. By May 1941 all had been returned bearing battle honour plaques in recognition of their service. Now it was Hull's turn to feel the pressure. After the devastating raids of 7th/8th May in which the Luftwaffe destroyed the central garage on Lombard Street, together with 43 buses, the remaining 65 per cent were stored in parks and suburban roads.

Pigeons

During World War Two a small Pigeon Corps was set up by the army at Kilham where message training was practised. From Brough the Blackburn Aircraft Company sent the Sopwith Baby – the Jabberwock – on reconnaissance sorties over Hornsea Mere, and the pilot carried a pair of pigeons for emergencies.

Voice of Britain

Little remains of this Ottringham site which from 1943 was the BBC's Voice of Britain to occupied Europe. Eight masts were set up on concrete bases rising 500 feet above this flattish Holderness landscape. Equipment including aircraft radar links was housed underground under thick concrete covers with steel reinforcements.

An all-too-credible tale is told of its planning in those dark days after the Dunkirk evacuation in 1940. Government officials turned up on the proposed site without a word to the owner, who covered them with a shotgun and handed them over to the police. It was late that night before they were cleared and released.

The importance of the Beacon's role in keeping up morale on the Continent is incalculable. Despite becoming something of a landmark it avoided bombs, except for one near miss. After the war it was simply abandoned. Storm damage in the 1960s caused the collapse of two masts, and in the 1970s it was dismantled.

Lucky Letters

In his History of Sutton in Holderness (1896) Thomas Blashill described some of the vagaries of the pre-Victorian postal arrangements. Carriers would bring letters from the Hull post office if they were confident the recipients would repay them the postage, as was the custom before the penny post, 1840. He added, "There was a chance that somebody would see your letter stuck in the window of the post office and it is amazing how rumour will fly".

Fit at the Post

Retired postman Charles Ireland died at Christmas 1916, having spent 24 years walking a round that took him from Beverley through Bentley, Risby, Walkington and Little Weighton – 16 miles a day and an estimated 115,000 miles during his postal career.

Beverley Post Office

Green's Household Almanack, 1952 Year Book provides some intriguing facts about the service in mid-century. For example:

"The office is open on week-days from 8.30 am to 6.30pm, on Sundays, Christmas Day and Good Friday from 9 am to 10.30 am and on Bank Holidays from 9.30 am to 12 noon.

There are two deliveries in the town area at 7 am and 11 am, except on Good Friday and Christmas Day, when there is only one delivery beginning at 7.30 am and on Bank Holidays at 7.00 am".

Oyez, Oyez!

At a time when the East Yorkshire Council has re-appointed a town crier for civic functions, it is interesting to reflect on past practices. By their livery and stentorian professional voices, bell-men tended to be larger than life characters. One long remembered was Dicky Fletcher (1748-1827) of Bridlington who had his own style of facetious rhyming announcements, like:

"Taken up this forenoon, near north sands,
Tow keys, which I have in my hands.
Whoever has lost 'em mun just come to me,
An' they shall have 'em ageean, an we can agree!"

Nonagenarian Pedal-Power

By the 1930s Miss Whitaker was in her 90s, and still demonstrating to the folk of Hessle that she was a lady of independent means, as she rode her tricycle around the village.

Beverley Bar Buses

Beverley's North Bar is the only survivor of five medieval gates, and was built in 1409-10 at a cost of £96 0s 11½d, using 112,300 bricks. Its low arch has presented obvious problems for tall vehicles, not least double-decker buses. From 1934 until the 1960s East Yorkshire Motor Services designed special "Beverley Bar Buses", en route to Driffield and Bridlington, with roofs specially tapered to negotiate the restricted opening.

Miss Whitaker, pedalling on at 90 in Woodfield Lane, near her home in Hessle *(Courtesy of P. Howlett)*

A Beverley Bar bus safely negotiates the North Bar, c1961 *(Courtesy of G. Lumb)*

Chapter 13

Alfresco

Lake Dwellings

As the Skipsea Drain was being deepened in 1880 Thomas Boynton of Ulrome Grange became intrigued by the remains of antler picks and pieces of bone. Continuing excavations revealed more implements and, significantly, fragments of brushwood stakes, flint scrapers, pottery, jet armlets, bronze spearheads and the bones of such animals as dogs, otter, deer and horses. Most exciting of all was a layer of tree trunks constituting primitive platforms, and oak piles driven into the bed of an ancient lake. Here, then, was a prehistoric lake dwelling site, presumably with simple wooden houses walled with layers of wattle and clay and some form of roof thatching.

Hessleskew Amphitheatre

This remarkable hollow, 20 feet deep and some 200 yards in circumference, overgrown with elder and willow, is set mysteriously on this plateau of the Wolds. One plausible theory is that here was once a purpose-built Roman amphitheatre used for chariot racing and gladiatorial combat. It was conveniently situated near the Roman road to York from Brough, and nearby have been discovered animal bones, tumuli, bronze and iron weapons, chariot wheels, swords, spears and coins from the era of the Emperor Constantine (AD306-337).

The remarkable Hessleskew Hollow *(H. Peach)*

Underneath the Arches

At the beginning of the 14th-century Hull ladies of the night were allocated the Foreland Arches for the sum of £3 6s 8d per annum. But if apprehended by the town constables, they were fined by the magistrates.

Classic DMV

For over 40 years from 1950 the deserted medieval village (DMV) of Wharram Percy was excavated and studied by distinguished archaeologists Maurice Beresford and John Hurst. Their researches have traced the decline of the village from c1300, noting that by 1458 only 16 households were taxed, and by 1500 many cottages had been cleared to make a sheep run. Lords of the manor (Percy until 1403, then the Hiltons) were believed to have deliberately evicted peasants as sheep-rearing became profitable. By 1543 a grazier from outside was keeping 1,180 sheep in this isolated valley of the high Wolds.

Built on the chalk hill-tops were peasants' longhouses, with animal stalls at one end. About every 25 years these constructions of timber, clay and turf were re-sited at right-angles, and for reasons that are still speculative. The more durable manor house was built of sandstone. Remaining in occasional use until 1949, was the Church of St Martin, an 11th-century foundation. Among the artefacts found were wind instruments, dice and Nine Men's Morris (or Merrills, which survives).

Excavations, 1950. Prof. Michael Beresford is standing tall, feet apart. Mr Winstanley (Settrington School) points his finger. Keith Allison, author of 'Deserted Villages' (1970) is in the ditch.
(Courtesy of Miss M. Milner)

Shepherd Lord

Fought on Palm Sunday, 1461 the Battle of Towton brought the death of the infamous Butcher Clifford, John de Clifford of Skipton Castle, callous murderer of the young Duke of Rutland, son of Richard of York, at Wakefield the year before. Now that York had won, Lady Anne Clifford, fearful for her own seven-year-old son Henry, sent him into hiding on the family estate at Londesborough. Here, removed from the lordly Lancastrian upbringing that should have been his right, he lived as a simple shepherd lad. At 13 he was removed to Cumberland, still among the shepherd fraternity, though he was allowed to pursue certain private interests like astronomy.

Another battle – Bosworth in Leicestershire in 1485 – changed his fortunes again. His Lancastrian estates restored, Henry Clifford went to live at Barden Tower. Always a natural student and countryside lover, he won valour against the Scots at Flodden (1513) and died ten years later. Posterity has remembered him as "Shepherd Lord".

Whin Common

Most villages once had "pains" limiting where and when brushwood could be gathered. Sometimes concessions were made, as at Seaton where Whin Common survives. Here were a few acres where the poor could collect as much fallen wood as they could carry – though "whin", strictly speaking, meant gorse.

Nuisances

Many social offences have been repeated endlessly down the centuries. Eavesdropping, for instance, in 16th-century Hunmanby was likely to incur a fine of 5s. Dumping rubbish of various kinds has always been reprehensible, as with James Mattock, fined 4d by the Rectory Manor of Patrington in 1663 "for his mannor (manure) lying in the street". Nearer our own time, wartime girls were incurably attracted to military uniforms. At Barmby Moor c1916 one local lady was dubbed, possibly with good reason, as "the officers' groundsheet".

Testamentary Manure

Near the end of the 17th century William Hide, yeoman of Market Weighton, died leaving in addition to household goods and chattels:

> "six loads of manure lying in a certain place which did belong to
> him in his lifetime, and was valued at 1s 6d".

Woe Waters

Rising near Wharram Percy the Gypsey Race is a slow intermittent stream that makes its tortuous way, often underground, through villages like Burton Fleming, Rudston and Boynton before emerging finally into Bridlington harbour. "Gypsey" may derive from gupos (Greek) meaning chalk; or from gypa (Norse) – a gushing stream; or it may have been likened to the gipsy wanderer. Associated with the stream is a curious legend, centuries old, according to which drying up is rather a good sign, while a very strong flow was a portent of disaster, as allegedly happened in 1665, the year of the Great Plague; in 1926 and the General Strike; and in 1914 and 1939 when two world wars erupted. One story repeated by successive generations of local historians claims that as a result of the Race floods of 1776 the Burton Fleming – Foxholes road had to be re-sited.

Wolds Floods

In Chapter 12 some aspects of the watery history of Holderness were recorded. But the Wolds to the west and north also have produced some historic floods. In particular the village of Langtoft has experienced catastrophes as far back as 1657 (the Great Flood). During a tremendous thunderstorm in May 1853 three horses were struck dead and two ploughmen barely escaped with their lives. In June 1888 a waterspout brought down boulders into the main street; and four years later early July water levels in the streets rose to a height of 7½ feet.

Several places were overwhelmed by the floodwaters that poured off the Wolds on 20th May 1910. In Driffield torrents of yellowish water flooded houses to a depth of six feet, sweeping away a bridge. Boats were used to rescue trapped families; in Providence Place a child was drowned. Cowlam, too, suffered flash floods and lightning.

During the afternoon of 24th July 1912 Beverley was almost submerged by two inches of rain in 1½ hours. Boats and bathers were out in the streets.

Old Walkergate, Beverley, after the cloudburst on Wednesday 24th July 1912 *(Courtesy of East Riding of Yorkshire Council Library and Information Services)*

Saturday Market at the critical stage was under three feet of unprecedented water, and several adjacent pubs had barrels afloat in their cellars.

Lightning, snow and hail uprooted vegetation, drowned poultry and flooded houses at Wold Newton on 12th August 1938. The centre of Stamford Bridge has proved highly vulnerable when the River Derwent has risen to dangerous heights on so many occasions, as in 1931 and 1947; and for several weeks during the winters of 1998-99-2000 the village's plight made national television news.

Hornsea Hurricane

In February 1733 a hurricane swept through the town, blowing down 28 houses, together with innumerable sheds and outhouses. Collections were held in nearby parishes, Sigglesthorne raising £4 13s 11d for the "poor sufferers".

Merely Frozen

In February 1838 Hornsea Mere was so thickly frozen over as to allow ice parties, skating and shin-up, a version of hockey. Another severe winter was that of 1890-91, when there were sheep roastings and on St Stephen's Day (1890) a cricket match.

Inter-Village Football

As far back as 1472 at Market Weighton it was decreed that no-one should play football in the cemetery under penalty of 12d. The players here may well have been youngsters; but in centuries past epic contests were held – rough and raucous rampages – between enormous numbers of men when neighbouring villages met, like Hedon and Preston, Sutton and Wawne, Hornsea and Sigglesthorne. Played with a succession of pigs' bladders or tight bundles of rags, each team faced its own village, maybe a mile or more distant, and the idea was to get the ball somehow, anyhow, onto home territory. There was much drunkenness and bones were broken in the melee. Little regard was given to ordinary folk whose property stood in the way.

Legal whistles were blown about the year 1825. At Beverley the game had been a precursor to the Sunday races, but the constabulary bore down on it and it was never revived. Owing to strong Methodist influence the affair was banned at Kilham, where again it had taken place on a Sunday.

Town Bull

From the 18th century the Lords Feoffees of Bridlington had at their disposal a bull which could be made available to freeholders for breeding purposes. It became an additional responsibility of the town constable, who had to ensure that its flanks were well-branded with the Bridlington coat-of-arms. The branding iron has survived and is kept in the town chest in the Bayle Museum.

Robin Lythe

Re-popularised by R.D. Blackmore in 'Mary Anerley' in the 1880s, Robin Lythe was a semi-mythical smuggler who once operated around Flamborough. Apart from the incidents of the swashbuckling novel, his main associations are with the "hole" or cave ascribed to his activities. One account is of him being swept from a shipwreck into the cave where he managed to cling to a high projecting rock until the tide had ebbed. Others say he kept contraband goods on the higher ledges, where he also sheltered from the excise men. Predictably perhaps, a ghostly figure has been sighted hereabouts, unloading boxes and barrels from a small boat.

Robin Lythe's Hole, Flamborough *(Courtesy of Hull Central Library, Local Studies)*

Countryside Grave

Richard Laybourne, an outdoors gentleman of Nafferton, wanted to be buried "where ploughboys singing and calling to their horses would pass". On his death on 29th October 1820 at the age of 77, his wishes were respected, and his grave lies in a field called Windersome north-east of the Nafferton round-about. A plaque inside the church shows that Laybourne gave £50 for the maintenance of a family window; for the family tomb in the churchyard; and for keeping his own grave tidy.

Moby Dick Prototype

In April 1825 a whale washed up on Tunstall beach and removed to Burton Constable Hall (where some of the skeleton remains) was dissected by James Alderson (1795-1882), a rising young Hull physician from a distinguished medical family. The publication of his unusual anatomical research marked a step on the way to a glittering career culminating in the presidency of the Royal College of Physicians (1867) and a knighthood (1869). Further

Dr James Alderson *(Courtesy of Hull Museums)*

piquancy to the whale incident was added with the publication in 1851 of "Moby Dick" where in Chapter 102 Herbert Melville discussed the background in detail, acknowledging his indebtedness as a major source.

Cockfighting

As a public spectacle cockfighting drew followers from all social classes. Sir Francis Boynton (1777-1815) bred gamecocks and had a cockpit at Burton Agnes Hall. In the 18th and early 19th centuries newspapers like the York Courant advertised details of forthcoming bouts – and bets – in, for instance, Newton's pit in Beverley, or Foster's pit at the White Hart in Howden. Town bellmen shouted "Cockins tonight!' One Sancton clergyman was so obsessed by the prospect that, on being awakened by his parish clerk, he jumped to his feet, startling his congregation with "Guinea on the black cock!' Pocklington School still has a small bell dating from the 1660s, inscribed with the names of Thomas Ellison (1664-93) and John Clarke (master, 1660-64), who would certainly have initiated their boys into the refinements of the art.

The origin of the term "battle royal" lies in this sport where many birds, topped up with brandy and reinforced with metal spurs, were put into the same arena.

The Publicans Licensing Act of 1849 abolished cockfighting – officially, at least.

Lucky Storm Break

The impetus to one aspect of the fishing industry in Hull was due to a North Sea storm. By the 1840s the enterprising men of Devon, already entrenched in Ramsgate, were starting to explore the waters off Suffolk. In 1843 some Brixham trawlers were blown off course during a storm, and eventually letting down their nets south of the Dogger Bank, discovered an abundance of fish, especially at Silver Pits. So the smacks migrated northwards to Hull. With the coming of the railways an immense market was opened up towards London, as well as Yorkshire and the North Midlands; and Hull's fishing advanced as whaling declined.

Under the Brush

Held on Easter Monday, Whit Monday, 26th August and 19th September (or nearest) the Little Driffield fairs survived in vestigial form until 1918. It was unquestionably thirsty work exhibiting or inspecting horses, sheep, hardware, dishes, small farm tools etc. and a number of local householders on fair days hung a brush over their door as a sign that liquor was available to those applying within. Blind eyes seem to have been turned by the magistracy; and the Pie Powder Court, appointed to settle disputes, was doubtless well occupied, meeting as it did in the Red Lion at Driffield, possibly raising an occasional glass to the fair's continuing bonhomie.

A Prayerful Pair

Moved by the spiritual plight of Filey fishermen, and well known in nonconformist circles in the 1820s around Driffield, John Oxtoby took himself and the efficacy of prayer very seriously. Braced to live on potatoes and salt, and sleep on a board to pursue the Lord's work in redeeming Filey, he was often obliged, in his early days there, to turn the other cheek when his potential flock pelted him with fish. Nevertheless he made many converts. Invited to preach to a group of Primitive Methodists, he deeply impressed one listener who donated £300 for the Oxtoby cause.

Some miraculous cures were attributed to his prayers. A young child regained the ability to stand and walk. One Betty Ross, however, having recovered the use of her stiffened limbs, fell from the grace induced by Johnny, only to find that her complaints returned.

More permanent were the musical gains. Singers and musicians rallied to "Ranter" hymns, becoming popular in Bridlington, Scarborough and the West Riding. They eventually provided the nucleus of the Filey Fishermen's Choir.

Operating in the South Wolds and Beverley area Billy Nicholson was a more obviously flamboyant character. He sought attention by walking about carrying a red flag bearing the device "Salvation". From time to time he crossed thresholds uninvited, shouting "Glory!" and falling on his knees to pray for the household. He was a familiar sight in the streets of Beverley in Victorian times, getting himself locked up for railing against public figures and shouting "Beer is the devil's broth!" He was a ready target for jeers, missiles and even buckets of water.

Mixed Bathing

In 1864 Joseph Armytage Wade, civic big-wig in Hornsea, successfully urged his colleagues to rule that male and female bathers should be separated on the beach, the one machine to be located not less than 200 yards from the other. Mixed bathing became more acceptable in the 1890s.

Hero of the Humber

The son of a keelman, John Ellerthorpe became a superb swimmer as a boy, practising "playing the porpoise" by breaking water in unexpected places. After working in the coaster trade he spent the rest of his working life (1848-68) as foreman of the dock gates for the Hull Docks Company. During this time he saved 39 people from drowning. Several unusual adventures befell him while crossing the Humber. As a passenger on the Brough to

Winteringham ferry he shared public alarm when a load of cattle was thrown into the river. By shouting and gesturing, John managed to drive them safely onto the Lincolnshire shore. On another occasion en route to Barton an accident occurred to his small boat. Dressed in a suit and wellingtons, and with moneys entrusted to him secure in various pockets, he kept afloat until rescue came, but he vowed to leave his wellies behind next time.

"For repeated acts of gallantry" he was decorated by the Board of Trade, the Royal Humane Society and by Queen Victoria. At his death in July 1868, at the age of 61, John Ellerthorpe was given a public funeral, attended by thousands of Hull people.

Amateur Wolds Archaeologist

A lifelong lover of the Yorkshire Wolds, John Robert Mortimer was born into a farming family at Fimber in 1825. He became a youthful observer of the changing seasons, superstitions, dog fights and badger baiting. The discovery of a skull by soldiers on Acklam Wold turned his attention to pre-history. He too began to dig; and visits to the Great Exhibition and the British Museum in 1851 generated in his agile mind a new ferment of ideas. With his brother Robert he began to put together a museum at home for geological specimens and ancient artefacts.

Whenever his grain business in Driffield allowed, Mortimer turned to systematic excavation of likely sites on the Wolds; and 25 Lockwood Street gradually filled up with arrowheads, knives, beakers, jet buttons, bone pins, etc., all faithfully recorded and labelled. Assisted by his daughter Agnes, who added beautiful drawings, he investigated some 200 Romano-British and Anglo-Saxon cemeteries, notably at Garton Slack in 1866. His book "Forty Years Researches in British and Saxon Burial Mounds of East Yorkshire", published in 1905 immediately became a classic of archaeological investigation.

Wildfowler Extraordinary

Snowden Slights (1830-1913) was a legendary figure around the marshes and swamps of Wheldrake Ings near his home at East Cottingwith. His vast armoury for his remorseless onslaught against bird life included 28 guns, one made for his father by Akrill of Beverley weighing 140lb and with a 10 foot barrel. At forty yards distance he achieved a spread shot of some 12 yards, enabling him to kill, or maim, several birds at once. Over a long working life he calculated that he averaged six birds per shot. In 1892, his best year, he accounted for 926 birds with 106 shots. While he would get a few shillings for smaller birds like duck and green plover, a whooper swan could bring him seven.

But even such an experienced and well-prepared man could be overwhelmed by events. He told the story of a gun recoiling and throwing him into deep and icy water. He emerged and walked the two miles home with parts of his corduroy jacket and trousers cut away. Next day he was back at work.

The Umbrella Man

The inventor of the light steel-ribbed umbrella frame was a Sheffield ironworks entrepreneur, Samuel Fox (1815-87). Whenever possible he liked to escape to the quiet of the Cliffe estate, bought from Sir William Worsley; later (1844) he acquired Hotham Hall as a family residence. He founded St John's Church, unusual for its north-facing altar, and he was the first to be buried in the Cliffe churchyard.

Soutter the Shooter

For most of us a bull would seem an unreliable pet. For a time Dr James Soutter (1863-1934) kept one behind his Hedon surgery. But his control of the beast proved uncertain, and there were a few incidents, culminating in it trying to pin him against a wall. So he shot it. Market gardening proved a quieter and more profitable sideline.

That he lived on Soutter Gate in Hedon was no more than a curious coincidence. There was no family connection, for this had once been the medieval street of shoemakers.

DIY Outdoor-Type

Burnby Hall Gardens at Pocklington, attracting thousands of visitors every

summer, were the creation of a remarkable and versatile man – schoolmaster, soldier and big game hunter. Major Percy Marlborough Stewart (1871-1962) decided to settle in the town at whose ancient school he served as deputy headmaster. After buying the site he dug the Upper Water by hand in 1904 and concreted it, the Lower Water being added six years later. Here, amidst beautifully landscaped gardens, was to be developed the finest collection of water lilies in Europe. The adjacent museum contains many intriguing memorabilia of Major Stewart's travels, including a Rhodesian lioness, Burmese religious artefacts, Mexican sharks, African musical instruments, together with a plethora of trophies and curiosities.

Major P.M. Stewart *(Courtesy of Mrs D. Hughes)*

Floral Clock

A first for Bridlington was the floral clock, created in the gardens of the Pavilion, Royal Princes Parade in 1907. From a nearby bush a "cuckoo" marked the hour. With a diameter of 12 feet the dial was made up of hundreds of flowering plants. Repeated annually it became an interesting feature for tourists, soon to be imitated by other resorts. Later a floral staircase was added.

Holtby Homelands

Notwithstanding the title of "South Riding", her best known book, Winifred Holtby's novels were firmly based on the eastern side of this Riding. Place names have been changed but the location can readily be identified from the context. Anderby, for example, is Rudston where she was born (1898) and buried (1935). In "Anderby Wold" the account of the agricultural workers' strike echoed her father David's sad experience when disaffection amongst employees drove him to a quieter life in Cottingham. In "The Crowded Street" the cliffs and promenades of Hardrascliffe were of Bridlington, and the snobbish stifling atmosphere of Marshington was alas! Cottingham, overlooked by Miller's Rise – Skidby Mill and its environs.

To the south-east was the lonely Cold Harbour Colony i.e. Sunk Island, a wide Dutch landscape with indented banks, the rhythm of the tides, great ships gliding up to Kingsport (Hull) and, inevitably, mud. During the summer of 1934 Winifred rented a cottage on Waxholme Road, Withernsea to gain local colour for "South Riding". This town, raw, ugly but bustling, she called Kiplington.

The much more attractive town of Flintonbridge (i.e. Beverley) included a detailed description of the famous Saturday Market. Alderman Mrs. Beddows is thought to have resembled Winifred's own mother Alice, who in real life was the East Riding's first lady alderman in 1923. Thinking that too many people would recognise her she resigned.

On 29th September 1935, a month after finishing "South Riding" Winifred died of Bright's Disease in a London nursing home. She was laid to rest in her native churchyard on 2nd October. Her grave carries the carving of an open book inscribed:

Winifred Holtby's grave, Rudston *(H. Peach)*

> *"God give me work till my life shall end,*
> *And life till my work is done".*

Raising seemingly eternal issues like local government corruption, country-side problems and rural housing, "South Riding" has considerable resonance for our own times.

Harken, Whitehall!

Grist to Winifred Holtby's mill, though the events there must have exasper-ated her, was the cack-handed horticultural experiment set up on Sunk Island towards the end of the First World War, demonstrating once more that White-hall did not know best in implementing local change. In 1917 the Ministry of Agriculture and Fisheries took over five farms for the re-settlement of ex-soldiers, who were to work in smallholdings as part of a commune. At Channel Farm a Director of Planning was installed with an abundance of files and an expensive Brussels carpet. The following year 24 cottages were built and the land was turned over by an unskilled team of conscientious objectors, youths and land army girls.

The authorities, surprised that ex-soldiers were failing to apply for this leap into the unknown and untried, threw open the scheme more widely. A few inexperienced town folk were lured in, and were immediately at a loss. Local farmers kept their distance. A change of Director in 1922 brought no better response and the colony was closed down in 1927, a monumental failure of well-intentioned central planning imposed without local knowl-edge or consultation.

Last of the Pondmakers

Pondmakers tended to guard well the secrets of their esoteric art; and certainly Jack ("Pondy") Welburn was no exception. The exact composition of clay, lime mortar, straw, chalk, rubble, grass sods, etc. he kept to himself, though his sons, Billy and Ray, helped. Pondy liked to finish the job himself, sometimes under cover of darkness. He liked to make an early start: 6am was not unusual, having ridden his bike or trundled his barrow all the way from Fridaythorpe. Curiously, for all his experience and expertise, Pondy was convinced that it was dew and not rainwater that filled his ponds.

He was laid to rest in his native churchyard in 1951 at the age of 75. Sadly, none of his family wanted to carry on the business, which died with him.

Climmers

Extraordinarily brave and dedicated were those summer climbers who were lowered over the sheer 400 foot cliffs at Bempton to gather sea birds' eggs. More than a century ago they trusted to ropes and one another. By the 1930s the technology had been improved to include winches and pulleys. Even so it was a precarious livelihood, shooing away gulls and guillemots that suddenly flew up into their faces as they stored away their eggs in canvas bags before being hauled to safety. Some eggs were sold locally. Others were sent to the West Riding for industrial purposes, like making patent leather.

The "climmers" were a tremendous attraction to visitors – until the Protec-

Egg gatherers, Flamborough c1900 *(Courtesy of East Riding of Yorkshire Council Library and Information Services)*

tion of Birds Act made illegal their activities in 1954. A practitioner, Sam Leng, wrote his autobiography in "Experiences and Reminiscences of a Cliff Climber". Visitors still seek out the RSPB Reserve at Bempton, delighting in the puffins, razorbills and especially the gannets, whose only mainland colony is here.

Harbour Houdini

A favourite spectacle attracting hundreds of visitors in the 1930s was "Professor" Albert Gautier diving off Bridlington's north pier at high tide. This was bravery enough but this man submitted to various handicaps of manacles and chains. His repertoire included being tied into a sack and thrown into the harbour; and he once swam around the base of Scarborough Castle with hands and feet shackled. During the daytime he ran the swimming pool in Bridlington's Queen's Square. He died in 1940 at the age of 47.

Winter of '47

In so many areas these were the worst snows in living memory. Sunk Island was cut off for six weeks, winds being a tremendous problem to persistent snow-clearing teams. The Huggate – Uncleby area of the Wolds was cut off by vast drifts, and supplies had to be airlifted in. Combined forces were needed at Huggate. On Monday 10th February an RAF Mountain Rescue team from Topcliffe and Army bulldozers from Ripon took nearly 600lb of food, bread, margarine, tinned meat, fruit, flour etc. to Huggate. For many farmers the spring sowing was delayed by up to two months.

Chapter 14

Miscellany

Place Names

About one-third of East Yorkshire villages are named after Viking settlements. Thus, Sywardby (Sewerby) was the settlement of Syward. Approximately 120 were of Anglo-Saxon origin, ending in "-ton" (enclosure). "Burton" meant a fortified village. Burton Agnus was once Agnes Burton, and into the 18th century Burton Pidsea was Pidsea Burton. The "Burtone" of Domesday Book had "Fleming" added later, and by the 14th-century had become North Burton, a preference that lingered into modern times. Cherry Burton (or North Burton) was contrasted with Bishop Burton (South Burton), where the Archbishop of York held a manor house from the 13th century.

Some old names are wonderful to savour, like Penisthorpe, a lost village to the south of Welwick; or Wetwang – was it a "wet place"? The theory loses credence in a dry valley area. A likelier possibility is thought to be "vaet vangr", the field of summons for trial, Icelandic in origin. "Doncevale" in medieval times, Dunswell had by the 17th century degenerated to "Beerhouses" on account of two inns facing each other across the road.

A persistent misnomer is Danes Dyke, the 2½ mile long earthwork behind Flamborough Head. In many places the great ditch is 60 feet wide and 20 feet deep, with double ramparts. Certainly it has nothing to do with Danish invaders, but was established about 150 AD, presumably for the protection of local settlements.

Street Names

The Land of Green Ginger, in Hull's Old Town, has invited much guesswork as to its origin. Was ginger stored in warehouses here? Or processed here? Or conceivably grown in, say, greenhouse conditions? Could there really have been a family called Lindegroen, migrating here from Holland, whose name suggested Land of Green – plus "jonger" (i.e. children) transmuted by local tongues as "ginger"? Fanciful ... and improbable, no doubt. Could this street name have derived from a 17th-century boatbuilder called Moses Grenehinger?

During the 19th century Princes Avenue was called variously Mucky Pig Lane, Newland Tofts Lane and Princess Bank, but the royal connections are obscure. Park Street had such previous names as Rest House Lane, Dog Kennel Lane and, ominously, Cut Throat Lane. In medieval times an area of the town washed by the Humber tides became known as Dede Horsekirk

Garth, used as it was for burying dead horses. With the later dumping of rubbish including sewage it gained the reputation of "Foul South End."

Hedon, as well as having Fletchergate (butcher street) and Baxter Gate (street of female bakers) also had an intriguing Grope Lane, favoured by courting couples. Victorian prudery, it seems, insisted on a shift to Grape, which has remained. Both Hedon and Beverley had a Walkergate where new cloth was "walked" in water to assist thickening and shrinking. Hedon's became Church Gate, Beverley's is unchanged. Other reminders of past economic activity in the latter town are Dyer Lane and Toll Gavel, where strangers had to pay entrance fees. Near Beverley railway station the Trinities area is said to have originated with the medieval Manor of the Holy Trinity once owned by the Knights Hospitallers of the Order of St John of Jerusalem. Their house provided food and lodging for pilgrims and travellers.

Trade Names

Tracing them is an endlessly amusing occupation. In the 1860s Hedon had a blacksmith called Horseman, and Peter Herdsman of Kirk Ella was a "bullocky". In the same period the Bullocks were farming in Baythorpe – and the keeper of a beerhouse in Shady Lane, Driffield was Robert Dry.

Rotenherings

This was a renowned merchant family in 13th and 14th century Hull. John Rotenhering (died 1328), a king's warden, had his own wharf backing onto the River Hull, and his ship, the Goodyear carried Yorkshire wool to Flanders. There were family links with the de la Poles (see Chapter 2).

Nicknames

Older folk will remember how common nicknames once were in village life. According to a contemporary local historian, Robert Addison there were in Leavening in 1831 five Toms, with epithets deemed appropriate for ready reference, viz. Long Tom, Short Tom, Norton Tom, Hall Garth Tom and Butcher Tom.

Kaiser's Own

During the First World War some men of the East Yorkshire Regiment suffered a degree of teasing because of the Teutonic flavour of their surnames. And, indeed, a study of the lists in the regimental chapel in Beverley Minster includes the following: Sieber, Trier, Stein, Schneider, Meyerhoff, Waecker, Beervault, Schlechte and Hagestadt.

Et Tu, Florence

Florence Mary Scott Cavell, sister of the immortal Edith (shot by the Germans in 1915) was matron of the Withernsea Convalescent Hospital from 1913 to 1945, and is buried in St Nicholas Churchyard nearby, having died in 1950. It is said that she, too, in the footsteps of Miss F. Nightingale, liked to do her evening rounds carrying a lamp.

"P" for Pauper

Two women were brought from Doncaster in 1577 to teach some of the poor of Hull to knit. They were rewarded with £4 each, plus board and lodging. Six years later fishermen were hired from Yarmouth to develop the arts of angling – an odd event in the light of the town's subsequent pre-eminence in that industry. In 1769 Thomas Stutt, tailor of Patrington, was commissioned to make badges showing "P" for paupers to wear.

Officials occasionally went to extreme lengths to try to offload some of their responsibilities. At the Beverley Quarter Sessions, July 1822 two overseers from Thearne were charged with conspiring to procure the marriage of a female pauper with a vagrant from another parish, which would then have become liable for the joint welfare of the couple.

Peppercorn Rents

During the 14th century Hawise, Prioress of Swine granted to Robert the Clerk of Brandesburton two oxgangs of land at the yearly rent of a pound of pepper.

In the time of Edward I Thomas Hildyard held pasturage for a thousand sheep at Sutton, Sculcoates and Drypool in exchange for a pair of gloves at Easter to John Sutton.

From 1422 John Wenslagh of Kilham was granted by Beatrice Cross a house and eight acres of land for the annual rent of a rose.

Town's Tag Price

By the Great Town Deed of 6th May 1636 Bridlington was taken over by the Lords Feoffees, a group of 13 men who controlled all administrative affairs until the Local Government Act of 1863 superseded them. Payment was made to the Crown of £3260, enabling the town to buy what it previously had rented.

Eight and Forty

In the Wallingfen district a medieval legend had grown of 48 witches who lived on their wits, engaging in poaching and drunken debauches. Their song included the chorus:

"We're eight and forty jolly girls, though witches we may be,
We live upon the best of food and, like the air, we're free".

Loosely associated with this tale was a curious system of local government which preceded the enclosures of 1777. Since 1426 some 48 local "townships" (often no more than hamlets) had sent representatives to meetings held at a house near St Stephen's Church, Newport in order to regulate such customary matters as land usage, drainage, crops, harvesting, taking of turfs, grazing, fish and fowl, etc. There was an organised system of pains and forfeits against offenders. It seems likely that this arrangement, focused on a limited, marshy domain, grew from a communal need for order and protection against marauding spirits, witches or otherwise.

Share That Among You!

Dr Dobson, a later 18th century Driffield general practitioner, enjoyed a party. On one occasion after joining friends for a few drinks, he eventually fell to belabouring a companion with an unwieldy parcel. As the wrappings disintegrated a human leg dropped onto the table, scattering the glasses. Having come straight from performing an amputation at Garton, the good doctor was taking the free limb home for an exercise in dissection.

Long Servers

This Riding has been blessed with some remarkably faithful Church servants, like Henry Barr, chorister at Sigglesthorne for 75 years. John Healey Bromby was Vicar at Holy Trinity Church, Hull for 70 years, starting in 1797. At North Cave William Hicks was a bellringer for 62 years. At Walkington, Harold Lythe served as organist from 1903 to 1967, apart from 2½ years of war service with the Royal Engineers. But the career of Thomas Smith of Nafferton takes some capping. A memorial in the south aisle of the Church records his work as schoolmaster for 58 years, overlapping with his role as parish clerk for 36 years. He died in 1856 at the age of 94.

A Brontë Elbow

One cleric could be forgiven for a shorter stay. The Rev. Henry Nussey, curate at Burton Agnes, proposed marriage to Charlotte Brontë during her visit in the spring of 1839. But she turned him down, preferring in the short term a trip to Bridlington with his sister Ellen, and in the longer term matrimony with another parson, Arthur Nicholls. Henry may have been the model for the dull parson, St John Rivers who was sweet on Jane Eyre.

Ribald Reverend

For six years (1823-29) that celebrated caustic wit, Sydney Smith was priest-in-charge at Foston, near York, and Londesborough. His verbal gems are still widely quoted. For example, his reply to a countryman whom he had just worsted in an argument but who wanted the last word:

"If I had a son who was an idiot I'd make him a parson".

To which Smith retorted, "Very probably – but I see your father was of a different opinion".

To the fair sex he could be charming. When a lady, conducting him round her garden, regretted that she couldn't bring perfection to her sweet pea, Smith took her hand and gently said:

"Permit me, then, madam, to take perfection to the pea".

He was well aware of clerical limitations:

"As the French say, there are three sexes – men, women and clergymen".

Not So Simple

Tom Moman (1720-1823) was generally regarded as Lutton's village idiot. But Tom was deeper than many suspected. When a farmer at Malton market asked him to drive some cows back to their village, Tom agreed but asked for two shillings in advance. This was agreed. On arrival he told the foreman that the master, not having the right money on him, had urged that he be paid, cows on delivery. This too was done. Tom next assured the farmer's wife that the master had promised him two shillings plus a dinner and a quart of ale and tobacco if he drove the new herd home safely. Having been rewarded yet again, Tom thought it prudent to return home quickly.

Cheers

On 12th November 1759 Beverley Corporation granted the sum of five guineas to the town militia to drink the health of His Majesty King George II. A timely gesture, for he died within the year.

Swanland Hangover

Sir James Reckitt (1834-1924), distinguished Hull industrialist and public benefactor went on to provide many more amenities after moving to Swanland Manor. But his Quaker misgivings about public houses seemed justified when during Christmas festivities in 1897 a local labourer died after imbibing too many whiskies. In the resulting court case the landlord of the White Horse lost his licence. The premises were sold off as a shop. Sir James saw to it that during his lifetime no other hostelry opened in the village. Indeed a teetotal atmosphere prevailed until the Swan and Cygnet opened in 1980.

Hull's First Bank

A pioneering venture in Yorkshire banking took place in 1754 when Joseph Pease (1688-1774) set up a deposit house at 18 High Street, Hull. He had made a modest fortune in shipping, and was to reach further prosperity in the development of the oil and seed-crushing industry. His institution was taken over in 1894 by the York Union Banking Corporation, and ultimately by Barclays. Account holders in Pease's bank eventually included such luminaries as Benjamin and Hugh Blaydes (shipbuilders) and Henry Ellerington and Samuel Standidge, merchants.

The Whaling Century

After a preliminary survey which brought back just one whale (and 300 seal skins) Samuel Standidge sent three whalers to Greenland waters in 1768. They prospered; and shortly at Sculcoates and Wilmington, along the River Hull, there developed the Greenland Yards where blubber was cut up and boiled for oil, a product still in use for street lighting until replaced by gas in 1830. But the Yards became a byword for noxious fumes and pollution.

Sir Samuel Standidge *(Courtesy of Hull Museums)*

Meanwhile, Standidge was five times elected as Warden of Trinity House, Hull, and the year 1795 brought him the mayoralty and a knighthood.

New customs arose. Outgoing whalers tied to their masts garlanded hoops given by wives and sweethearts. These lucky mascots, bleached white, were reclaimed on the vessel's return, when whale tusks and other decorative bones were dismantled.

The peak was reached in 1820 when 64 Hull whalers made 688 catches. Thereafter came a rapid run-down, and by 1860 the infamous Greenland Yards had closed down. With the wreck of the last whaler, Diana (See Chapter 5) at Donna Nook, near Grimsby, in 1868 the industry was dead.

Century Makers

Two East Yorkshire railways also lasted a hundred years. The Market Weighton – Beverley line began operations in 1865; was closed to passengers in 1959; and under the Beeching Axe was finally closed in 1965. The Hull – Hornsea line, opened on 28th March 1864, was likewise deemed to be uneconomic, ceasing operations on 19th November 1964.

Swine School lasted a century to the day. Henry Goodyear welcomed his first pupils on 16th July 1868, and Frank Pinfold signed off in the official log book on the same date of the month in 1968.

Lady Blacksmiths

Hooping wheel at Millington, once used by smiths and wheelwrights for shaping the rims of cart wheels *(H. Peach)*

In the 1820s Elizabeth Marshall ran the Kirk Ella smithy, and at South Cave Rachel Levitt had her forge opposite the church. During the 1850s Ann Milner shod horses at Sproatley, as did Mary Goodwill at Weston. At Wold Newton Harriet Haw worked into the 1920s. There were occasional female wheelwrights, too, Elizabeth Pearson soldering on at Hotham until 1901 when she reached the age of 75.

Chamber Emptier

Notorious for long dull speeches was David Hartley (1729-1813), MP for Hull 1774-80 and 1782 to 1784. His very rising to speak worked like a dinner bell. He went on for hours – five, even seven, especially when holding forth on his favourite topics of the abolition of slavery and the folly of war with the American colonies.

One day the celebrated Whig parliamentarian Edmund Burke was anxious to speak, but Hartley refused to yield. Burke seized his moment when DH urged the need to read the Riot Act. Waving his arm all round the chamber, the great man remonstrated:

"Why read the Act now? They have dispersed already!"

Nevertheless, Hartley was a man of probity and perseverance, and as a patient diplomat at the Paris talks in 1783 he helped to draw up a peace settlement with the emergent United States of America.

Butlin's at Filey

Billy Butlin had meant to open the Filey camp for the summer of 1940, but the RAF took over the premises for the duration of World War Two. With peace coming in May 1945 events moved fast. The parade ground soon became a boating lake, and Butlin's was back. Great days lay ahead.

The French Bar, 198 feet long and fitted with 20 pumps made the *Guinness Book of Records* until 1973 when it was reduced to make way for the Princes Bar. The Gaiety Theatre held an audience of 2,500. Many popular entertainers appeared – Des 0'Connor knew life here as a Redcoat!

During the 1950s Maurice Fogel drew large crowds as an unorthodox mind-reader. For a one-off stunt he promised to eat a camper alive in the Regency Bar. The packed house didn't believe him .. and tension rose as a white-coated assistant began to apply a solution from a large bottle marked ETHER to the shoulder of a volunteer who had stripped to the waist.

Maurice looked all around, assured himself that all was ready – then bit hard. The victim's yell could probably have been heard in Humanby village a mile or two down the road. He left on the trot.

Maurice apologised for being unable to continue, and called for fresh volunteers. As there were none he reverted to mind-reading, which at worst was no more than psychologically painful.

Calumnies and Compliments

Odo, first Lord of Holderness, described his Seignory to William the Conqueror as "barren, unfruitful and brought nothing but wild oats." This might have been true of the marshlands of the 11th century but in more recent times this area has been highly productive agriculturally.

Surprisingly, perhaps, Hull has attracted much praise, as well as censure. The actor-manager, Tate Wilkinson applauded (1790) its hospitality. At the same period Charles Dibdin, novelist and song writer, echoed Arthur Young (1770) in finding the streets wide and handsome. But there are inconsistencies in Young. It is hard to reconcile his earlier tribute to the town's cleanliness with his later finding (1797) of dirt and ugliness. Perhaps the intervening 'close-building' put him off or what Dorothy Wordsworth was to call ' brick-housey'. In her Journal of 16th July 1802 the poet's sister, while savouring the romance of the night lights on the river, hated the squalor and vulgarity of Hull's commerce. Nearly 30 years later the radical writer William Cobbett delighted in the port's cleanliness and pretty gardens, finding them comparable to the best parts of London.

Last Wills

Will Hickington, son of the vicar of South Cave and educated at Cambridge, became a local poet and critic of the establishment and various worthies. Dying in 1772 he was buried at South Cave and left the following versified testament:

> *"This is my last will,*
> *I insist on it still,*
> *So sneer on and welcome,*
> *And e'en laugh your fill.*
> *I, William Hickington,*
> *Poet of Pocklington,*
> *Do give and bequeath*
> *As free as I breathe*
> *To thee, Mary Jarum,*
> *The Queen of my Harum,*
> *My cash and my cattle*
> *With every chattel*
> *To have and to hold,*
> *Come heat or come cold*
> *Sans hindrance or strife,*
> *Tho thou art not my wife,*
> *As witness my hand*
> *Just here as I stand,*
> *The twelfth day of July*
> *In the year seventy".*

In due course the will was proved at the Deanery Court in York.

James Snaith of Tunstall left in his will, 1866, a replacement cow, should any villager's beast die, leaving the owner bereft of a livelihood.

Final Warning

Companion notices on the wall of the Kilnsea Heritage Centre confirm that over a century and a half the sea has encroached by some 340 yards. This Holderness coastline, unfortunately, shows the fastest rate of erosion in Europe. The old adage, "Go west, young man" has special relevance here.

The sea gives notice at Kilnsea *(H. Peach)*

Perhaps in full geological time this former "German Ocean" may once more lap at the foothills of the Wolds.

But doon't thoo fret, pet: happen somebody somewheer'll think o' summat!

Bibliography

R. Addison *Leavening* (1831)

W. Andrews *Yorkshire in Olden Times* (Brown, Hull, 1890)

T. Blashill *History of Sutton in Holderness* (Brown, Hull, 1896)

H.B. Browne *Story of the East Riding of Yorkshire* (Brown, Hull, 1912)

S. Caunce *Amongst Farm Horses: The Horse Lads of East Yorkshire* (Sutton, 1991)

M. Craven *A New and Complete History of Hedon* (Ridings Publishing Co., Driffield, 1972)

A. Crowther *Yorkshire Customs – Traditions and Folk Lore of Old Yorkshire* (Dalesman, 1974)

J. and P. Crowther *The Diary of Robert Sharp of South Cave: Life in a Yorkshire Village 1812 – 37* (OUP for British Academy, 1997)

A.G. Cox & D. Stather *History of the Parish of Market Weighton and District* (1957)

J. Dawes & T.G. Wilson *Barmby Moor: the History of a Village and its People* (1996)

East Yorkshire Federation of Women's Institutes and Countryside Books: *East Yorkshire Within Living Memory* (1998)

B. English *The Lords of Holderness* (Hull University Press, 1991)

M. Fearon *Filey from Fishing Village to Edwardian Resort* (Hutton Press, 1990)

H.L. Gee *Tales they tell in Yorkshire* (Methuen, 1954)

E. Gillett *The Humber Region in the Nineteenth Century* (University of Hull Department of Adult Education, 1982)

E. Gutch *Folk Lore concerning the East Riding of Yorkshire* (D. Nutt, London, 1912)

G. Hadley *History of Hull* (T. Briggs, Hull, 1788)

R. Heathcote *Anlaby: the History of an East Yorkshire Village 867-1999* (Beagle Publications, 1999)

Hessle Local History Society *Hessle Cottage Homes*

W. Hickington *Poems on Various Subjects* (J. Easton, 1821)

J.E. Hobson *A Sketch of Hornsea* (1974)

C. Holderness *Some Driffield Incidents of 117 Years Ago* (1909)

A. Jarratt *Lang Sermons* (East Riding Dialect Society, 1992)

J. Johnson *The Story of the Sinking of the Edith Cavell* (1996)

C. Ketchell *Showmen of the Past – Chicken Joe, the Man you all Know* (Tweedale New Era Publications, 1999)

Kingston upon Hull Publications *700 Years as a Royal Borough* (Walton, 1999)

I. Leatham *A General View of the Agriculture of the East Riding* (1794)

J. Markham *Nineteenth Century Parliamentary Elections in East Yorkshire* (East Yorkshire Local History Society, 1982)

J. Markham *Colourful Characters* (Highgate Publications, 1992)

M.C.F. Morris *Nunburnholme: its History and Antiquities* (H. Froude, 1901)

M.C.F. Morris *Yorkshire Folk Talk* (A. Brown, 1911)

M.C.F. Morris *Yorkshire Reminiscences* (CUP, 1922)

D. Neave *Pocklington 1660 - 1914: A Small East Riding Market Town* (W & C Forth, 1993)

G. Nellist *The Yorkshire Wolds of Yesteryear* (Horsley & Dawson, 1981)

J. Nicholson *Folk Speech of East Yorkshire* (A. Brown, 1889)

L. Owston *History of Humanby* (1948)

N. Pevsner & D. Neave *Yorkshire: York and the East Riding – The Buildings of England series* (Penguin Books, 1995)

G. Poulson *The History and Antiquities of the Seignory of Holderness* (1841)

E. Rennison *In Search of the Unusual in East Yorkshire and the Yorkshire Coast* (Hutton Press, 1997)

P. Robinson *Third Book of Ghosts* (Hutton Press, 1993)

F. Ross *Celebrities of the Wolds* (Trubner and Co., 1877)

R.M. Scrowston *A Hundred Years of Education in Walkington 1876-1976* (School Governors, 1976)

M. Sewell *Joseph Armytage Wade – The King of Hornsea* (Hornsea Museum, 1996)

T. Sheppard *Lost Towns of the Yorkshire Coast* (1912 – reprinted by Mr Pye Books, Howden, 1986)

J. Sibree *FiftyYears Recollections of Hull* (1882)

N. Stockton ed. *East Riding Dialect Dictionary* (East Riding Dialect Society, 1999)

L. Thorpe *In the Distance Enchanted* (Gwenora Books, 1998)

W.R. Watkinson *The Relieving Officer Looks Back* (Lunn, Withernsea, 1950)

E. Whelan ed. *The Oral Tradition of and District* (Pocklington & District Civic Society, 1986)

W. White *A Month in Yorkshire* (Chapman & Hall, 1858)

T. Wildridge *Old and New Hull* (M.C. Peck, Hull, 1884)

Also of interest . . .

CURIOUS TALES OF OLD WEST YORKSHIRE

Marie Campbell

"A fascinating collection of odd tales of occult doings, curious clergymen, eccentrics and the allsorts of society's fringes." NORTHERN EARTH 1999 "In this fascinating, entertaining, bustling...package of oddities, Marie Campbell ranges far and wide." BRADFORD TELEGRAPH & ARGUS
This compendium of 'curious tales' from old West Yorkshire is a first for our times. There has been nothing quite like it since the nineteenth century, when gentleman antiquarians and ghost-hunters took to travelling the country, unearthing the unexplained and the supernatural, and recording their incredible findings as they went. £7.95

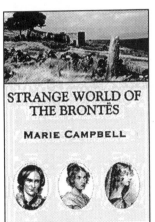

THE STRANGE WORLD OF THE BRONTËS

Marie Campbell

A comprehensive examination of new and little known material concerning the famous Brontë family and their involvement with occult practices. Foreword by Peter Underwood, President and Chief Investigator of the Ghost Club for over 30 years, and a fellow of the Royal Society of Arts. See the Brontës in a different light, their stranger/darker side; explore new material and fresh evidence about the Ripper case; digest new information about 'The Golden Dawn' - a Victorian occult group in Bradford; examine the Brontë birth charts. £7.95

TOWN & VILLAGE DISCOVERY TRAILS: Yorkshire Dales

Elizabeth Fowler

From simple village walks to longer adventures around larger towns, this book is a pure education! Many of the towns and villages are recorded in the Domesday book, and each has a story to tell.
"Leisurely but satisfying walks around some of the most attractive villages in the Dales... a compact well-set out book which should be carried by motorists whenever they visit the area." WHARFEDALE & AIREDALE OBSERVER
£6.95

WALKS IN THE MYSTERIOUS YORKSHIRE DALES

Graham Dugdale

A new approach to walking in this popular region, with 30 routes which unravel the many varied mysteries of the Yorkshire Dales. These tales dig deep into the region's history and folklore, follow in the macabre footsteps of the Swaledale corpse bearers, challenge the Penhill Giant in his own domain and listen for ghostly revelry at Ribblehead. The author provides his own decorative and extremely detailed maps. This is the fourth in Graham Dugdale's series of guides that transport walkers and armchair travellers into the enigmatic world of mystery and imagination. £6.95

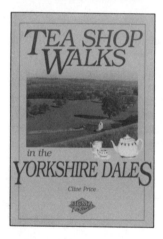

BEST TEA SHOP WALKS IN THE YORKSHIRE DALES

Clive Price

Enjoy a stroll in the Yorkshire Dales rounded off with afternoon tea in a specially selected teashop. "A tantalising mixture of walks and eating places... a delightful concoction of exercise and culinary indulgence."
£6.95